ASA 5047

1

EP 2/01 24.45

D1568283

Bill W. and Mr. Wilson

Bill W. and Mr. Wilson

THE LEGEND AND LIFE OF A.A.'S COFOUNDER

Matthew J. Raphael

UNIVERSITY OF MASSACHUSETTS PRESS

AMHERST

Printed in the United States of America
LC 99-086304
ISBN 1-55849-245-3
Designed by Dennis Anderson
Set in Adobe Dante by Graphic Composition, Inc.
Printed and bound by Thomson-Shore, Inc.

Library of Congress Cataloging-in-Publication Data

Raphael, Matthew J.
Bill W. and Mr. Wilson : the legend and life of A.A.'s cofounder / Matthew J. Raphael.
    p. cm.
Includes bibliographical references.
ISBN 1-55849-245-3 (alk. paper)
1. W., Bill. 2. Alcoholics—Biography. 3. Alcoholics Anonymous. I. Title.
HV5032.W19 R36 2000
362.292′86′092—dc21
[B]   99-086304

British Library Cataloguing in Publication data are available

For my sons

As a matter of personal preference, I'd rather there never would be any biography, because A.A. has been such a benign conspiracy of God and so many other people, that I should certainly be over-rated.

Bill W. to Max W., 25 September 1961

And again, and again, in secret communion with my own spirit, would I demand the questions, "Who is he?—whence came he?—and what are his objects?"

Edgar Allan Poe, "William Wilson"

Contents

Preface

It is an intriguing coincidence that William (Griffith) Wilson bore the same name as the title character of a well-known tale by Edgar Allan Poe, whose notoriety as a hopeless drunkard in the nineteenth century compares to Bill W.'s celebrity as a recovered alcoholic in the twentieth.

In "William Wilson," Poe explores the idea of the *Doppelgänger,* the shadowy double, who haunts the story's dissolute and frequently inebriated narrator with his unaccountable and progressively insufferable materializations—to the point where the nameless narrator is maddened to murder what turns out to be an imago of his own conscientiously sober self. Poe's William Wilson is, in fact, an uncanny prototype of "Bill W."!

The idea of doubleness also governs my treatment of the other William Wilson, the fusion of whose personal identity with A.A. history has tended to obscure whoever may have lived behind the legendary persona. Although *Bill W. and Mr. Wilson* is by no means a comprehensive biography of its elusive subject, it does represent a type of life writing that is epitomized by A. J. A. Symons's classic *The Quest for Corvo* (1934), the progenitor of the "quest biography" genre in which the life of the biographical subject is linked to the vicissitudes of the biographer.

Bill W. and Mr. Wilson is a book of personal impressions and ruminations, for which no one else is ultimately accountable. Although I am very grateful for the cooperation of archivists at A.A.'s New York Headquarters and at Stepping Stones—respectively, Judit Santon and Eileen Guiliani—this book does not in any way speak for them or for Alcoholics Anonymous.

I am indebted as well to previous work on Bill Wilson and especially to the three excellent studies from which I have drawn the most: Robert Thomsen's *Bill W.*, Ernest Kurtz's *Not-God*, and the anonymous A.A. biography *'Pass It On.'*

For reasons that I think will become apparent, I have chosen not to break my own A.A. anonymity. "Matthew J. Raphael" is a pseudonym.

Abbreviations

AA   *Alcoholics Anonymous: The Story of How Many Thousands of Men and Women Have Recovered from Alcoholism.* 3d ed. New York: Alcoholics Anonymous World Services, 1976. (I am using the third rather than the 1939 first edition of *Alcoholics Anonymous* for the convenience of the reader; although the text of the first part is virtually identical in both editions, they have different pagination.)

AACA   *Alcoholics Anonymous Comes of Age: A Brief History of A.A.* New York: Alcoholics Anonymous Publishing, 1957.

BW   Robert Thomsen. *Bill W.* New York: Harper and Row, 1975.

DB   *Dr. Bob and the Good Oldtimers: A Biography, With Recollections of Early A.A. in the Midwest.* New York: Alcoholics Anonymous World Services, 1980.

LH   *The Language of the Heart: Bill W.'s Grapevine Writings.* New York: AA Grapevine, 1988.

LR   *Lois Remembers: Memoirs of the Co-Founder of Al-Anon and Wife of the Co-Founder of Alcoholics Anonymous.* New York: Al-Anon Family Group Headquarters, 1979.

PIO   *'Pass It On': The Story of Bill Wilson and How the A.A. Message Reached the World.* New York: Alcoholics Anonymous World Services, 1984.

VRE   William James. *The Varieties of Religious Experience: A Study in Human Nature.* Edited by Martin E. Marty. New York: Penguin Books, 1982. (This is a facsimile reprint of the first edition of 1902.)

Bill W. and Mr. Wilson

Founders' Day 1998

It takes ten minutes for the bikers all to pass. This, I am told, is the customary windup to Founders' Day, the annual birthday party for Alcoholics Anonymous, born here in Akron, Ohio, in the spring of 1935. A procession of motorcycles, with hundreds of sober riders astride, roars out to Mount Peace Cemetery, the burial site of Robert Holbrook Smith, M.D., cofounder of A.A. One biker has brought along bagpipes to drone at the graveside ceremony. Throughout this June weekend's activities many alcoholics, less conspicuously than the bikers, have sought out Dr. Bob's headstone. As a sign of their gratitude, some leave behind their chips, the brass medallions given by A.A. groups to mark sobriety anniversaries.

I am not going to the cemetery this year, my thirteenth of sobriety and my first at Founders' Day. But I make a point of rising early enough to catch the parade, which is supposed to begin (but does not) at 7:30 sharp. I am standing near the head of the lengthening motorcade, at the corner of South College and East Main Streets, on the campus perimeter of the University of Akron, host to the festivities. It is a cloudy Sunday morning with sprays of rain, and spectators are sparse. The bikers, their engines now at rest, are visiting among themselves. A few are "sensibly" dressed in plastic raingear. Most are not; a scowl is their umbrella.

The leaders, I realize, must have been chilling here for hours in

1

order to hold the coveted vanguard they have seized. These point men (a few women follow close behind) all belong either to the "Fifth Chapter" or to the "Messengers," national A.A. biker groups. One of them, the coolest dude I have seen, hails from my own environs in upstate New York. A muscular man of average height, thirty-something, with a handlebar mustache and shoulder-length dark hair capped by a knotted red bandanna, he is decked out in blue and black. A sleeveless denim vest, with "The Fifth Chapter" emblazoned on the back, covers a black leather jacket. Black leather chaps cover faded jeans. The contrasting colors and textures emphasize the cut of the chaps, how they cradle his virilia, leaving him suggestively exposed. So far this attire is nothing extraordinary: merely mainstream biker wear. But my upstate neighbor has gone the extra mile sartorially. He also sports a silver nose stud, linked by a chain to another stud in his left ear, from which depends a small silver cross. The chain is perfectly draped to follow the curve of his chiseled cheekbone. On his left boot only he wears a silver spur, with the rowel removed. In his right hand he fingers a petit corona, which he may well have been saving to smoke on just this occasion.

The dude, like most of the bikers, affects a tough obliviousness to the spectators. But down the line one brother, who obligingly poses for a snapshot, asks the sidewalk photographer, "Do you want mean-looking or nice?" The offer of this choice reassures me that the cyclists compose not some pack of road ragers hell-bent for leather, but rather a benignly wild bunch of recovering alcoholics who celebrate the fellowship we all believe is keeping us sober, if not always "nice." The signal comes to move it out, and hundreds of engines rev up. If the din isn't quite loud enough to raise the dead, it may be enough to get Dr. Bob's posthumous attention. After the lithe cycles roar past, the rear is carried up by five lumbering buses.

I was riding in one of those buses yesterday for the A.A. shrine circuit of Akron. The tour includes drive-by glimpses of the Mayflower Hotel, where William Griffith Wilson, the other A.A. cofounder, famously picked up the phone instead of a drink and saved his own sobriety by finding another drunk to talk to; the gatehouse at Stan Hywet, the estate of Goodyear's founder, where Bill W. and Dr. Bob first met through the good offices of Henrietta Seiberling; Saint Thomas Hospital, where Dr. Bob practiced proctology and where the resourceful Sister Mary Ignatia, a nun who seems to have stepped out of *The Bells of Saint Mary's,* abetted the surreptitious admission of alcoholics for treatment; the King School, home for many years of the first established A.A. meeting, Akron's Group Number One; the Smith home where Bill and Dr. Bob fervently planned an expansive future for their new partnership.

By car I later return for a closer look at Dr. Bob's house. Perched on a small corner lot in the gracefully aging suburb of Highland Square, where the streets are still paved with bricks, 855 Ardmore is a six-room, four-square, plain frame house of the sort endemic to midwestern towns. "Welcome home!" is the official greeting for every visitor, as if all of us were Akron prodigals. Three rooms down (parlor, dining room, kitchen) and three small bedrooms up, plus a bath, a full basement, and a gabled attic. The only exterior frill is a wide front porch, the large peaked roof of which is supported by brick columns. The interior, which has been restored to resemble its state in 1935, is nondescriptly furnished in late Victorian style. There is a touch of luxury in the brick fireplace at the end of the long parlor, which runs from the front to the rear of the house, and in the oaken molding and ceiling beams in the dining room.

This house, neither modest nor opulent, speaks of unadorned respectability. It recalls that Dr. Bob shared the stolidly simple ways of his Vermont ancestors, including their moral and verbal austerity. A video titled *Dawn of Hope* is screened for homecomers in the bedroom that once belonged to Bob's son, Smitty, who was often displaced to the attic during A.A.'s early days by the drunks his father brought home for aid and comfort. In a taped interview Smitty chucklingly recalls his first and only lesson from the doctor on sex education: "Flies spread disease, keep yours buttoned." Equally terse was the father's verdict on his son's adolescent infatuations: "You're not in love, you're in heat!" Such blunt sayings jibe with "Keep it simple," Dr. Bob's famous last words to Bill W. at their meeting, in this very house, during the summer of 1950.

A few days earlier, dying of prostate cancer, Dr. Bob had delivered the same message to an A.A. convocation in Cleveland. He got a "big thrill," he said, from surveying the sea of faces "with a feeling that possibly some small thing that I did a number of years ago played an infinitely small part in making this meeting possible." He was also

thrilled to realize that all the A.A.'s present had gotten "the same results in proportion to our zeal and enthusiasm and stick-to-itiveness."
Above all else, Dr. Bob stressed the pragmatic simplicity of the program, its bedrock of mutual love and service. "Let's not louse it all up
with Freudian complexes," he implored, "and things that are interesting to the scientific mind, but have very little to do with our actual
A.A. work."[1]

Dr. Bob's house is filled nearly beyond capacity now as bus after bus
rolls in. Pilgrims arrive here in all seasons, but denizens of this quiet
neighborhood must especially dread the horde for Founders' Day. (I
later heard that many leave town for that weekend.) Fraying tempers
are not in evidence, however, either among the residents or among
the curious alcoholics, who practice the patience and tolerance requisite for serenity amid so suffocating a swarm. The crowd is not
so thick in the backyard, where hot dogs and the ubiquitous A.A.
coffeepot may be found. The Akron Archives displays the mother of
all such pots, the one used by Anne Smith (Mrs. Dr. Bob) to make
coffee for the first A.A. meetings in their home.

While ancient A.A. history lives within Dr. Bob's house, modern
A.A. commerce thrives outside. The basement and detached garage
have been converted into souvenir shops full of recovery paraphrena-
lia. The proceeds go toward restoration and maintenance of 855 Ardmore, but the line of goods resembles that of the freelance profiteers
who surround the main parking lot back on campus and ply their
trade from the back of pickups and station wagons.

There, laid out on long tables, under plastic wrap when it sprinkles,
are heaps of caps, shirts, and sweats, stamped with A.A. slogans or
encoded with cryptic signs (for example, "Wilson-Smith University,
School of Hard Knocks") that are readily decipherable by true "Friends
of Bill." Unsold merchandise is, doubtless, recycled from year to year,
as A.A. sayings do not date. Some peddlers offer medallions and other
jewelry, some of it bearing the erstwhile A.A. symbol of a triangle
inscribed within a circle.[2] Amethyst, one hawker tells the prospective
buyer of a high-end item, is "the A.A. stone." This strikes me as shameless hype until I look up the word when I get home and discover that
"amethyst" literally means "against drunkenness."

Although Akron is Bob Smith's territory and although there is no
lack of reverence for him among the throngs who are touring his

house today, such devotion may border on the perfunctory for some
of the pilgrims. At the dorm this morning an Irish rummy from Manhattan, whose mental clock still seemed set to the New York minute,
urged me to hustle out to 855 Ardmore before it was overrun by bus
tourists. "I got all that over with yesterday," he exulted, as if honoring
Dr. Bob were merely obligatory.

And, indeed, the stiff and self-effacing Dr. Bob does not fire the A.A.
imagination as does his fellow Vermonter, the far more garrulous and
flamboyant Bill W. At the old-timers meeting that kicks off Founders'
Day on Friday evening—staged in the hallowed space of the University
of Akron's basketball arena—large portrait photographs of Bill and
Bob (and also Sister Ignatia) flank the speakers' platform. It looks a
bit like a cold-war Communist Party congress conducted under the
overbearing visages of Marx and Lenin, except that the A.A. portraits
are placed on the floor rather than hung imposingly from above. None
of the three women speakers, who range in sobriety age from thirty-
one to forty years, ever mentions Dr. Bob.

Having all-female "leads" (those who tell their stories) is an innova-
tion for this Founders' Day: a concession, perhaps, to the common
criticism that A.A. from the start has been predominantly male and
often sexist. Two of the speakers, extolling their A.A. "sponsors" (men-
tors), recall how difficult it was in the old days to find a woman for the
job. Twelve-Step wisdom calls for men to sponsor men and women to
sponsor women, lest an intimate relationship based on trust succumb
to the "Thirteenth Step" of mutual seduction. So the older men who
solicitously took younger female members in tow during the 1950s
warned them to guard their reputations carefully, to keep predatory
male members (a.k.a. "chicken pluckers") at arm's length. One of the
speakers was told that although it was quite all right for her to ride
with the men to distant meetings, she should never be the last to be
dropped off back at home.

Women in A.A. were expected to sit, this speaker muses, not with
the men, but rather with the nonalcoholic wives, who often attended
meetings in the days before Al-Anon, a program founded by Bill's wife,
Lois Burnham Wilson, for the independent recovery of "co-alcoholic"
mates. Apparently, A.A. wives did not always see much difference between the women they eyeballed in the A.A. rooms and the floosies
they suspected of inveigling their men in the barrooms. Of necessity,

then, the virtue of early A.A. women was proved by their becoming unthreatening gal pals to the old boys, much like the unsexed sidekicks to the romantic heroines of 1940s movies.

Two of the three women leads, as well as the female chair, brag of their long-standing marriages (up to half a century), and then make amiably feeble jokes about their hapless husbands. The third old-timer, who prefers the euphemism "long-timer," speaks instead of her enduring relationship to Bill Wilson himself. Formerly a member of the New York group, Joan B. recalls her 1966 meeting with the charismatic leader. Temporarily tending bar at a golf club in Montreal, she observed the arrival of a tall dark stranger, the letters on whose New York license plates disclosed his origins in suburban Westchester. The young woman, martini in hand, offered the guest a drink. "I haven't had a drink since 1934," says he. "Are you in A.A.?" says she. Says he, "I'm the founder!"

That Wilson's characteristic hyperbole—he was merely the *co*founder, after all—goes unchallenged at an A.A. anniversary in Smith's hometown is an indication of how fully Dr. Bob has been eclipsed by Bill W., at least in some A.A. circles. In the case of Joan B., Bill captured her loyal devotion for life. Later, in sobriety, she often consulted the (co)founder for advice about her work in alcoholism treatment. If not her sponsor exactly, Bill W. became for her, as for many others, an A.A. father figure, to be revered both in life and in death. Present at Bill's burial in 1971, Joan B. still makes an annual pilgrimage to the gravesite in East Dorset, Vermont. She also attends Founders' Day religiously. (At dinner earlier that evening I overheard a man propose that Founders' Day is like the hajj: at least once in a lifetime every alcoholic ought make a pilgrimage to A.A.'s Mecca.)

At the Saturday night meeting, which is the culminating event, the lead is Tom I., one of the celebrity speakers who retail their well-polished stories at A.A. gatherings from coast to coast. He echoes the truism that the fellowship brings together people who would ordinarily have little or nothing to do with each other and teaches them about their common humanity. The pilgrims to Akron *are,* in truth, remarkably diverse, considering the program's original homogeneity: middle-class, middle-aged, white men. There are significant numbers not only of bikers, but also of African Americans, of Spanish-speaking citizens (who hold their own meetings here), and of non-Americans.

Racial tension seems to have been suspended for the occasion, even when an Asian man on the tour bus ineptly jokes to two black men, as they head toward the only remaining seats in the rear, about their sitting in the back of the bus. "That's over," one of them firmly but peaceably retorts, as he nevertheless takes the last spot. "We don't do that anymore."

Disabled persons are fully accommodated at Founders' Day. So are smokers. These days, in fact, when people who light up are often put down, A.A. is one of the last refuges for the American smoker. (I myself finally quit six years ago.) Although tobacco prohibition is enforced to some extent by the University of Akron, especially in the dormitories where many of the visitors are staying, ashtrays have been laid out in the major public spaces, and the cloud of smoke in the cafeteria recalls the toxic levels at some windowless A.A. meetings I used to attend before most of them went smokeless under pressure from their landlords (who, most often, are churches willing to rent out their basements).

Aside from nicotine, the main drug of choice in A.A. is, of course, caffeine; and so it's deliciously ironic when the coffeemaker for the huge Saturday night meeting fails to show up, leaving a single belatedly brewed pot to serve a stadium full of patrons, some of whom are not amused by the oversight, or by the tight restrictions on smoking in the "open" air. For this climactic occasion, a crowd of ten thousand or more has assembled at Canal Park, Akron's brand-new downtown baseball stadium, home of the Aeros. This is the first time, in fact, that it has been possible to fit everyone attending Founders' Day into a single place at one time. In the past the campus basketball court was hooked up with remote sites by closed-circuit television.

Standing at a podium near second base, Tom I., the celebrity lead, recalls the excitement of his own first visit to Akron many years ago. What he most remembers, he says, is trying to put himself in Bill Wilson's shoes as he paced the lobby of the Mayflower Hotel on the eve of Mother's Day in 1935. One of the foundational legends of A.A., the tale of the Mayflower lobby was frequently retold by Bill W. himself, as well as by biographers and A.A. historians.

In its original 1939 version, which did not identify the experience as Wilson's own, the story went like this. Having lost a proxy fight that would have put his derailed business career back on the fast track, the newly sober Bill Wilson found himself marooned at the Mayflower Hotel with ten dollars in his pocket.

> One dismal afternoon he paced a hotel lobby wondering how his bill was to be paid. At one end of the room stood a glass covered directory of local churches. Down the lobby a door opened into an attractive bar. He could see the gay crowd inside. In there he would find companionship and release. . . .
>
> He was on thin ice. Again it was the old, insidious insanity—that first drink. With a shiver, he turned away and walked down the lobby to the church directory. Music and gay chatter still floated to him from the bar. (*AA*, 154)

Here is Wilson's later version, as published in his 1957 history of A.A.:

> On Saturday, Mother's Day eve, I was pacing up and down the hotel lobby, wondering what I could do. The bar at one end of my beat was filling up rapidly. I could hear the familiar buzz of conversation in there. Down at the other end of the lobby I found myself pausing before a church directory. Then I was seized with a thought: I am going to get drunk. Or no, maybe I won't get drunk; maybe I'll just go into that bar and drink some ginger ale and scrape up an acquaintance. Then I panicked. That was really a gift! I had never panicked before at the threat of alcohol. Maybe this meant that my sanity *had* been restored. I remembered that in trying to help other people, I had stayed sober myself. For the first time I *deeply* realized it. I thought, "You need another alcoholic to talk to. You need another alcoholic just as much as he needs you!" (*AACA*, 65–66)

Hence the redeeming urge to use the church directory to find a local member of the Oxford Group, the First-Century Christian Fellowship, in which Bill had gotten sober and to which he had tried to attract other alcoholics. One call led to another and ultimately to the fateful meeting the next evening, 12 May 1935, between Wilson and Smith.

For now, however, let's dwell on Bill W.'s turning point in the lobby. As Ernest Kurtz remarks, this incident and its aftermath constitute "the self-consciously supreme moment of A.A. history—often lengthily and romantically described" (*NG*, 258 n. 62). Nan Robertson similarly remarks: "Bill's recounting of this scene and all the events of the crucial weeks that followed form part of the oral history and shared legend of Alcoholics Anonymous. It is like A.A.'s own Christmas story, familiar and loved, which never palls in the retelling."[3]

First written down four years after the fact and frequently retold thereafter, the story was inevitably embroidered. Here, for instance, is Robert Thomsen's version, from his semiofficial 1975 biography:

> For a long while he sat considering his next move, then he rose and began to pace the lobby, from the elevators past the manager's desk to a row of telephones, then back along the same route.
>
> Directly across from his path of march was the entrance to the Mayflower Bar, and with every step he took he was growing more aware of the cool inviting darkness just beyond the entrance, the low din of male voices, occasionally interrupted by a girl's happy laugh, or the sweet crackling sound of ice in a cocktail shaker. Then came—as he may have always known they would—the words: Why not? Who would know? And what harm could one drink do? (BW, 235)

Obviously, the scene is more fully imagined here than it is in Wilson's relatively bare account. The "familiar buzz of conversation" has been elaborated into a mouthwatering evocation of intriguing voices and crackling cocktails. Bill's motives are also more fully psychologized, in an attempt to verbalize the thoughts that led him to prefer (barely!) the phone bank to the bar stool.

The same scene becomes even more deeply interiorized in a later authorized biography:

> Bill faced a solitary weekend in a strange city where he had just sustained a colossal disappointment. He had time on his hands and bitterness in his heart; fate had suddenly turned against him. His self-pity and resentment began to rise. He was lonely. He did not even have his colleagues as weekend company. Saturday noon found him pacing up and down the lobby of the Mayflower Hotel in extreme agitation, wondering how to pass the weekend. He had about ten dollars in his pocket.
>
> Now began the personal crisis that was to set in motion a series of life-changing events for Bill. There was a bar at one end of the lobby, and Bill felt himself drawn to it. Should he have a ginger ale or two, perhaps scrape up an acquaintance? What could be the harm in that? (PIO, 135)

Although this version hews to the original by borrowing Bill's exact language, the emphasis falls, as in Thomsen's account, on a fictive rendering of what Bill must have been thinking and feeling that afternoon.

After leaving the ballpark, I join some other pilgrims at the Mayflower Hotel, which is across the way, a couple of blocks from Bowery Street! Like Tom I., I am trying to put myself in Wilson's place as he prowled the lobby that long ago May Saturday. I am amazed to realize, however, that there is something slightly wrong with what I have always envisioned of the scene, the picture I have been led to draw by the narratives just quoted. Perhaps because they lay such stress on the internal contours of Bill W.'s crisis, all the stories, including Wilson's, overlook the topographical facts of the matter. There is a discrepancy between the original layout of the lobby and Bill's recollections.

Now a residential hotel, the Mayflower was once the jewel of Akron, whose present downtown has that vacant look so typical of commercially abandoned urban cores. A tall structure in art deco style, the building has two street entrances. From the canopied doors facing east toward South Main Street, one must climb a steep stairway to the lobby; on the southern State Street side, however, where the building follows the grade of a sharply rising hill, the ascent to the lobby is only a few steps. The lobby itself is octagonal, much smaller than I had expected, with a T-shaped extension, opposite the State Street door, leading toward the elevators; and there's a mezzanine level over the Main Street entrance.

I am confused when I first enter the lobby and try to get my bearings, in part because things have been moved around. The old church directory, for instance, is still hanging, but not in its original position. The main desk and the telephones have long since been removed. Fortunately, someone has taped up hand-lettered signs to indicate what was where in 1935. The front desk, which has been supplanted by a large painting of the nautical *Mayflower,* once stood opposite the stairway from the Main Street entrance. Thus in 1935 a guest reaching the lobby by those steps would have seen the desk straight ahead, the doors to the hotel dining room at the near left of the desk, the steps down to the State Street entrance at the far left, and, to the far right, the lobby extension leading to the elevators. The telephones were located on the eastern wall of the lobby extension; the church directory hung on the adjacent octagonal panel of the main lobby. Wilson would have seen the directory to his right just before he reached the phones, walking toward the elevators. If he had turned around at the top of the Main Street steps, he would have noticed a divided stairway rising half a level to the cigarette stand (now gone) and off to the right, in the front corner of the building, the Merryman Tavern (also gone, the space now soberly subdivided between the Buckeye Room for business meetings and the Shamrock Room for fitness machinery).

None of the several narratives of Bill W.'s moment of truth conforms to the actual configuration of the lobby in 1935. They all misleadingly depict Bill crossing between the elevator bank and the bar at opposite ends. Given the deployment of furniture in 1935 (according to an old photograph), so as to leave an aisle to the desk from the Main Street stairs, the only possible path for Bill to have paced ran north and south across the width of the lobby, with the elevators at one end. But what stood at the other end, past the desk in the middle, was the State Street entrance. *There was no bar on the same lobby level as the elevators.* It lay neither "down the lobby" (*AA*) nor "at one end of my beat" (*AACA*) nor "at one end of the lobby" (*PIO*) nor "directly across from his path of march" (*BW*). To enter the Merryman Tavern, Wilson would have had to climb seven steps to the mezzanine level, and he could not have seen inside without such an ascent. (This may account for the otherwise inexplicable emphasis in the accounts on bar *sounds* rather than alluring smells or sights.) Once Wilson had picked up the phone, moreover, a pillar would have blocked his view of the mezzanine. The phone bank, tucked around a corner of the lobby extension, would have provided him a sanctuary from ocular temptation.

These facts subtly but significantly change the psychology of the "self-consciously supreme moment of A.A. history." In the standard accounts, the battle between the drink and the phone is figured as a psychomachia, as if a good and a bad angel were perched on Bill's shoulders, vying for his very soul. That Wilson was pacing on a different level from the bar suggests to me that his succumbing to temptation would have required, *however slightly,* more decisiveness than it would had the bar been set right in his path, threatening to suck him through the doors.

Most recovering alcoholics in A.A. make a point of removing all the bottles from their homes, so that if the urge to drink ever comes over them, there will be nothing close at hand. The tedious business of fetching booze from the market or the package store can buy a drunk critical moments in such a pinch: time (*pace* T. S. Eliot) for a hundred indecisions, for a hundred visions and revisions, before the taking of a gin and tonic. Meanwhile the dreadful compulsion may safely pass. Likewise for Bill W. in 1935, the bilevel layout of the Mayflower lobby may have afforded him a slim psychological margin that might have tipped the balance in favor of his continued sobriety.

My point here is not to "debunk" the Mayflower story or to suggest that Wilson was not telling the whole truth about his own experience, strength, and hope. For one thing, he probably misremembered the scene in perfectly good faith, unknowingly deceiving himself as much as anyone else about the small details. Like his father before him, Bill W. was a spellbinding storyteller; and, as Robertson observes, he had a "lifelong penchant for embroidering the facts while accurately summarizing the gist of an event."[4] Thus his factual liberties may be regarded as acts of poetic license. Bill's imaginative rearrangement of the Mayflower lobby had the effect, whether intentional or not, of improving upon the facts: simplifying the narrative, intensifying its conflict, and heightening its suspense.

What is often forgotten about Wilson is that once he had retired from Wall Street and dedicated himself completely to Alcoholics Anonymous, he was primarily a writer. "Over the past twenty-five years," he proudly stated in the foreword to *As Bill Sees It* (1967), "it has been my privilege to write these books about A.A.: the text of 'Alcoholics Anonymous,' 'Twelve Steps and Twelve Traditions,' 'Alcoholics Anonymous Comes of Age,' and 'Twelve Concepts for World Service,' the last as part of our 'Third Legacy Manual.'" He goes on to say that, in addition, he has written many columns for the A.A. *Grapevine* and kept up "a large correspondence" with A.A. groups and individuals.[5]

Wilson was born in 1895, within two years either way of such writers and fellow drunks as Dorothy Parker, Dashiell Hammett, James Thurber, Edmund Wilson, F. Scott Fitzgerald, and William Faulkner. He was, after all, a member in good standing of the "lost generation" that came of age during Prohibition and revolutionized American literature, in part by their jaunty attitude toward drinking. Thus *Alcohol-*

ics *Anonymous* (1939), including "Bill's Story," belongs in the context of such alcoholic novels as Ernest Hemingway's *The Sun Also Rises* (1926), F. Scott Fitzgerald's *Tender Is the Night* (1934), John O'Hara's *Appointment in Samarra* (1934), Charles Jackson's *The Lost Weekend* (1944), and Malcolm Lowry's *Under the Volcano* (1947).

Although Wilson, a voracious reader, might have had some familiarity with the work of his modernist contemporaries, his own style remained decidedly late-Victorian, with a dash or two of the peppy business slang satirized with devastating effect by Sinclair Lewis in *Babbitt* (1922) and *The Man Who Knew Coolidge* (1926). As the first 164 pages of *Alcoholics Anonymous* have remained essentially unchanged from one edition to the next—stuck in time, as if it were sacrilege to tamper with this originary text—Bill's old-fashioned style continues to shape new members' perceptions of A.A. It is worth recalling that the Big Book was written early in the history of A.A., when there were only about a hundred members and when Wilson, the first of them to stop drinking, had only four years' sobriety. So recently himself on the road to excess, he had not, perhaps, fully entered the palace of wisdom.

Some members of A.A. may find such heretical thoughts about the cofounder and his first book to be as offensive as my deconstruction of Bill W.'s crisis in the Mayflower lobby. I am not advocating, however, that A.A.'s foundational legends be henceforth regarded as myth. Wherever the bar may have been on 11 May 1935, the heart of this story remains the reality of Bill's torment in fighting off a drink and his saving faith in talking to another drunk.

The (discarded) working title of this book, *In Quest of the Historical Bill W.,* echoed that of Albert Schweitzer's celebrated book, *The Quest of the Historical Jesus* (1906), in which he studied the unsettling efforts of French and German scholars in the nineteenth century to search out the Jesus of history, as distinct from the Jesus of faith. (Today the Jesus Seminar, which unravels New Testament fabric into its constituent threads, stirs up the same sort of controversy.) For Schweitzer, a believer, regrounding faith in recoverable historical facts was necessary to revitalizing Christian theology in the secular modern age. The quest of the historical Jesus also moved the Oxford Group to emulate, as far as possible, the practices of first-century Christians. And insofar as Bill Wilson, who was initially inspired by the Oxford Group, modeled A.A. on their example, Alcoholics Anonymous itself may also be said to have sprung from the root of biblical Higher Criticism.

In appropriating Schweitzer's title, my idea was not to suggest some blasphemous equivalence of Bill W. and Jesus Christ; rather to point out the similar evolution of a charismatic leader into an object of belief. What I suggest is that just as there is a gap between the historical and the divine Jesus, so there is a gap between the historical William Griffith Wilson and the legendary Bill W., who even in his lifetime, as Robertson points out, had become "a cult figure within the movement, a role he both dreaded and secretly desired . . . the Grand Poohbah of Alcoholics Anonymous."[6]

This book is an effort to rehumanize the cult figure, to reclaim Bill W. from A.A.'s fundamentalist tendencies to apotheosize the cofounder, to sacralize the Big Book, and thus to encumber the program with ecclesiastical trappings. Dr. Bob's admonition "Keep it simple!" leads me to a contrary desire: to recover, along with Bill Wilson himself, the unchurchly and often irreverent spirit of the A.A. fellowship during its apostolic era.

PART ONE

What We Used to Be Like

Bill's Elusive Childhood

When A.A. speakers tell their stories, they ordinarily follow the triadic formula suggested in "How It Works," a passage, often read at meetings, from the fifth chapter of the Big Book: "Our stories disclose in a general way what we used to be like, what happened, and what we are like now" (*AA*, 58). One measure of "recovery" in A.A. is how a given speaker adjusts the proportions among the three parts. "What we used to be like" is often the most colorful portion of an alcoholic's career, especially when the drunken years featured blackouts, prodigious hangovers, marital combat, death-defying car wrecks, drunken driving arrests, and the like. But dwelling too long on one's "drunkalog" is thought to suggest a lack of true sobriety; the battle of the bottle, however sensational in the retelling, lies in the past; the present focus should be attaining a purposefully *un*dramatic life without booze. Therefore those more advanced in A.A., whose bad old days are increasingly behind them, tend to foreshorten their narratives. A brief drunkalog serves only as a prelude to "what happened" (the turning point that led to A.A.) and "what we are like now" (the development of soberly spiritual values).

In the case of William Griffith Wilson, what he "used to be like" scarcely exists outside "Bill's Story," the account he first gave in *Alcoholics Anonymous* (1939) and then repeated often, with refinements and variations, at A.A. meetings throughout his life. About 1954, Wilson, along with other old-timers, also recorded his autobiography for the A.A. Archives. As Ernest Kurtz remarked in 1979, Bill's taped remembrances of things past (also available at one time in a hundred-page transcript)[1] "is virtually the only source for biographical data on the details of Wilson's life before 1934" (NG, 342); that is, before the conversion experience, early in Bill's fortieth year, that led directly to the foundation of Alcoholics Anonymous. Robert Thomsen, author of *Bill W.* (1975), and Nell Wing, A.A.'s first archivist, made, according to Kurtz, "large efforts productive of frustratingly small results to check and verify these autobiographical reminiscences in any case where such seemed possible" (NG, 342). The paper trail had nearly vanished; Wilson's past was largely lost to memory.

The situation improved a bit in 1984, with the publication of '*Pass It On*' (1984), an A.A.-sanctioned and anonymously written biography of Bill W. that contained a few new scraps, including childhood letters to his mother, recollections from relatives, and clippings from local Vermont newspapers. It remains unlikely, however, that Bill's youth and early manhood will ever be known in much more detail than he himself supplied. We are left, consequently, with a sketchy and partial portrait of the pre-A.A. Wilson, who closely guarded his private life during his public career, even as he seemed to bare his soul at A.A. meetings. Most of what *is* known, moreover, has been filtered through Bill W.'s not entirely reliable memory, and inevitably distorted by his legendary status as A.A.'s cofounder.

A dearth of information about a subject's childhood, or any other period, leads to gaps in the life-historical record, gaps that trouble the scrupulous researcher. "It is gaps that tempt the fledgling biographer to speculate, the 'artistic' biographer to invent, the scholarly biographer to give a lecture on history," cautions Paul Murray Kendall. "To fill gaps by wondering aloud, lying, padding—or simply to leave them for the reader to tumble into—is not to fill the shoes of a true biographer."[2]

A biographer is damned if he does and damned if he doesn't, Kendall implies. He has no choice but to fill the gaps, as artfully and truthfully as possible; but the tricks of the biographical trade, even in pursuit of veracity, introduce falsity as well. It matters, then, just how the gaps are "filled," for biography always teeters on the edge of becoming fiction. At the limit of wondering, lying, and padding, it is sometimes hard to tell the genres apart, to find much difference between fictual and factual stories, especially when the narrative does not merely chronicle a subject's transit from cradle to grave, but also gives shape and implicit meaning to his or her life's course.

In the earliest Wilson biography, for instance, Bill W.'s heroic role in A.A. has clearly affected Robert Thomsen's reconstruction of the cofounder's life, often by fictional devices. Although *Bill W.* adheres to Wilson's own taped memoirs, Thomsen does not hesitate to exceed the bare facts, entering his subject's mind at will and presenting events from his supposed point of view. That the book contains neither documentation nor index reinforces the notion that *Bill W.* is more of a biographical novel than a biography.

Thus Thomsen's first chapter, meant to set the prevailing tone of Wilson's youth (and, indeed, of his entire life), begins with a Hemingwayesque scene of male bonding in the face of boyish fears:

> When he stood beside his father Bill Wilson never felt too tall. He never felt skinny then or thought his ears stuck out too far and he was never afraid that he was going to do something awkward that would make people laugh and call him Beanpole. And now he was realizing this had been true whether they were walking in town, playing catch or—he turned to glance back at the little light shining from the shed at the quarry's entrance—whether he was just standing, waiting. If his father was nearby there was nothing to fear. But tonight—he couldn't help it—tonight everything was different, wild and dangerous and whatever his father was doing, he wished he'd hurry, come out and join him. (*BW*, 3)

Thrown into young Wilson's life at a critical juncture, the reader does not immediately grasp what is happening. All that's clear is Billy's severe self-consciousness, especially about his ungainly appearance, and his dependence on his father for emotional support.[3] Thomsen wants us to experience the boy's mounting anxiety about his father's mysterious absence, as well as his self-assuring reliance on paternal companionship and protection. Waiting outside the shed, at the mouth of the Rutland-Florence marble quarry near East Dorset, Vermont, where (as we learn) Gilman Wilson was the manager, the boy takes small comfort from the faint light that proves his father is still inside, going about his obscure business.

What's so "wild and dangerous" about this night is suggested by the boy's realization (in the second paragraph) that "never in his life had he been awake and out riding through the night when everyone else was sleeping." The manly thrill of flouting womanly rules— "many times he had been warned by his mother that God did not approve of nine-year-old boys being up past bedtime"—coexists, however, with a dread that such pious warnings may apply all too well in this situation, where "his mother and God had no connection with what was happening" (*BW*, 3).

Thomsen's opening pages strongly recall Ernest Hemingway's early fiction, particularly "Indian Camp," in which we witness the initiation of an innocent boy (Nick Adams) into adult experience. Hemingway thought he could gain intensity in his stories through radical editorial surgery, by lopping off their beginnings and/or endings, which, like amputated limbs, would remain somehow sensible even in their absence. In accordance with this strategy, he dropped the opening three pages of "Indian Camp" in which young Nick, like Billy Wilson, slowly succumbs to the illusive threats of the midnight hour away from home.

Left alone in the woods while his father and uncle go fishing, Nick gives way to irrepressible panic and fires the three alarm shots that he knows will summon the men to his aid. They suspect the boy's fears are imaginary, but they nonetheless indulge his weakness. At the root of Nick's terror, as "Three Shots" discloses, is his newly awakened sense of mortality. In church recently, a line from an old hymn ("Some day the silver cord will break") suddenly brought the boy to "realize that some day he must die. It made him feel quite sick. It was the first time he had ever realized that he himself would have to die sometime."[4]

Less explicitly, this same fear haunts "Indian Camp" in its (amputated) published form. Watching his father, a doctor, improvise a Caesarian delivery with a jackknife and fishing line, Nick also hears the Indian mother's horrific screams. It is just too much for her husband, who is discovered to have slit his own throat during the operation. Nick learns, in grim Hemingway fashion, about the simultaneity of birth and death. But he seeks to deny this dark knowledge by taking refuge in his father's comforting lie. "Is dying hard, Daddy?" "No, I think it's pretty easy, Nick. It all depends." At least under the special circumstances of father-son intimacy, fear of death can be held at bay: "In the early morning on the lake sitting in the stern of the boat with his father rowing, he felt quite sure that he would never die."[5]

For Billy Wilson, standing outside his father's shack (in about the same year in which "Indian Camp" is set), the immediate threat is not literal death so much as a mortal blow to childish faith and security. The emotional contours of Hemingway's fiction resemble those of Thomsen's "true" story. Both depict a nervous boy whose journey with his father into the wild leads to primal fear and an elemental revelation about life's tragedy—the proper response to which is seen to be manly stoicism. Thomsen reads Billy's mind as his father finally emerges from the shed, liquor jug in hand:

> His father was silent now as he had been before his mother, and Billy could see his silence was not weakness, it was strength. If he talked, if he'd felt he must put it all into words, it would have stirred up the ugliness, made it live again. Women and little children put everything into words. They had to. Men didn't. What was more, this silence, this acceptance, in no way changed his father or made him less. And suddenly, looking at the plain bony face in the moonlight, Billy was filled with a huge and beautiful emotion. He felt closer to his father than he'd ever felt to anyone; he felt a part of him. (BW, 9)

In this passage, told from the boy's point of view, there seems to be little or no ironic distance between the child's and the adult narrator's sense of values. Like Hemingway, Thomsen glorifies the modernist manly ideals of emotional withdrawal and disciplined silence. Exactly how the jug fits into this ideal is left implicit, but drinking is clearly associated with masculine bonding, the fusion of father and son in the face of cosmic fatality.[6]

Billy has no choice but to accept his fate, one way or another. The boy has often seen his mother's nagging exasperation with his father's drinking and lassitude. But this time, as the boy senses from his mother's tone, the quarreling is more ominous than usual.[7] "Something was going to happen and it had to do with him, with his father, and with the fact that no one in the world knew that they were here" (BW, 5). His father, it dawns on Billy, is preparing to leave home. "Gilly" Wilson, a taciturn Yankee, has stolen into his son's room and silently summoned him upon a midnight ride in order, again silently, to bid him

fond farewell. And also to charge him with becoming the new man of
the house. "You'll take care of her, won't you Billy?" Gilly is said to
have said, without really giving the boy any choice in the matter.
"You'll be good to your mother, and to little Dotty too" (BW, 8). De-
prived of paternal comfort and prematurely weighted with the mill-
stone of responsibility, the boy is also consumed by guilt. His parents'
quarreling and their separation must be, as Billy sees it, ultimately *his*
fault. Yet he has nowhere to turn except to the same father whose
inexplicable desertion has traumatized him. Riding the buggy home
in the wee hours, Billy, exhausted by the emotional upheaval, clings
to his father and falls asleep. He will never forget, Thomsen says, "the
feel of his father's coat" (BW, 11).

   Bill W. effectively mitigates the elder Wilson's actions—which from
another angle might be seen as grossly negligent and irresponsible—
by seeming to participate in his misogyny: the stubborn resistance,
passed from father to son, to female authority, deemed all the more
oppressive for its godliness, domesticity, and sober propriety. In Thomsen's view, which ultimately derives from Bill W.'s, Emily Wilson resembles the formidable Grace Hemingway, who became in Ernest's
memory an archetype of the castrating bitch-mother, a bloodsucking,
manipulative dominatrix who had ruthlessly brought her husband
whimperingly to heel and who had similar designs on her son's
manhood.

   Although Thomsen tries to be "fair" to Wilson's mother—explaining that her temperament unfortunately clashed with her husband's and that "she was perhaps constitutionally incapable of giving
the unquestioning adulation he and all Wilson men needed from their
women, and that indeed may have been all they needed" (BW, 17)—
still Thomsen's portrait of the marriage, faithfully following Bill W.'s
own bias, places Emily Wilson in a less than flattering light. Gilly's
message to his son, in so many words, seems to have been: if you were
married to that shrew, you'd drink too!

   Some time after Gilly's departure for British Columbia, where he
had secured another job in mining management, Emily took her children on a picnic to Dorset Pond (a.k.a. Emerald Lake) in order to
break the news as gently as possible that their father "wouldn't be
coming back—ever." Billy Wilson, in Thomsen's interiorized rendering, reacts to this announcement at first with denial—"He could hear

but he literally could not accept what she was saying"—and then with anger and resentment:

> Once when she rose to hand him a sandwich he turned and looked up at her, but now—it was the strangest thing—he wasn't seeing her as she was, standing above him, tall, handsome, with the afternoon sun shining on her hair; he was seeing her as she had been that evening when she'd taken him out behind the shed and had thrashed him with her hairbrush, when she had made him drop his trousers down so his bare bottom was exposed before her. He couldn't ever remember what he'd done to provoke that thrashing, but he remembered the wild anger in her eyes and his own impotent terror as he was forced to stretch his body out, awkward, naked and ashamed, across his mother's lap.[8] (*BW*, 20)

This primal scene of humiliation at the hands of a woman is used by Thomsen to epitomize Billy Wilson's relationship with his mother. No wonder that his first reaction to her devastating announcement is to find a way to reaffirm his own potency. Billy heads for the tallest tree in East Dorset, a giant oak, and climbs it higher than he's ever gone. Billy has never climbed this tree before, and he never will again. But from that night on, says Thomsen, "the feeling of the ancient oak, the sense of being sheltered in its arms, was seldom completely absent from his mind." It remained for him "a sort of symbol . . . a place he knew he could run to if and when this might be necessary" (*BW*, 22).

It could be argued that in such passages, Thomsen recognizes that Billy's anger was partially or wholly *displaced* from his father to his mother, anger that arose not only from the desertion, but also from the boy's resentment of the adult responsibilities laid upon his shoulders ("You'll take care of her, won't you, Billy?"). But the narrator gives no indication of differing from his subject's point of view. Thus although loss and abandonment are the keynotes of Bill Wilson's childhood, according to Thomsen, the biographer places much of the blame not on the errant father, but rather on the mother who found it necessary soon after the divorce to leave her children behind, to be raised by her own parents in East Dorset while she moved on to Boston to pursue a career in osteopathic medicine.

As Thomsen's narrative flashes back from the opening scene at the quarry to a brief family history, his aim is to suggest the fundamental and insuperable incompatibility of Bill Wilson's parents, who had little in common, after all, except their long Yankee lineages and their growing up together. This was a case, it seems, of opposites attracting and then colliding. The Wilsons, of Irish extraction, were a gregarious clan whose men, generation after generation, worked the quarries around East Dorset. The Griffiths, of Welsh extraction, were smart, hard-driving "loners" who sought professional success, which earned them respectability but never popularity. True to her Griffith heritage, Emily was a proud woman; she was also, Thomsen implies, a high-strung, hard, and unforgiving one, who increasingly soured on her husband's free and easy ways. By contrast, Emily seemed determined, with "her superior knowledge and training," to "analyze and then in some way dominate her circumstances" (BW, 16).

With her marriage in ruins, Emily Wilson remained "calm and completely herself, completely a Griffith," as she struck out on her own. A bright and determined woman of thirty-five—she had taught school before her marriage—"she could study, start over again and launch herself on a brand-new career." The unpleasant past could be touched up, if not entirely erased. She quietly obtained a divorce, using the services of a city lawyer, and she understated the grounds, making genteel reference only to her husband's "utter irresponsibility" (BW, 18). Of course, one part of the past could never be left behind her: the two children.

Emily's behavior may have been "impeccable"—"Everything she did, everything she said, was above reproach" (BW, 17)—but leaving Billy and Dorothy in the care of her parents for months at a time must have compounded their sense of loss. At least that is how it appears from a late-twentieth-century perspective, after decades of experience with proliferating divorce and its often dejected offspring. In 1905, in a small village such as East Dorset, where the Wilson children were nurtured both by close relatives and concerned friends and neighbors, it may be that the emotional damage was minimized. Kurtz points out that, in fact, "little evidence remains of how the lad interpreted his next separation—nor even, indeed, that it was necessarily traumatic at the time" (NG, 10). The lack of such evidence may be one reason Thomsen does not dwell on the matter, once he has shuffled Emily Wilson offstage to Boston. He focuses instead on young Bill's developing relationship with his grandfather, Fayette Griffith.

Before moving on to that, however, let's see how the other biography of Bill W. deals with the same formative period of his life. It should be noted, first, that *Pass It On* is far less fictive and interpretive than *Bill W.* Although the unnamed narrator's voice occasionally offers judgments, the book strives to be both anonymous in its authorship (which may, indeed, have been collective) and disinterested in its retelling of what Bill sardonically called his "bedtime story." *Pass It On* unlike *Bill W.,* identifies its sources, including some new ones, and provides proper documentation. Although this plain and slightly academic book may lack the imaginative flair of Thomsen's, it may also be more reliable.[9]

Despite Thomsen's liberties with the facts, his reading of Bill Wilson's relationships to his parents is generally supported by *Pass It On.'* Bill and his father were very close, it seems, but his attachment to his mother was quite another matter. *Pass It On,'* like *Bill W.,* mitigates Emily Wilson's decision to leave her children in order to pursue her education: "The effect on her family notwithstanding, this was a courageous undertaking for a woman of her age, in her time" (*PIO*, 27). But the book also paints her as forbidding and "disturbed." *Pass It On'* opens, in fact, with her painful recollection of Bill's birth on 26 November 1895. (It has become biographically obligatory to note the irony that Bill W. was born *behind the bar* of the Wilson House, a village inn run by his widowed grandmother.) In Emily's account the pain was no less than searing:

> When they brought you to me, you were cold and discolored and nearly dead, and so also was I, you from asphyxiation and I from painful lacerations and loss of blood, but I held you to me, close in my arms, and so we were both warmed and comforted—and so we both lived, but the memory of it all could not be clearer in my consciousness if it had been seared into my brain with a red-hot branding iron, for I was given no anesthetic while those huge instruments were clamped onto your head.[10] (*PIO*, 13)

However loving her intentions may have been in this letter, Emily implicitly blames her son for all her own suffering.

The young mother's ambivalence about childbearing—something quite reasonably to be feared in rural America in 1895—also comes through in a poem she wrote during her pregnancy. "A Welcome

Guest," which Emily sent to her sister and her mother, shows her trying to convince herself that the imminent infantile guest really *is* welcome. "When Baby comes!" reads one verse, "Methinks I see / The winsome face that is to be, / And old-time doubts and haunting fears / Are lost in dreams of happier years / Smiles follow tears" (*PIO*, 14). Emily offers no explanation of her "old-time doubts and haunting fears." But *'Pass It On'* conveys Bill's sense of her neuroticism: "my mother was having what they said were nervous breakdowns, sometimes requiring that she go away for extended periods to the seashore, and on one occasion to the sanitarium" (*PIO*, 24). Thus long before the parental rift became visible to the children, they lived under the cloud of their mother's female maladies: the severe depression (to which Bill became heir) that would likely have been diagnosed at the time as hysteria or neurasthenia, the standard treatments for which were travel and a rest cure.

Under the circumstances, Bill might well have perceived a gulf opening between himself and his frequently absent mother. Wilson's childhood letters to Emily, first printed in *'Pass It On,'* tend to support this hypothesis. In the earliest one, dated February 1902, the six-year-old Willie misses his mother, who at the time was spending more than six months in Florida with Dotty: "I would like to go too. If Papa would let me go with you." Willie's later letters press home the point: "I guess you will not know me when you come home . . . . When are you coming home?" (*PIO*, 19–20).

After the marital separation, Bill later said, he had "remained depressed for almost a year" (*PIO*, 25). He also stressed the severity of his psychic injury. He still shivered, he admitted, every time he thought about that picnic at Emerald Lake: "It was an agonizing experience for one who apparently had the emotional sensitivity that I did. I hid the wound, however, and never talked about it with anybody, even my sister" (*PIO*, 24). *'Pass It On'* speculates that "the divorce must have been painful beyond imagining." In a small and conservative New England town, "feelings of shame and disgrace" were probably aroused. Bill's wife Lois later claimed that it had "made him feel set apart and inferior to youngsters who lived with a mother and father" (*PIO*, 27).

After 1905, young Bill Wilson's life was recentered on his mother's parents rather than his own: Ella and Gardner Fayette Griffith. Uncle Fayette, as he was known, was a Civil War veteran who had struck it rich in the lumber business and also prospered from rental property in

East Dorset, as well as ownership of the village waterworks. Griffith's arrogance and affluence did not endear him to his neighbors, by whom (according to a cousin) "he was popularly considered a rather smug person" (*PIO*, 27). This tightfisted Yankee trader seemed a poor substitute for the affable Gilly Wilson; but Fayette Griffith, who had lost his only son to consumption in 1894, did his duty in providing his grandson with male example and comradery. An avid reader himself, Fayette encouraged Will to explore the world of books. Most of all he fostered the boy's scientific curiosity and gave him confidence in his intelligence. "Uncle Fayette thought Will was the smartest person that ever was," a relative recalled (*PIO*, 29). By setting the boy increasingly difficult challenges, the grandfather pushed him to ever greater feats of ingenuity.

The most famous of Will's experiments, which became an integral part of Bill W.'s A.A. stump speech, involved his construction of a boomerang. Intending to goad Will (then in his twelfth year), Fayette told him that "it says in this book that nobody but an Australian can make and throw a boomerang" (*PIO*, 29). The boy immediately rose to the bait and spent the next few months fiddling with a variety of designs and materials for the first American boomerang. His absorption in the project—this is one lesson of the anecdote—was developing into an obsession. Bill's grandmother, says Thomsen, was concerned about his neglect of chores and his plummeting grades at school. *'Pass It On'* quotes Bill W.'s own perception of the event: "But mine was a power drive that kept on for six months, and I did nothing else during all that time but whittle on those infernal boomerangs. I sawed the headboard out of my bed to get just the right piece of wood, and out in the old workshop at night by the light of the lantern I whittled away" (*PIO*, 30). Such single-mindedness seems to bear on Bill Wilson's later drinking career: the alcoholic adult was the lengthened shadow of the obsessive-compulsive child; even as a boy, Bill Wilson was prone to "power drives."

This tendency to excess bears also on the rest of the boomerang episode, the main point of which lies in its triumphal consummation and its emotional aftermath. All that planning and whittling led ultimately to a boomerang that really worked, as the boy deliriously demonstrated for his grandfather. Fayette celebrated Will's success by bragging about him all over town: "The very first American to do it. Our Willie. The number-one man" (*BW*, 36).

Bill reveled in all the approbation: "I remember how ecstatically happy and stimulated I was by this crowning success. I had become a Number One man." The mature Bill W. would see in this incident how "my willpower and yearning for distinction, later to keynote my entire life, were developed" (*PIO*, 30). Emotionally, he perceived, he "had begun the fashioning of another sort of boomerang, one that almost killed me later on":

> In that early period I had to be an athlete because I was not an athlete. I had to be a musician because I could not carry a tune. I had to be president of my class in boarding school. I had to be first in everything because in my perverse heart I felt myself the least of God's creatures. I could not accept this deep sense of inferiority, and so I did become captain of the baseball team, and I did learn to play the fiddle well enough to lead the high-school orchestra, even though it was a terribly bad band. I was the leader and lead I must—or else. So it went. All or nothing. I must be Number One. (*AACA*, 53)

Bill's understanding of his drive to be Number One seems to have derived from the idea, usually attributed to the Freudian apostate Alfred Adler, of the "inferiority complex" and its compensatory counterpart, the "superiority complex." Although feelings of inferiority are humanly universal, according to Adler, there are certain persons (neurotics) who have a magnified sense of inferiority that "permeates the whole personality." In such cases, "It is more than a complex, it is almost a disease whose ravages vary under different circumstances." The damage is done by a vicious psychological circle. Human beings cannot endure feelings of inferiority for very long. And if there are no realistic means to alleviate such feelings through some kind of action, then the chronically "inferior" person will seek other, self-destructive, remedies:

> His goal is still "to be superior to difficulties," but instead of overcoming obstacles he will try to hypnotize himself, or autointoxicate himself, into *feeling* superior. Meanwhile his feelings of inferiority will accumulate, because the situation which produces them remains unaltered. The provocation is still there. Every step he takes will lead him farther into self-deception, and all his problems will press in upon him with greater and greater urgency. The real feelings of inferiority will remain . . . .They will be the lasting undercurrent of his psychic life.

In striving to be "superior to difficulties," a sufferer from an "inferiority complex" may spin out escapist fantasies of personal supremacy that constitute the "superiority complex." "He assumes that he is superior when he is not, and this false success compensates him for the state of inferiority which he cannot bear."[11]

It is possible that the bookish Wilson encountered these notions in Adler's best-selling popularizations of his theories, published during the late 1920s and early 1930s, when Bill W. himself was sinking ever deeper into "autointoxication." He could easily, in any case, have picked up the inferiority/superiority idea at second hand. Whether psychoanalysis really did hold the key to his "whole personality," the biographies of Bill W. adopt Adler's theory as if it had explanatory power—thus gainsaying Dr. Bob's deathbed wisdom for A.A.: "Let's not louse it all up with Freudian [or Adlerian!] complexes."

Of course, insofar as any biography may attempt to explain its subject's "interiority," a biographer must depend on one or another psychological theory, including the psychoanalytic concepts that were seeping into American popular consciousness during Wilson's lifetime. The point here is simply that his own idea of alcoholism was tightly bound up with Adler's idea of the inferiority and superiority complexes. To smash the vicious circle of autointoxication, Bill W. would later realize, required what he called (claiming to borrow the term from William James) "deflation at depth": a shrinkage of the self-aggrandizing ego that would produce a realistic and more positive assessment of self-worth.

As Wilson pointed out, his youthful self-esteem was raised not only by scientific triumphs, and later by athletic and musical exploits, but also ("despite my homely face and awkward figure" [PIO, 35]) by adolescent romance. In the fall of 1909, Bill had entered Burr and Burton Academy, a boarding school in the resort town of Manchester, Vermont. During the spring of his junior year in 1912, Bill fell "ecstatically in love," as he said, with Bertha Bamford, a classmate and the daughter of the local Episcopal minister (PIO, 35).[12] A beautiful, brainy, and popular girl, Bertha must have seemed well out of reach for the "homely" Bill Wilson, but they proved to be soul mates. Bertha's parents warmed to Bill just as he warmed to them. Here at last came the perfect fulfillment of a young man's fancies. The older Wilson psychologized the moment in Adlerian terms:

Well, you see, at this period, now that I am in love, I am fully compensated on all these primary instinctual drives. I have all the prestige there is to have in school. I excel—indeed, I'm Number One where I choose to be. Consequently, I am emotionally secure; my grandfather is my protector and is generous with my spending money; and now, I love and am loved completely for the first time in my life. Therefore, I am deliriously happy and am a success according to my own specifications. (*PIO*, 35)

In *Bill W.* Thomsen exploits this youthful romance for all its heart-rending sentiment. Taking off from Bill's meager description, Thomsen puts us inside the feverish mind of the young lover as he experiences a cosmic consciousness he has felt before only in the presence of his star-gazing father. Too excited to sleep, Bill supposedly went to his window, looked upon the empty streets, and contemplated his neighbors: "He knew them all and he loved them in a way he'd never known or loved before. For now, through a process that had nothing to do with thinking, he realized they were people who themselves had once loved, who like him were filled with hungers and desire" (*BW*, 60). This passage, reminiscent of George Willard's adolescent attitudinizing in Sherwood Anderson's *Winesburg, Ohio* (1919), is entirely fictive. Thomsen continues in the same vein, tenderly ventriloquizing Bill's point of view. Here the young Wilson becomes a Whitmanesque seer afoot with his vision:

And some nights his imaginings would lead him even beyond the town. He could see his mother in Boston, shut in her room, sitting at a table, poring over her books, and to the west, his father walking in the night, always walking, walking and wanting more. Now he could even picture people he didn't know: young men in cities studying, lost in the agonies of concentration, and some out on lonely farms and ranches, others crossing the continent on trains, riding through the night, all wanting more. (*BW*, 60)

Thomsen builds up Bill's love affair with Bertha Bamford so as to maximize the impact of its tragic denouement: what '*Pass It On*' calls "a blow as cruel and unexpected as the separation of his parents" (*PIO*, 35). Bill, whom no one thought to tell privately, in advance of the public announcement, received the devastating news along with everyone else at Burr and Burton in daily chapel on 19 November 1912:

Bertha had died the night before, following routine surgery in a New York City hospital.

Thomsen treats the tragedy poetically, in light of *Romeo and Juliet*, the supreme literary expression of young love lost. He places Bill at Bertha's crypt, trying "to recall the ending of the play. Romeo, thinking Juliet was dead, had killed himself, but then Juliet awakened and . . . his mind went blank; he couldn't remember" (*BW*, 62). The version in '*Pass It On*,' following Wilson's own guarded telling of the story, is notably more restrained and prosaic. This, he reflected, was "simply a cataclysm of such anguish as I've since had but two or three times." As Bill's grief settled into unrelieved despair, he suffered "an old-fashioned nervous breakdown, which meant, I now realize, a tremendous depression" (*PIO*, 35).

Young Wilson also felt all his faith in providence slipping away. He had discovered, according to *Bill W.*, that all his loving "didn't matter a good goddamn"; it "meant nothing to the terrible ongoing forces of creation" (*BW*, 63). He had discovered his radical powerlessness over his own and others' destinies. He had also discovered his proclivity for depression and begun his search for an emotional anodyne.

Bill's First Drink

T W O

Many an A.A. testimony begins with the speaker's remembrance of taking the first drink—which, of course, was also the first step on the slippery slope that led to the "bottom" that is deemed prerequisite to "recovery." The sober alcoholic's first drink, then, recalls the Christian paradox of the fortunate Fall (*felix culpa*). Without the original sin of Adam and Eve and their expulsion from the Garden, there would have been no need for divine redemption and thus no possibility of a heavenly city that transcends the edenic paradise lost. When some A.A.s introduce themselves as "grateful recovering alcoholics," what they mean is that without the fall into alcoholism, there would have been no salvation in sobriety; without the nightmare of drinking, they would never have found a life in Alcoholics Anonymous that is, as the A.A. maxim has it, "beyond our wildest dreams." In that sense, then, they are truly grateful not only to be "recovering," but also to be "alcoholics."

Given its symbolic importance in A.A., it might be supposed that an alcoholic's memory of his or her first drink would be indelible. But the immensity of the event is perceived only in retrospect; and, in fact, many A.A.s have no exact idea when they started, often because they were raised in an environment so saturated with alcohol that drinking seemed as unremarkably natural as breathing. For many drunks the memory of their first drink is analogous to what Freud called a "screen

33

memory," a recollection that has been unconsciously reworked. It's not that A.A. speakers routinely lie about their past; it's that they respond to strong peer pressure to recall their first drink by producing an appropriate memory.

In my own case, for instance, I have no idea when I first imbibed. Although I didn't hang out with the drinking crowd in my suburban high school (which, as I learned much later, was located just a few miles from Bill and Lois Wilson's home), it must have been during those years that I first sampled beer. For all I remember, I may have tried hard liquor, too. But I drank very sparingly, and I don't recall ever getting drunk. In *my* A.A. story, I usually gloss over these foggy and prosaic origins of my drinking career and focus instead on a narratively superior version of my first drink.

I was barely unpacked at a certain Ivy League campus, I say, when I attended a cocktail party given by my official faculty adviser, a notorious drunk, for incoming freshmen. On this occasion, as on many others, he had concocted a potent bourbon-based punch, the secret recipe for which he freely dispensed to inquirers. (One New Year's Eve, when I was in graduate school, I mixed up a batch that laid everyone low.) The punch introduced me to whiskey. More to the point, it was also my entree to what I then envisioned as the glamorous ambiance of the drinking world, in which true collegiate sophistication seemed to consist of suavity about all things alcoholic. I soon learned, for example, that scotch should be my drink of choice because it would not "sneak up" on me as gin or vodka could. You always know where you are with scotch, I was told; so you can always "control" your state of inebriation. (After a decade of drinking it, however, knowing where I was did not deter me from moving on to wherever another scotch might take me.) I was only seventeen at the time of this cocktail party—that is, below the legal drinking age in that state—but I deeply felt, as indeed I was meant to feel, transformed by my double initiation into booze and boola boola.

In the first biography of Bill Wilson, there is a certain ambiguity about his alcoholic initiation. Robert Thomsen devotes most of a chapter to Wilson's first encounter with a barroom. This occurred during his early adolescence, in the company of Mark Whalon, a boon companion who was ten years older than Bill.[1] Mark, a college boy given to cracker-barrel philosophizing, evinced the sophistication, intellectual and otherwise, to which Bill aspired. The friends often rode along together in Mark's delivery wagon, spelling each other in deep conversation. Mark was especially talkative about the rigid class structure of their home town, a topic in which Bill took keen interest because of his own sense of exclusion at boarding school.

One lazy summer Saturday, late in the afternoon, on the way home from making a delivery in Denby, Vermont, Mark suggested that they stop off at a wayside inn to have a drink. Once Bill had adjusted to the dim lighting and boisterous banter, he felt remarkably well at ease: "As they stepped through the door they were greeted by the warm, friendly smell of wet sawdust, spilled beer and whiskey" (BW, 49). More important, he was immediately swept up into a cheerful male comradery that seemed oblivious of class or other divisive distinctions. Here was an idyll of American democracy: a New England town meeting purged of politics and pesky womenfolk. Bill, according to Thomsen, fit right in:

> They stayed on in the tavern for maybe a couple of hours. It was already getting dark when they went outside, but Bill felt nothing but a crazy happy feeling of lightness. He had laughed so hard and so much, the muscles of his stomach ached, but his whole being was relaxed. Mark was a little drunk, he guessed, but that didn't matter; the horse knew the way and the night was crisp and this new happiness lasted all the way back to East Dorset.
>
> Just as a song may sometimes leave an echo and keep returning for no discernible reason, Bill kept remembering that afternoon and his feeling of being at home, his feeling for the men. Sometimes he could think of nothing else. He wanted it again. (BW, 51)

While Mark got "a little drunk," Bill reached a comparable state of intoxication apparently without benefit of alcohol. Thomsen reports that someone "handed Bill a mug of cider" as he entered the tavern (BW, 49), but he leaves the proof of the cider unspecified.

Thomsen distinguishes, in effect, between picking up a drink and feeling intoxicated. With an alcoholic beverage, of course, one may lead to the other in a direct causal sequence; but just as consuming alcohol does not always result in drunkenness, so intoxication may exist in the absence of alcohol. Bill's quaffing cider, whether hard or soft, may have been less important than his drinking it in the barroom setting. What was "addictive" for young Bill—what left him so obsessed that "sometimes he could think of nothing else"—were the tavern's comfortingly homey atmosphere and its radically democratic ethos. These same features, not coincidentally, were later to characterize Alcoholics Anonymous.

The conclusion to be reached from Thomsen's account is, evidently, that Bill Wilson's alcoholism was founded on his psychological insecurities. An unusually unsettled childhood had left him vulnerable to alcohol, which promised instantly to relieve his awkwardness, his loneliness, and his depression; in short, to cure his inferiority complex. In principle, Thomsen implies, Bill might not have become alcoholic if he had found some other means to fill his emotional needs, some natural high to satisfy his cravings for the intoxication of the barroom.

Given the prominence of this tavern episode in Thomsen's account, it is surprising to find it omitted entirely from the official A.A. biography, 'Pass It On,' in which we are told merely that Mark Whalon was a "sort of uncle or father" to Bill, with whom he worked, hunted, fished, and talked together. "Later, they would drink together, although Mark's drinking never progressed into alcoholism" (PIO, 49). In fact, 'Pass It On' emphatically denies that Bill touched a drop before 1917; that is, before his hitch in the U.S. Army. "Until that time, he had never had a drink. The Griffiths did not drink, and there was a family memory of what alcohol had done to some of the Wilsons. Bill, who thought it may have been one of the reasons for his parents' divorce, was afraid of liquor" (PIO, 55).

The logic here seems shaky. There are plenty of drunks whose lives have been ravaged by parental alcoholism who nevertheless (consequently?) experiment with drinking. Given the demonstrably strong linkage of bibulous fathers and sons—a theme that Thomsen stresses in Bill W.—it would seem likely, despite protestations to the contrary, that young Bill did try drinking sometime during his adolescence.

In any event, Bill's initial experience of alcoholic intoxication was preceded by the ecstasy of romance. Bill's loss of his alcoholic virginity coincided, in fact, with the beginning of his married life.

In her memoirs, Lois Burnham Wilson recalls how a nodding acquaintance with Bill Wilson, who was four years her junior, blossomed into love during the summer of 1914. A year later Bill was prompted to pop the question when a rival suitor arrived in Vermont, but the couple kept their betrothal secret for a while. The eldest child of a prominent and wealthy New York physician, Lois would accompany her big happy family to their upcountry "camp" on Emerald Lake. Doctor Burnham's practice was divided between Brooklyn and East Dorset, and many of his urban patients annually followed him, for months at a time, into rustication.

Lois, therefore, was one of the "summer people": those set apart from (and to some degree set above) the natives, even those, like Bill Wilson, who belonged by birth to what passed for gentry by local standards. "She represented areas in which I had always felt a great inferiority," Bill later said, exaggerating the contrast between Miss Burnham's refinement and the crudity of his neighbors. "She had social graces of which I knew nothing. People still ate with their knives around me; the back door step was still a lavatory. So her encouragement of me and her interest in me did a tremendous amount to buck me up" (PIO, 39). In terms of social standing, Lois Burnham was even a notch or two higher than Bill's first love, Bertha Bamford, daughter of a Manchester clergyman. Bill's courtship of Lois was, in effect, an avenue to his upward mobility; winning the hand of the rich doctor's daughter would be one more way to prove himself a Number One man.

But Bill's chief attraction to Lois was obviously emotional. He fell in love with a beautiful, vivacious, and highly educated young woman (Packer Collegiate Institute in Brooklyn, plus two years of art school in New York), who not only handed him the key to her heart, but also opened a door to the nurturing family life he was lacking. Her parents and five siblings embraced Bill as one of their own, and he basked in the glow of their acceptance. "From my parents' standpoint," Lois recalled, "Bill was hardly a brilliant prospect as a son-in-law. He was only twenty years old, still in college, with no profession in view except the Army. But they liked him. Everybody did. And they loved me, their daughter, and respected my choice. When we told them about our engagement, they seemed surprised but happy" (LR, 16).

Bill's romance with Lois came at a time when he had been severely depressed: "She lifted me out of this despond, and we fell very deeply in love, and I was cured temporarily, because now I loved and was loved and there was hope again" (PIO, 40). Wilson's dark mood may have been accountable in part to his lingering grief over Bertha Bamford; but throughout his life, even in sobriety, he suffered crushing periodic depressions that were not merely situational. During the summer of 1914, when he first courted Lois he was unable to bear the thought of returning to school.

Bill's grades had slipped during his troubled final year at Burr and Burton, but he had managed to graduate in 1913 by making up some failed courses. After a trip with his grandfather to a reunion of Civil War veterans, upon the fiftieth anniversary of Gettysburg, he then joined his mother and sister in the Boston suburb of Arlington, where Doctor Emily Wilson was now practicing osteopathic medicine. Bill enrolled in the Arlington high school during 1913–14, taking a special curriculum designed to prepare him for the entrance examinations then required by the elite colleges to which he, with maternal prodding, aspired. Emily assumed that her scientifically gifted son was destined to become an engineer, and so Bill dutifully took the demanding tests for the Massachusetts Institute of Technology. He performed so poorly, however, that he quickly retreated from the heights of MIT to the lowlands of Norwich University, a strict but unprepossessing military academy not far from home in Northfield, Vermont.

Just before Bill's freshman year began, in the shadow of impending world war, he spanned the continent by train, traveling to British Columbia to visit his father for the first time in eight years; for the first time, that is, since he had been a child. Gilman Wilson had remade his life, rising to a position of authority in the mining business. He was so well liked and respected that some of his old hands from Vermont had gone west to work for him again. Bill's visit ostensibly went smoothly, at least according to his upbeat letters to Grandmother Wilson. The prodigal Gilly seemed delighted to see his son, eager to mend their damaged relationship. Despite the inevitable ambivalence he felt toward his father, Bill was undoubtedly happy to rejoin him.

The visit, however, was also fraught with anxiety for the introverted Bill, whose childhood bond to Gilly had been cemented by their common weakness in the face of Emily Wilson's forbidding strength. Bill, according to Thomsen, found he could not confide in his father as he used to do. He felt alienated from Gilly's bluff optimism, his unreflecting contentment and, above all, his new self-possession, which contrasted so painfully with the young man's gloomy insecurity. "Gilly was a man in charge now, in charge of his men, his place in the world, and in charge of himself. And possibly it was this that Bill had not expected" (*BW*, 72). Whereas the formerly hangdog husband had escaped the termagant for good, her son clearly had not. During their last night together, the father confided his plans for remarriage: to Christine Bock, "an attractive, round-faced woman just Gilly's age, who had been a schoolteacher" (*BW*, 73). Reaching out to his father and then withdrawing to Vermont must have revived Bill's sense of abandonment and intensified his desire for consoling male intimacy.

In this emotionally charged context, it was particularly painful for Bill to suffer a difficult transition into college. Having been a somebody in high school (concertmaster of the orchestra, star pitcher of the baseball team, president of his class), he was now a nobody who lacked the musical, athletic, and personal gifts to compete at this level. It was especially galling that, as Bill W. later remembered, he had been passed over by every fraternity at a fraternity-centered school.

There is some doubt about this memory, however. Without attempting to explain the discrepancy, *'Pass It On'* finds "a very different picture" in Bill's letters to his mother from the fall of 1914. To her he boasted that no fewer than four fraternities were beating down his door; three had already made bids. But he had decided to hold out for a while, to get the lay of the land socially. Months later he wrote: "Can't seem to get away from being popular. Have had second invitations to all the frats. But think it policy to stall. Just the minute you join a frat, you join more or less of a clique." Bill reasoned that since fraternity networks often proved instrumental to advancing one's later military career, he would be better off playing the field and not joining any single house. Instead he would "stand more on his own merits" and take advantage of his general popularity "with men of the strongest frats here" (*PIO*, 44).

So which is it? Was Bill Wilson the lion or the leper of his freshman class at Norwich? It is certainly possible that he was putting on a false front in these letters, masking failure from a mother who expected (in fact, demanded) only reports of success. According to Thomsen, Bill was constantly reminded that "life had not treated Emily Wilson gently." Having herself prevailed over her misfortunes, she expected no less from her son than "the proper mental attitude"; indeed, "whenever they happened to be separated during this period, she wrote Bill long letters with the word 'succeed' in every paragraph" (*BW*, 71). The gambit about strategically choosing *not* to join a fraternity may well have been a face-saving rationalization. Or, perhaps, the older Bill W. painted his youthful experience blacker than it really had been. The truth here, as in many aspects of Wilson's life, will remain elusive, for lack of corroborating evidence.

What matters most is that although Bill was thriving academically,[2] he was unhappy at Norwich; and his misery was manifested in physical symptoms (heart palpitations, shortness of breath, indigestion) that proved to have no somatic basis. The symptoms were classically "hysterical." Bill's problems began when he slipped on some ice and fractured his elbow. As bones were his mother's specialty, he naturally turned to her for treatment and then recuperated at her Arlington home. But when it was time to go back to Norwich, Bill suddenly developed his "heart" attacks, which persisted for weeks after his return. By February 1915, he could carry on no longer, and it was agreed that he would postpone his education for a year. Wilson was remanded to the care of his mother's parents in East Dorset, where his debility lingered. Bill W. later wrote that "it required no profound knowledge of psychiatry to understand what had been going on. He saw no reason to live; a part of him wanted to die; but another part was terrified by the thought of death" (*BW*, 76).

This was the "despond" from which Lois rescued Bill during the summer of 1915. The following winter of 1916, he reentered Norwich University, only to be suspended for the term, along with his classmates, as the result of a hazing incident in which he was only peripherally involved. Because no one would take responsibility, and no one would finger the perpetrators, the entire class was punished. In June 1916, however, when the Mexican Revolution led to border troubles, Bill's class was suddenly mobilized as part of the Vermont National Guard and thus fortuitously reinstated at Norwich.

During the balance of his college career, curtailed by a year when the United States entered the Great War in 1917, Bill became an increasingly bigger man on campus. He was gratified to have his leadership qualities finally recognized by military promotions. But when called to active duty, he vacillated between soldierly zeal and private dread of putting himself in jeopardy just when he finally had something to live for: "the thing that scared me most was that I might never live my life out with Lois, with whom I was in love." In order to minimize his risk, Bill volunteered for the Coast Artillery, reputedly "one of the safer branches of military service" (*PIO*, 54). (He never quite forgave himself for what later seemed to him an expedient and cowardly choice.) After officer's training school at remote Plattsburgh, New York, Wilson received more instruction at Fort Monroe, Virginia, where he was commissioned a second lieutenant and then assigned to Fort Rodman, Rhode Island, over the state border from New Bedford, Massachusetts.

It was here, so the story goes, that Bill Wilson picked up his first drink late in 1917. "War fever" in this seaport town blurred the sharp class lines that Bill used to discuss with Mark Whalon. Amid public adulation of the doughboys in their valiant mission of saving democracy from the Hun, high-toned parlors that were ordinarily closed to the likes of rustic Bill Wilson now were opened to Lieutenant Wilson, the noble warrior. "We were flattered," he recalled, "when the first citizens took us to their homes, making us feel heroic. Here was love, applause, war; moments sublime with intervals hilarious" (*AA*, 1).

In the home of one such leading family, the Grinnells, Bill was offered a heady Bronx cocktail, which he downed nonchalantly, despite his ingrained fear of drinking:

> Well, my self-consciousness was such that I simply had to take that drink. So I took it, and another one, and then, lo, the miracle! That strange barrier that had existed between me and all men and women seemed to instantly go down. I felt that I belonged where I was, belonged to life; I belonged to the universe; I was a part of things at last. Oh, the magic of those first three or four drinks! I became the life of the party. I actually could please the guests; I could talk freely, volubly; I could talk well. (*PIO*, 56)

When Wilson retouched this oral testimony for publication in 1957, the revised account placed even greater stress on the power of alcohol to dissolve his isolation, to relieve his excruciating self-consciousness, and to transport him into the social mainstream. "Ah, what magic! I had found the elixir of life! Down went that strange barrier that had always stood between me and people around me. My new companions drew near to me and I drew near to them. I was part of life at last. I could talk easily, I could communicate. Here was the missing link!" (AACA, 54).

As Wilson recalled, he had gotten "thoroughly drunk" from those initiatory cocktails, and "within the next time or two, I passed out completely" (*PIO*, 56). His drinking, that is, immediately became habitual and excessive; and although heavy boozing was certainly not untypical among his comrades-in-arms, Bill's drunkenness was still conspicuous. During one visit to New Bedford, Lois was horrified to learn how Bill, who moderated his consumption in her presence, had fallen unconscious during a spree: "his Army buddies told me they had dragged him home and put him to bed. There I found him, dead to the world, with a bucket by his head." During their engagement, Bill sometimes had "gone with the boys to the saloons, but while they drank beer, he sipped ginger ale, sarsaparilla or birch beer." Now he was more than keeping pace at the bar. Although Lois was alarmed, she was "only slightly unhappy," convinced that after their marriage she would "persuade him to return to his former abstinence. I could 'fix' him" (*LR*, 22–23).

Bill later suggested, in a moment of psychoanalytical self-analysis, that a maternal element lay at the heart of his relationship with Lois. "At the unconscious level, I have no doubt she was already becoming my mother, and I haven't any question that that was a very heavy component in her interest in me. . . . I think Lois came along and picked me up as tenderly as a mother does a child" (*PIO*, 40). This view accords with the classical Freudian "explanation" of alcoholism as an "oral fixation," a regressive desire for the mother's nurturance.[3] Whatever the marital dynamics, the Wilsons were burdened from the start with Bill's drinking.

The wedding ceremony, originally planned for 1 February 1918, was moved up a week when rumors flew of the impending embarkation of Bill's unit, the 66th Coast Artillery. As it turned out, the couple had six rapturous months together, mostly at Fort Adams near Newport, Rhode Island, before Bill was finally shipped overseas in July. While her new husband was abroad, Lois Wilson did her own part on the home front. She enrolled for training as an occupational therapist, a new profession at the time. She was assigned to the shell-shock ward in Washington's Walter Reed Hospital, where she became all too familiar with "what war does to young men" as she wondered "what it was doing to Bill" (*LR*, 26).

There was really no cause for concern; Lieutenant Wilson never saw combat. After his battery was detained in England because of the influenza epidemic of 1918, Bill arrived in France during the final weeks of the war. Posted to a mountain village far from the front, he was in considerably less danger from the enemy than from his own errant gunners, who once nearly blew him up during target practice. Wilson stayed in place when the armistice was signed in November and remained on active duty until May 1919.

Unlike some members of the lost generation—particularly the literary cohort that included Ernest Hemingway, John Dos Passos, William March, and Edmund Wilson—Bill Wilson escaped the soul-searing carnage in the trenches; and he felt no urge to question either his own patriotism or the wisdom of the political elders, whom the modernist writers denounced as cynical warmongers. To Bill, stuck in his mountain village, all such serious matters were irrelevant. The challenge was merely to fend off boredom; and with so much time on his hands and so much wine in the local cellars, Bill took full advantage of the situation. Although his drinking did not, Lois believed, "interfere much with his military career," it did "prevent his writing as many letters as I longed for" (*LR*, 26 and 27).

After Bill was mustered out, he moved with Lois into her parents' brick row house at 182 Clinton Street, Brooklyn, and prepared to launch what he assumed would be a glorious career at something-or-other. "I fancied myself a leader," he later said, mocking his own youthful conceit, "for had not the men of my battery given me a special token of appreciation? My talent for leadership, I imagined, would place me at the head of vast enterprises which I would manage with the utmost assurance" (*AA*, 1). Lacking a college degree or any vocational skills, Wilson found himself floundering in the tough postwar job market.

During his troubled adjustment to civilian life, Wilson was moved to question the same corporate order of American life that aroused the wrath of his modernist contemporaries in their bitter postwar writings. Bill strained so hard against his conservative Yankee grain, in fact, that he briefly fancied himself a socialist. His next step was actually to join the proletariat, laboring with a sledgehammer on the New York Central Railroad's piers for sixty-one cents an hour. But when he was pressured to join the union, he balked: "Well, I wasn't so socialistic now . . . and I left the job rather than join the union." His drinking, all the while, "had been crawling up" (PIO, 63).

On one memorable occasion when he was just out of the army, Bill and fellow veteran Rogers Burnham (his brother-in-law and best man at his wedding) guzzled their way through a stockpile of bottles presented to Doctor Burnham by his grateful patients. "Rogers seldom got drunk," Lois recalled, "but this day he and Bill made a shambles of the cellar and got deathly sick. It upset the whole household, but the returned heroes were readily forgiven" (LR, 27). Although Lois shared her family's indulgence of Bill's increasingly obnoxious habits, she worried enough about his drinking to advocate what's called in A.A. a "geographical cure." They would simply and literally take a hike far from the barrooms and think things over as they tramped the mountain trails from Maine to Vermont.

After a recreative month in the woods during the fall of 1919, both the Wilsons resolved to find work. Lois joined the Red Cross at Brooklyn Naval Hospital, continuing the career in occupational therapy she had started while Bill was away. Her well-connected father arranged for Bill to work as an insurance clerk with the New York Central, where another Burnham son-in-law was already employed. Meanwhile the Wilsons made their first home together: a furnished room at 24 State Street, near her parents' home in Brooklyn Heights. In 1922, when Lois found a better-paying job in the women's psychiatric ward at Bellevue Hospital, they moved up to a charming three-room flat on nearby Amity Street.

Meanwhile, at his grandfather Fayette's urging, Bill enrolled for night courses at the Brooklyn Law School, a branch of Saint Lawrence University in upstate Canton, New York. Bill persevered in his legal studies until 1924, but he never saw the diploma for which he had paid fifteen dollars in advance. "He was too drunk to leave the apartment the next day to pick it up," Lois recalled. "He never bothered to get it. It could still be there" (LR, 31). Bill gave a different version of the same events. The problem, he said, was that he was too drunk to pass one of his final exams, which he was allowed to make up the following fall. But when he then demanded his diploma on the spot, he was required to wait until the next commencement in June. "But I never appeared, and my diploma as a graduate lawyer still rests in the Brooklyn Law

School. I never went back for it. I must do that before I die" (*PIO*, 67). (He didn't.)

Wilson, in any case, never took the bar exam. He realized he lacked a judicial temperament. He wanted a more exciting and improvisatory kind of work. The erstwhile Lieutenant Wilson, moreover, hated taking orders instead of giving them. The role of underling, he thought, was infra dig, and so he soon quit the railroad in self-righteous disgust. During the summer of 1921, he found a better job with United States Fidelity and Guaranty Company, as an investigator of firms defaulting on the stock exchange. Wilson soon was pulled into the Wall Street maelstrom, into a business whirl that was the counterpart to his alcoholic vertigo.

It's worth pondering, perhaps, what might have happened if Wilson had followed a road not taken: in the spring of 1921, Bill tested his mental mettle against the exacting standards of Thomas Alva Edison, the god of American invention. Answering Edison Laboratories' want ad for well-informed young men, Wilson went out to East Orange, New Jersey, to take the required test, which Edison himself administered to small groups of aspirants. Bill sweated over the hundreds of questions, all requiring a short and specific response; he was the last in his group to hand in a (still incomplete) exam. So he was surprised a few weeks later when, after he had already signed on with Fidelity and Guaranty, Edison belatedly offered him a job.

Wilson then became embroiled in a teapot tempest over Edison's denigration of American higher education, a controversy that uncannily foreshadowed the debate over "cultural literacy" during the 1980s. Edison told the *New York Times* that he found the results of his "efficiency and intelligence test," the same one Bill had passed satisfactorily, to be "surprisingly disappointing": "Men who have gone through college I find to be amazingly ignorant. They don't seem to know anything. When I discover that any one fails to come up to the standard I set, I give him a week's pay and fire him."[4]

Nonsense! indignantly editorialized the *Times,* sensing the potential for at least a mild public sensation. The purely factual kind of questions favored by Edison were arbitrary and asinine, such things as What is copra? What is zinc? How did Cleopatra die? Where is Madgalena Bay? What is the greatest depth of ocean? What are felt hats made of? What fabric is used in auto tires? Such certified geniuses as

John Milton and Henry Ford would certainly have been stumped by such arcane queries. The *Times* claimed that Edison's insulting grade, "XYZ," which he reserved for "those who fail completely," betrayed only his own ignorance and insensitivity:

> Can't Mr. Edison understand that the young graduate whose mind is dwelling on the long roll of the hexameter or, more probably, on the uncovenanted caperings of free verse doesn't care to know the ingredients of felt hats or automobile tires? Has it never been brought to his attention that not a few college men who would be entirely willing to be inscribed temporarily upon his payroll nevertheless look upon his shops, his factories, his materials, his processes, as the mere dross and slag of life, not to be compared with the lofty things to which they aspire?[5]

The editorial inspired a raft of letters from an aroused public, and by 11 May, the paper was reporting the results of its own publicity stunt. "Edison Questions Stir Up A Storm," howled the headline on an inside page. "'Victims' of Test Say Only 'a Walking Encyclopedia' Could Answer Questionnaire." This "victim," one of the hopeless XYZ cases, was still bright enough to recall 141 of Edison's secret questions, which the *Times* deemed news fit to print. The paper challenged its readers to try the questions themselves.

The public soon got into the carnivalesque spirit of the imbroglio. Everyone seemed to be having fun except, perhaps, Edison himself, whose sourpuss spokesman refused to verify the authenticity of the 141 questions. (Other "victims," meanwhile, were racking their brains to remember more of them.) Publication of the questionnaire had evidently "caused more perturbation among newspaper readers yesterday than publication of the names of alleged draft dodgers." All over town, together or alone, people were poring over Edison's baffling brainteasers. Two men on the Seventh Avenue subway became so absorbed that they missed their stop and ended up in Brooklyn. Out at the University of Chicago, twenty-five randomly chosen students all failed badly: "The average answered correctly by the men of the university was about 35 per cent., while the women answered only about 28 per cent. correctly." There was apparently even more at risk than bruised egos: a New York bus driver worried that those taking the exam literally in stride might obliviously step off the sidewalk into the path of destruction. In Holyoke, Massachusetts, one youth, allegedly "crazed" by the test, demanded police protection—from whom or what it was not clear![6]

Too bad this fellow had not attended the prep school that capitalized on the ruckus by running a clever ad in the *Times*. A beaming, well-scrubbed boy is shown exulting: "I can answer most of those questions, Mr. Edison, and so can any number of other school boys and girls. I'm just a regular boy, but my father and mother have given me the biggest educational advantage anybody ever had." The *Times* gleefully kept the story rolling for days, retaining experts to provide definitive answers to the test, now appended to 146 items. The man and woman on the street, along with everyone who was anyone, weighed in with an opinion.

For Bill Wilson, the affair afforded a first taste of fame outside his small hometown. A *Times* reporter ascertained somehow that Wilson was among the elite thirty (out of hundreds) who had passed the original test. (As its integrity had been compromised by all the publicity, Edison had since dashed off a new one, supposedly in just a few minutes.) "Found Questionnaire Easy" reads the subhead. (In a later version of this story, however, Bill W. recalled how Edison had walked over to his desk and asked him if he "found the exam difficult"; and he had replied: "yes, he thought it very difficult" [*BW*, 136]). "I think I answered most of them," Bill said, "not from the knowledge I acquired at school, but from reading, hearsay and observation after I left school. I have read a great deal on economic and scientific subjects."[7]

In this respect, Bill had much in common with Edison himself, one of his idols since boyhood. The Wizard of Menlo Park, whose reading ranged from technical journals to the *Police Gazette,* claimed to devour eighty pounds of periodicals a week, in addition to "a great deal of history and travel, some fiction and some poetry."[8] Bill's mind may not have been quite so well-stocked as Edison's, but still it was crammed with potentially useful information. It was, he once said, "like his grandfather's toolshed, a spot where random objects could be stored that one day might come in handy" (*BW*, 136).

More important, Wilson was in tune with Edison's bluntly practical and empirical outlook. Bill would likely, in fact, have become a Number One man at Edison Laboratories had he not passed up this golden opportunity and kept a job he soon came to detest. He could have read his own possible future in the company's claim that all those hired after passing the test were still making the grade as factory inspectors: "The plan is to advance those men to executive and administrative positions if their future progress is satisfactory."[9] When Bill W. did ascend to an executive role, it was atop his own organization, one that took a relentlessly pragmatic approach to (drinking) problems that Edison himself would certainly have approved.

On one point, however, these brilliantly inventive men did not see eye to eye. "I think chewing tobacco acts as a good stimulant upon anyone engaged in laborious brain work," Edison had opined, in answer to an 1882 survey of the drug habits of prominent writers and scientists. "Smoking, although pleasant, is too violent in its action; and the same remark applies to alcoholic liquors."[10] Bill preferred alcoholic stimulants, the violent effects of which were beginning to drag him down. The damage was subtle during the years that Bill made his success on Wall Street. But the "first drink" led him inexorably to another and another, until it got past counting.

Bill's Roaring Twenties

Alcoholics Anonymous was a brainchild of modernity. It reflected the life course of a particular group of Americans: a generational cohort of professional, Protestant, white men born late in the nineteenth century. Men such as Bill Wilson, whose coming of age coincided with Prohibition, whose excessive drinking paralleled the speculative binge of the 1920s stock market, and whose drunken misery bottomed out during the Great Depression, in the depths of which A.A. itself was born.

The linking of private history to public events is made explicit in *Alcoholics Anonymous,* where "Bill's Story" asserts that the "inviting maelstrom of Wall Street" held him as tightly in its grip as alcohol ever did (*AA,* 2). "The great boom of the late twenties was seething and swelling. Drink was taking an important and exhilarating part in my life" (*AA,* 3). Making oblique reference to the boomerang incident of his childhood—an incident not revealed until *Alcoholics Anonymous Comes of Age* (1957)—Wilson suggests how his twin intoxications delivered a double whammy. "Out of this alloy of drink and speculation, I commenced to forge the weapon that one day would turn in its flight like a boomerang and all but cut me to ribbons" (*AA,* 2).

At this stage of Bill W.'s story, we reach the point where a typical A.A. speaker, especially one with a "low bottom," might rehearse his or her riotous and harrowing adventures with booze in a drunkalog.

49

In the life of an alcoholic, as Mark Schorer discovered with Sinclair Lewis (born just a decade before Bill Wilson), the sheer number of drunken incidents, as well as their monotony, poses a narrative problem. How much to tell? How much is enough when, as Tolstoy might have said, drunks, happy or unhappy, are all alike? Schorer reported that some readers of his massive *Sinclair Lewis: An American Life* (1961)

> do not think that I selected drastically enough and others think that I did not select at all; the fact is that I did not, for example, report on every drunken rumpus, as one reviewer has complained, but only on, I suppose, some six or ten of them, whereas there must have been at least ten times ten and possibly one hundred times six of them. But if from my mention of six or ten, my exhausted reader has some sense of the exhausting intemperance to which Sinclair Lewis, in long stretches of his life, was addicted, I am at least partially vindicated.[1]

In light of Bill Wilson's celebrity, what's unexpected about his drinking career is that so little is known about it. Whereas some A.A. members revel in telling their "war stories," trumping each other's vainest exploits, Bill W. was decidedly reticent. The gritty details of his deterioration during the 1920s are so scarce and so poorly documented, in fact, that one recent study proposes, astonishingly, that Wilson never fit the textbook definition of an "alcoholic" until the last two years of his drinking.

Before that, John J. Rumbarger contends, "such drinking as he did is best characterized as sporadic and opportunistic." Later Bill evolved into a "social" drinker who sometimes overindulged, but "there is no evidence, beyond Thomsen's unsupported assertions, to suggest Bill W drank on a regular basis, much less exhibited E. M. Jellinek's 'pre-alcoholic' symptoms of alcoholic disease":

> Can we say that Bill W's life from 1917 to 1934 exhibits a pattern of "progressively worsening"—i.e., *increasing*—drinking? Does his drinking history reveal regularly increasing amounts of alcohol consumed, regardless of circumstances, necessarily accompanied by regularly increasing amounts of time and money devoted to its consumption? Do we find evidence of the necessary consequences of regular excessively heavy drinking—including regular intoxication and debilitating illness—that interferes with what we take to be normal, healthy living?
>
> In short, the answer to these questions for the years 1917–32 appears to be "no."[2]

Rumbarger rightly remarks that what is known about the worst of Bill W.'s drinking is "only what he told us" and, furthermore, that the other major sources (the two official biographies and Lois Wilson's memoirs) largely derive from Bill himself and reflect his artful shaping of his own life narrative for the exemplary purposes of Alcoholics Anonymous. All the sources are thus "more or less involved with the assumption of the literal truth of his personal witness to the fate he believes befell him, which he subsequently crafted into a saving message to the audience of alcoholic drinkers then supposed to be filling the country, and so in different ways are crucially dependent upon that assumption."[3] "Bill's Story" may therefore be read as a didactic fiction, a homiletic distortion of the historical record in the interests of building up A.A.

Although I think Rumbarger's conclusions are finally unwarranted, it is not entirely unreasonable, given the paucity and limitations of the available evidence, to question whether Bill Wilson was an alcoholic during the 1920s. But the problem with this approach is that it construes a dearth of facts about Wilson's "alcoholic" drinking as proof it didn't happen; that is, Bill's drunkalog seems so tame because his drinking was not really so bad, at least not before 1932.

Let's consider, however, some reasons why Wilson's drunken depredations may *purposefully* have been understated in "Bill's Story." Perhaps blackouts had rendered many of them literally unmemorable. Perhaps as a skillful teller of tales Wilson recognized, much as Schorer did, that less is more. (One A.A. old-timer I know has boiled down his drunkalog to a three-act, nine-word tragicomedy: "got drunk, had no fun, went directly to detox.") Perhaps, as the original old-timer, Bill W. realized that dwelling on the past is counterproductive; the high drama of sobriety lies not in reliving alcoholic escapades, but in cherishing the good life without booze. In any event, although the Big Book treats Wilson's drinking cursorily, other sources do compensate for what he left unsaid, providing more than enough particulars to prove, though not perhaps beyond *any* reasonable doubt, the alcoholic nature of his drinking during the 1920s.

On the second page of "Bill's Story," after recalling his postwar arrival in New York, Wilson tells of the bright idea that then made his fortune: the theory "that most people lost money in stocks through ignorance of markets" (*AA,* 2). It followed that knowledge was the way to wealth; inside information about investment properties could cut the risks and hike the profits of stock speculation. So Bill and Lois quit their jobs, stashed their gear in the sidecar of their Harley-Davidson, and hit the road on an intelligence mission. Traveling light and camping out along the way, doing farmwork for a month when their cash ran low, the Wilsons crisscrossed the Atlantic seaboard from Canada to Florida.

The objective was surreptitious scrutiny of a few targeted companies, "sleepers," whose undervalued stock promised a handsome return on investment. Wilson applied his keen investigative skills, sometimes plying his informants with a few drinks. The resulting field reports earned him notice on Wall Street; he was offered a berth in a brokerage house, along with an elastic expense account and generous stock options. "I had arrived," he put it baldly in "Bill's Story." "My judgment and ideas were followed by many to the tune of paper millions" (*AA*, 3). When Wilson once visited his grandparents in Vermont, preening in the role of hometown-boy-made-good, one local banker watched him "whirl fat checks in and out of his till with amused skepticism" (*AA*, 4).

Unfortunately, Wilson's drinking, like his bankroll, "assumed more serious proportions"; it continued "all day and almost every night" (*AA*, 3). In "Bill's Story," his downfall during the 1920s, passes in a blur. The later part of the decade is recalled summarily in three sentences: "The remonstrances of my friends terminated in a row and I became a lone wolf. There were many unhappy scenes in our sumptuous apartment. There had been no real infidelity, for loyalty to my wife, helped at times by extreme drunkenness, kept me out of those scrapes" (*AA*, 3). Then, without transition, the narrative jumps to 1929, when "hell broke loose" on the stock exchange and Wilson reached the nadir of his alcoholism (*AA*, 4). At the same time it makes a connection between the economic collapse and Wilson's personal collapse, "Bill's Story" also abridges the history, both public and private, of the 1920s.

Before retracing Wilson's crash after 1929, it is useful to fill in some blanks in the Big Book and give a fuller version of Bill's story than he himself preferred to tell. Let me begin by unpacking those three cryptic sentences. The first leads to the inference that Bill's drinking problem was evident to his friends; otherwise he would not have rebuffed their concern and become such a "lone wolf." For Wilson as a solitary drinker, alcohol lost its original value as a means to male comradery. The second sentence implies that as Bill spent more and more of his waking hours in bars (becoming nevertheless more alone), his wife inevitably felt abandoned and aggrieved; there were numerous domestic "scenes" in their "sumptuous" apartment. In the third sentence, Wilson gingerly touches on an issue later addressed in the Big Book, an issue that remained problematic even in his sober life: philandering.

There had been "no real infidelity," Bill avers, leaving the reader to ponder the implications of that fig-leafy word, "real." Sounding a bit like Bill C. in the tortuous parsing of his intercourse with Monica L., Bill W. hints that, despite his technical innocence, something at least imaginably adulterous *did* occur, and more than once.[4] Marital loyalty, albeit alloyed by "extreme drunkenness," had always stopped him short of a "real" affair. But it must have been cold comfort for Lois to realize that Bill's fidelity in these "scrapes" had hinged on the anti-aphrodisiacal effects of booze (stupor and/or impotence).

In fact, the calamitous impact of Wilson's drinking during the 1920s appears less in his own writings than in those of his long-suffering wife, whose memories are all the more devastating for their unflinching, but astoundingly unresentful, candor. Consider, for example, Lois's recollection of her heartrending ectopic pregnancies (three of them between 1921 and 1923), which ultimately led to radical surgery.

> By then [May 1923] both tubes and the complete cystic ovary had been removed. A small portion of the other ovary was kept so that I might retain my feminine characteristics, it was said. Bill was often too drunk, for days at a time, to come to see me in the hospital.
>
> We had both deeply desired a family. But after my second ectopic, Bill and I knew positively that we could never have children. . . . Bill, even when drunk, took this overwhelming disappointment with grace and with kindness to me. But his drinking had been increasing steadily. It seemed that after all hope of having children had died, his bouts with alcohol had become even more frequent. (*LR,* 34–35)

Then, speaking for so many of those, mostly women, who would join her in Al-Anon, Lois goes on to describe the lacerating conflicts of life with an alcoholic spouse: the alternation of hope and hopelessness, empathy and anger, love and hatred:

> I knew I had done nothing to prevent our having children; yet somehow I could not help feeling guilty. So how could I blame him for the increase in his drinking?

> This kind of thinking made me try harder to understand him and
> to be tolerant when he was drunk. But there were many times when I
> lost my temper. He never hit me, but I hit him. I remember with shame
> one time toward the end of his drinking, when I was so angry as he lay
> drunk on the bed that I beat his chest with both my fists as hard as I
> could. (*LR*, 35)

Lois's compassion for Bill does not disguise the cruelty of his derelic-
tion. Perhaps his worst abuse of her came when her mother was dying
painfully of bone cancer. Although Bill truly loved and respected Mrs.
Burnham, he was missing in action throughout the ordeal of her radia-
tion treatments; when she finally died on Christmas Day in 1930, Bill
could provide no comfort to his grieving wife and family. He even
missed the funeral. As Lois wrote, with crushing simplicity, "Bill was
drunk then and for days before and after" (*LR*, 82).

Things had initially begun to turn sour during the early 1920s, when
Bill's dedication to the courtroom had succumbed to his affinity for
the barroom. With Prohibition now in force, consuming alcohol was
an illicit activity, but only theoretically: New York City had a speakeasy
on every corner, and the law was openly flouted. Like many others in
the rising generation, Wilson might have imagined his drinking as an
act of protest against the victorious Drys, a youthful nose-thumbing at
the puritanical elders, the kind of prissy stiffs who were stereotypically
associated with the Women's Christian Temperance Union and the
Anti-Saloon League. Prohibition, as A. J. Liebling once quipped, "was
the only period during which a fellow could be smug and slopped con-
currently." Robin Room points out that the drinking of the lost generation, especially among its urban intellectuals, constituted "an act of
political dissent" insofar as it resisted the entrenched values of Victorian America.[5]

Bill Wilson put on no such dignifying airs about his drinking. He
drank simply because he loved what alcohol did for him. He was, in
fact, the ideological opposite to those American modernists (a large
majority of whom were also alcoholics) who protested the iniquity of
American capitalism during the 1920s and then drifted leftward during
the 1930s, often becoming fellow travelers or card-carrying members
of the Communist Party. A rock-ribbed Yankee conservative, who
later fulminated against F. D. R. and the New Deal,[6] Wilson formed
his identity around what was anathema to his more "progressive" con-

temporaries. Nor was he interested, like F. Scott Fitzgerald, in thinking the American Dream through to a tragic conclusion. Rather he was trying, like Jay Gatsby, to live it to the hilt at a time when, as Robert Thomsen says, "having fun and making your fortune became a mass movement" (*BW*, 157).

Although Alcoholics Anonymous, a quintessentially bourgeois institution, would bear some striking organizational resemblances to the underground wing of the Communist Party (most notably in the role of anonymity and autonomous "cells"), Wilson never saw the reformation of individual drunks as part of any collectivist movement. The only kind of revolution he advocated was an "inside job": a quasi-religious conversion experience. In this respect, too, his vision was more residually Victorian than that of his rebellious contemporaries.

"Bill's Story" treats excessive drinking not as a structural or social problem—as another product, arguably, of industrial capitalism itself—but rather as a failure of "character," a psychological and spiritual dis-ease for which, despite the A.A. rhetoric of "powerlessness," individual drunks are held personally accountable once they have regained their sobriety. As Edmund B. O'Reilly perceives:

> The role of social pathologies in the genesis of individual alienation will never become a powerful theme in AA: the restoration and maintenance of sobriety and the development of autonomous moral responsibility are reckoned sufficiently formidable tasks from which, within the framework of the group, engagement with social and political critique could only prove a distraction.

A.A. members have not necessarily been discouraged from social activism, but there has always been a potent quietist element in the fellowship. Surviving the passage through active alcoholism, O'Reilly says, "renders humble acquiescence to everyday life contrastingly so superior to dissonance of any sort that willful disruption is, for many, wholly unthinkable."[7]

From a more rigorously Marxist perspective, Craig Reinarman argues that whereas A.A. members "proudly proclaim that their ideology is stringently apolitical" and exclude discussion of social factors (race, class, gender, poverty, marital or job stress) as "outside issues" and/or as "*prima facie* evidence of 'denial,'" A.A.'s culture is "objectively" reactionary. "Rather than transforming private troubles into public issues or at least linking the two, 12-Step ideology tends to sever this link or to transform what might be understood as public issues into private troubles."[8]

Bill W.'s first biographer recognized the Wilsons' implication in the materialism of the 1920s. Bill and Lois shared the excitement of surfing the seemingly endless waves of prosperity. There were times "when it seemed enough just to keep abreast and adjust to the whirling sense of change. And wasn't this all that really mattered?" (BW, 159). Robert Thomsen nevertheless takes pains to place Bill's alcoholism in a larger historical context and to credit him with a rudimentary social conscience. He argues that the Wilsons did not join altogether thoughtlessly in the "carnival spirit"; they were at least subliminally aware of the poverty and "savage injustice" they encountered during their cross-country expeditions (BW, 158). Thomsen portrays Wilson after 1930 as having gained—much like Hurstwood, in Dreiser's Sister Carrie (1900)—a new compassion for the downcast and a detestation of the complacently rich:

> Bill was beginning to see that something had changed irrevocably. He saw it in the quiet dignity of men standing around the street, waiting. . . . He saw it in the offended eyes of men who slept on park benches, in bus depots and railway stations, men with newspapers for blankets, boys with no shoes to change. As the months passed and the winter grew sharper, he knew that some of these boys were spending their nights curled up on the dank floors of subway lavatories, and in time the acrid stench of urine worked its way in to become a permanent part of his memories" (BW, 176–77).

No such social awareness or moral conviction attaches, however, to Wilson as he is presented in the official A.A. biography, 'Pass It On.' In general Bill and Lois kept their distance from those less fortunate, and they never construed their own poverty, when it came, as anything other than the direct result of Bill's drinking, which effectively blighted his American Dream and disqualified him from the success he had earlier enjoyed—and to which he still felt destined, despite his self-inflicted disability. Only with the benefit of hindsight, as even Thomsen concedes, could Wilson fully recognize the role of "denial" in the binge mentality of the twenties:

Only later, years later, would he be able to look back and discover the curious parallel between what was happening to him and what had happened around him. It was not in his nature to admit there was anything wrong with the system, with his country or with himself. With the kind of superhuman power he and the country had, they would prevail. He would keep going and somehow he would show them. He would show them all. (*BW,* 168)

By 1923 the hot air was beginning to leak from Wilson's braggadocio. His Christmas gift to Lois that year was a pledge that "no liquor will pass my lips for one year. I'll make the effort to keep my word and make you happy" (*BW,* 141). Not only did Bill fail to keep his word; he also proved incapable of waiting for his own dandelion wine and bathtub gin to mature. "It was always raw when he drank it," Lois recalled. "It made him sick as well as drunk." She was all the more receptive, therefore, to the idea of touring around the country in 1925. "I was so concerned about Bill's drinking that I wanted to get him away from New York and its bars. I felt sure that during a year in the open I would be able to straighten him out" (*LR,* 37). Life on the road was, in fact, tonic for Bill's intemperance, except for a few alcoholic interludes. In one of these Lois tried to provide a sobering object lesson by getting drunk herself. He missed the point, while she suffered a walloping hangover.

Back in New York during the spring of 1926, Bill immediately reverted to his old habits. Frenetic wheeling and dealing, which involved his own speculation in stocks bought on margin, provided an ironclad excuse to drink his way uptown every day after work, soothing his tensions as the sun set. Having sold Frank Shaw, a high-rolling broker, on the value of his insider tips, Bill had joined a leading firm, J. K. Rice and Company; and the Wilsons were living in unwonted affluence. During a business junket to Havana in 1927, they stayed at the swank Hotel Sevilla, which placed a car, a driver, and a speedboat at their disposal. While Bill looked into Cuban sugar plantations, he also acquainted himself with the island's bars, often in the company of a convivially drunken official from the U.S. embassy. Lois was so frustrated by Bill's drinking that she tried to sabotage him one day by flinging his shoe out the window. Bill calmly had a porter recover it from an adjoining roof, and he was soon installed, as usual, at the bar downstairs.

Although Bill had pledged in January that "there will be no booze in 1927" (*LR,* 69), his consumption was heavier than ever; and Lois believed that his work was beginning to suffer: "because of the drinking, Cuban sugar was not one of his most successful investigations" (*LR,* 71). In a September letter to Frank Shaw, Bill swore he had definitely sworn off the sauce:

> I have never said anything to you about the liquor question, but now that you mention it and also for the good reason that you are investing your perfectly good money in me, I am at last very happy to say that I have had a final showdown (with myself) on the matter. It has always been a very serious handicap to me, so that you can appreciate how glad I am to be finally rid of it. It got to the point where I had to decide whether to be a monkey or a man. I know it is going to be a tough job, but nevertheless the best thing I ever did for myself and everybody concerned. That is that, so let us now forget about it. (*PIO,* 80)

Despite Wilson's resolve, he proved to be all too simian; his alcoholic monkeyshines persisted, keeping pace with ever higher levels of affluence and conspicuous consumption. Upon their return to New York from Cuba, the Wilsons moved out of Dr. Burnham's house and rented a huge apartment at 38 Livingston Street, in an even better Brooklyn neighborhood. After annexing an adjoining flat and knocking out some walls, they possessed "two bedrooms, two baths, two kitchens, and one tremendous living room. That was the point of it all—Bill loved big living rooms" (*LR,* 71). It was furnished in high style, with a $1,600 Mason and Hamblin baby grand piano as the centerpiece. As one of Bill's business associates fondly recalled this period: "Up to the historic crash of 1929, everybody and his uncle seemed to be floating along to riches on the sweet euphoria of paper profits" (*PIO,* 78).

Although Bill was still riding high—he would soon move to another investment house, Tobey and Kirk—his personal life reflected what John Kenneth Galbraith has called "the mood of unreality, gargantuan excess and hovering disaster of the months before the crash."[9] Lois stood by helplessly as Bill steadily lost control of his drinking; night after night, she had to help him to bed or else let him lie where he passed out, just inside the door. In her diary, she poured out her grief, praying that God might cure Bill through her own abiding love.

Bill, meanwhile, swaggered and staggered through the financial inferno. In October 1929, while some timorous speculators leaped "from the towers of High Finance" (*AA,* 4), Wilson, who had also plunged into the red with $60,000 in margin arrears, defiantly hunkered down in the barrooms. He soon arranged a move to Montreal, where financial prospects were brighter, and there he temporarily recovered his high standard of living. "I felt like Napoleon returning from Elba," he said in "Bill's Story." "No St. Helena for me!" (*AA,* 4). Booze proved to be Wilson's Waterloo, however. He was fired for drinking by the friend at Greenshields and Company who had kindly hired him, and he was forced to retreat from Canada back to the Burnham house in Brooklyn, without any job in sight.

Now his own great depression really set in. "Mercifully," as Wilson recalled, "no one could guess that I was to have no real employment for five years, or hardly draw a sober breath" (*AA,* 4). Liquor became not a luxury but a necessity, and things inexorably "got worse" (*AA,* 5). "Bill's Story" mentions "a brawl with a taxi driver" and a "prodigious bender" that ruined his last chance to recover his financial footing. He became a "hanger-on at brokerage places," begging for scraps from men who once had fawned on him. He recalls the steady alternation of binges and sober respites, which cruelly raised and then dashed his wife's hopes (*AA,* 4–5).

The depth of Bill's bottom was abysmal, far worse than he chose to reveal in the Big Book (or in the even sketchier account in *Alcoholics Anonymous Comes of Age*). One must turn to the official biographies and to Lois Wilson's memoirs to get the fuller story and also to get it straight. As Thomsen says, Wilson lost more than a few weekends in his blackouts. Times and places got jumbled in his mind. His life became like the "rough cut" of a movie, which

> may contain a group of scenes, beautifully photographed, clear and perfect in every detail, and then suddenly all will go blank on the screen or a title may appear, "Scene Missing," and after that only bits and pieces, fragments complete in themselves but unrelated to anything that has gone before; or the camera may have moved in on a tight shot and remained fixed on it for what seems endless minutes. (*BW,* 171)

Among these fragments were a brawl with a hotel detective, a night in jail, an aimless odyssey with a drunken stranger that ended up at

Emerald Lake. After he lost his briefcase in a barroom fight, Wilson was subjected to insinuating phone calls; and he had to wonder, anxiously but inconclusively, what he might have said or done in a blackout to make himself so vulnerable to threats of blackmail. He was "halfway to hell now," he told Lois in 1927, "and going strong" (*LR,* 72).

Bill's deepest shame arose from his abject failure to support his wife in the high style to which she had become accustomed. To his mind, formed as it was by the gender conventions of the period, this failure was disgracefully unmanly. As Bill's income shrank, the Wilsons were forced to take rent-free sanctuary with Dr. Burnham.[10] Bill scraped by on occasional stock deals, and early in 1931, he finally secured a steady job with Stanley Statistics, publisher of the *Standard and Poor's* index. But soon he was fired, apparently for a drunken incident, and Lois went to work at Macy's department store to provide for her insolvent husband.[11]

On one mortifying occasion, Bill came into Macy's drunk. In an attempt to propitiate Lois, he laid a bouquet of chrysanthemums at her feet, knelt before her, and handed over a check for a thousand dollars he had received as a grub stake from Joseph Hirshhorn, the Wall Street wizard who would later distinguish himself as an art collector. The next day Bill retrieved the check and soon thereafter squandered the money on bad investments.

One indicator of his growing powerlessness over alcohol was the increased frequency of his pledges to stop drinking. Between 20 October 1928 and 12 January 1929, on the flyleaf of Lois's family bible, Bill made three separate vows that he was "finished with drink forever." He entered another, equally futile, pledge of abstinence on 3 September 1930: "Finally and for a lifetime. Thank you for your love." Andrew and Thomas Delbanco point out that the ingenuousness of Bill's promises "is matched by a fear legible in the handwriting itself, which becomes increasingly spidery as it moves down the page."[12]

Thomsen hypothesizes that a signal change occurred in Wilson's drinking during this period. He crossed "an invisible line that every alcoholic crosses" into chronic inebriation (*BW,* 165). This was exactly the same time that the boom economy reached its crest. There was no better year to get rich than 1928, according to Galbraith. It was, indeed, "the last year in which Americans were buoyant, uninhibited, and utterly happy. It wasn't that 1928 was too good to last; it was only that it didn't last." Wilson was ostensibly on top of the world in 1928: inflated by his own success, intoxicated by what Galbraith calls "the pervasive sense of confidence and optimism and conviction that ordinary people were meant to be rich."[13]

Within a year, however, Wilson was plummeting along with the stock market, and the losses were not merely material. Just as the Great Crash deflated the ebullient mood of the twenties, inciting psychic panic as profound as the economic depression, so Bill's financial losses drained his mental and spiritual reserves as well.[14] First his moods became unpredictable. After a few drinks he began to exhibit uncharacteristic truculence, which led to verbal and sometimes physical assaults. The next morning, once the drunken rage had subsided, anxiety and melancholy ensued. Bill's dreadful hangovers recalled the debilitating "heart" attacks of his adolescence.

Lois noticed an edge of madness in Bill's intoxication; he was now afraid to leave their apartment "for fear the Brooklyn hoods or the police would get him" (LR, 86). As he himself later put it, "In those days, of course, I was drinking for paranoid reasons." He was also far gone into alcoholic grandiosity, which alienated his few remaining friends. "I was drinking to dream greater dreams of power, dreams of domination. Money to me was never a symbol of security. It was the symbol of prestige and power" (PIO, 81). Bill was still striving for success, determined to be recognized, once and for all, as a Number One man.

Having money, in other words, was the guarantor of Bill's identity, the sign of his sanctification in terms of the modern, secular version of the Protestant Work Ethic. Bankruptcy, by contrast, meant not merely fiscal but also psychic dissolution. Wilson took his failures personally, as the wages of sinful intemperance.

Rumbarger argues that Wilson's failure may have reflected "less the power of alcohol than the power of self-loathing in the face of what was to be expiated: failure in the marketplace." From this perspective, Wilson appears to have been a victim of his own worshipful prostration before what William James called "the bitch-goddess, *success*."[15] That is, the ideology of capitalism, which Wilson had imbibed since boyhood, led him to overestimate the role of drinking in his ruin, so as to suppress awareness of its external determinants. "It was not too much drink that consigned him to his fate," Rumbarger maintains, "but bad luck in a social system where luck derives from the earthly power that Bill W never had enough of." The result of Wilson's stigmatizing himself as an "alcoholic" and then convincing others to do the same was the creation of an institution, A.A., that "has played a major role in diverting attention from the social sources of individual dysfunction to the consequent afflictions of the individual's mind, body, and soul."[16] By taking such complete responsibility for his failure, Wilson paradoxically achieved a different kind of success, by reaffirming the efficacy of individual autonomy. Abstinence is understood, from this angle, as a kind of puritanical self-abuse designed to reinstantiate and reinforce the nefarious capitalist status quo.

Certainly, as commentators have often observed, Alcoholics Anonymous, despite its claims to the contrary, has a distinctly religious, if not a puritanical cast. As Reinarman says, Wilson "rhetorically recrafted words such as 'sin' and 'retribution' into 'character defects' and 'amends' so that they would resonate with modern, anti-clerical, and 'wet' (post-Prohibition) sensibilities." And however nondenominationally "spiritual" A.A. purports to be, its "original vision of recovery . . . was clearly modeled on religious conversion." From a secular and "progressive" perspective, this is exactly what's "wrong" with A.A. But, as Reinarman must acknowledge, the Twelve-Step ideology itself is not inevitably an "impediment to other collectivist movements." It may, in fact, "work *either* against the sorts of social change other movements seek or in concert with them," although the latter possibility has remained latent in A.A.[17]

The question begged by such materialist approaches is whether significant social change is ever possible through individual reform or through institutions composed of individuals collaborating in each other's reform. Is "conversion," religious or otherwise, invariably a matter of "mystification"? Can social change ever be *im*material?

The means of change for contemporary A.A.s remain essentially what they were for the cofounders: an epistemological reversal leading to a radical shift of values; "a spiritual quest for a new way of life and a new consciousness sharply different from those one had during active drinking."[18] Such a spiritual quest might effect material change only indirectly; nonetheless, if it had no social force whatsoever, then Alcoholics Anonymous and its innumerable Twelve-Step clones would never have flourished as they have since 1935, and especially in the last quarter-century.

It is important, however, to distinguish between A.A. and its (all too pale) imitations; it is precisely on the matter of individual agency that they differ most consequentially. Insofar as the spiritual integrity of A.A. is currently imperiled, it is not by Marxist critiques, but rather by the seepage into the program of a pop-psychological determinism (often tied to the "disease" concept of alcoholism) that dissolves personal responsibility in a wash of "powerlessness."

As Andrew and Thomas Delbanco define it, A.A.'s fundamental principle is

> that no one is responsible for the wreckage of the alcoholic's life except the alcoholic himself. No matter what has been done *to* you, members would be told, you are responsible for what is done *by* you. They would refuse to project evil onto some blamable cause, even though they might speak of alcoholism as (in the Big Book's words) an "illness" or "allergy," and of some people as alcoholic before they ever touched a drop, as if they were born tinctured by a poison activated by the first drink.

The Delbancos identify a powerful moral paradox at the core of Wilson's vision and of Alcoholics Anonymous: "that helplessness is a fact of human life, yet, at the same time, no one should be spared responsibility for his actions." They quote an elegant statement of this paradox—"responsibility despite inevitability"—that was formulated by the theologian Reinhold Niebuhr in 1939, the year the Big Book appeared.[19] So even if alcoholism is considered a "disease," it is not thereby an excuse for anything. Although alcoholism may have blamable external causes, natural and/or nurtural, its consequences are not predetermined.

While A.A.s have held themselves accountable for their actions, drunk or sober, most A.A. spin-offs (which may be grouped under the umbrella of "co-dependency") encourage their members—in fact, oblige them—to regard themselves as innocent victims. This essential difference is traced by John Steadman Rice to the roots of "co-dependency" in the "liberation psychotherapy" of the 1960s, a "revolutionary" discourse that preached the radical priority of the individual over society: "the claim that every person has a right to autonomy from social and cultural proprieties."[20]

Liberation psychotherapy failed to provide for communal action and purpose, but "co-dependency" forged a new type of community among its adherents, who embrace the binding premise of their common victimization, commonly conceived as the abandonment and abuse of the "inner child" by tyrannical parents who have been brainwashed by a repressive American society. (In this way "co-dependency" is unexpectedly allied with Marxism in an emphasis on social as well as psychological determinants.) The strength of this community hinges, however, on the power of its analogical reasoning: "our problems are 'like' alcoholism—and without that analogy, the common ground disappears." In effect, the "disease" of "co-dependency" is a "dis-ease"; "co-dependency" is not something one *has* but, rather, something one *believes*. It relies on a *symbolic* understanding of "disease" in which "addiction" describes a psychological process rather than a physiological condition: "the addiction itself is now a rhetorical rather than a biological category." Like other sociologists, Rice uses the term "process addiction" to differentiate "co-dependency" as a "learned disease" from addictions that are more demonstrably physical, such as those to alcohol or narcotics.[21]

In light of these later developments, Bill Wilson's wariness about the rhetoric of "disease" (a term he avoided in the Big Book) now seems all the wiser, if also all the more old-fashioned. Although Wilson was very much a modern in his frantic pursuit of material success, his moral universe remained unabashedly Victorian. If his belief in individualism marks him as a "reactionary" in a political sense, his belief in free will makes him a "reactionary" in a theological sense.

PART TWO

What Happened

Bill and the Oxford Group

F O U R

It is a common belief in Alcoholics Anonymous that the program sprang full-blown from the brow of Bill W., with obstetrical assistance from Dr. Bob, in 1935. But A.A.'s creation myth is less Greek, after all, than Judeo-Christian. The founders are seen to resemble not Zeus giving forth Athena so much as latter-day prophets retrieving the tablets (inscribed with the Twelve Steps) that Moses carelessly dropped on the way down Mount Sinai. The entire Big Book, trailing streams of glory from above, is sometimes said to be "divinely inspired" and its quasi-biblical text thought to be as sacred as the Scripture it has supplemented or supplanted. That's one big reason why A.A.'s leaders, acting as trusted servants of the membership at large, have steadfastly resisted—Wilson's contrary preference notwithstanding—any revision of the first, and increasingly dated, section of *Alcoholics Anonymous:* its Old Testament, so to speak.

True believers prefer not to recognize that the Big Book, as Emerson famously observed of Whitman's *Leaves of Grass,* "must have had a long foreground somewhere, for such a start."[1] In fact, nearly all the constitutive elements of the A.A. Program were in place a century before Bill W. ever set foot in Akron. As William L. White says, in his magisterial history of addiction treatment in America, it is "clearly not the case" that mutual support groups for inebriates began with A.A.:

From the Washingtonian Movement through the fraternal temperance societies, the reform clubs, the Ollapod Club, the Keeley Leagues, the United Order of Ex-Boozers, the Jacoby Club of the Emmanuel Clinic, and so on to the Oxford Group, alcoholics struggling to get sober and stay sober found places to band together for mutual support.[2]

Bill Wilson himself came to recognize that the fellowship's historical taproot reached down to the Washington Temperance Society, which had revolutionized attitudes toward drunkards in the mid-nineteenth century. The temperance crusade, which began late in the eighteenth century, was instigated by the clerical, legal, medical, mercantile, and political establishments as a means to regulate drunkenness among the lower orders. In time, with moral impetus from the revivalism of the Second Great Awakening, the movement became a vehicle for self-improvement as well as social reform: a path to individual uplift and middle-class respectability.

When the Washington Temperance Society was founded in 1840, by six Baltimore artisans who pledged total abstinence, vowed mutual assistance, and recruited other drunkards to attend their meetings, the balance of power briefly shifted from sober reformers to drunkards themselves. The Washingtonians proved that even those in thrall to Demon Rum might be emancipated through the empathic aid of recovered inebriates. By February 1841, the Baltimoreans had enrolled twelve hundred men, with another fifteen hundred women and children in auxiliary groups. The Washingtonian gospel, disseminated by traveling "delegates" (as the Society called their proselytizers), then blazed a path across the country. Throngs of pledge-signers raised national membership at the acme to half a million intemperate drinkers, plus another hundred thousand confirmed drunkards.[3]

At the heart of Washingtonianism were the open meetings at which drunkards gave mutual help through the plain and honest telling of their own life stories. Some of these temperance narratives were published as books during the 1840s.[4] One early historian of the movement described the mountain-moving force of the drunkards' testimonials:

How much more influence then has the man, who stands before an audience to persuade them to abandon the use of strong drink, when he can himself tell them of its ruinous and blasting effects on his own life and character—trace the progress of his own habits of intemperance,—and warn others to avoid the rock on which he split. A reformed man has the best access to a drunkard's mind and heart, because he best knows, and can enter into all a drunkard's feelings. And such appeals from such sources, properly directed, can rarely fail of entire success.[5]

Like other evangelical blazes during the nineteenth century, Washingtonianism soon burned itself out. Membership fell as exponentially as it once had risen; and although a few scattered chapters persisted through the 1850s, the Society as a national movement was moribund by 1845, giving up the ghost as suddenly as it had materialized. While some Washingtonian practices were adopted by male fraternal organizations after the Civil War, these fellowships put little or no emphasis on public testimony; although a few temperance narratives were published intermittently until World War I, the sobering synergy of speech and writing, as briefly attained during the early 1840s, was lost.

Lost, that is, until the embers of the Washingtonian spirit were rekindled in Alcoholics Anonymous. A century after the Society had collapsed, Bill Wilson was "startled, then sobered" to learn of the astonishing parallels between A.A. and this now obscure temperance group. The similarities had been brought to his attention by a letter to the *Grapevine,* A.A.'s newly founded monthly magazine. "It was hard for us to believe," Bill confessed in his column for August 1945, "that a hundred years ago the newspapers of this country were carrying enthusiastic accounts about a hundred thousand alcoholics who were helping each other stay sober; that today the influence of this good work has so completely disappeared that few of us had ever heard of it" (*LH,* 4–5). Wilson wished thereafter to keep the Washingtonians in view, if only to provide a valuable object lesson for A.A.'s future. "We are sure," he continued, "that if the original Washingtonians could return to this planet they would be glad to see us learning from their mistakes" (*LH,* 5).[6]

Historians Leonard U. Blumberg and William L. Pittman find many features in common between these institutions: a focus on inebriates themselves, moral suasion, total abstinence, experience meetings, mutual help, traveling speakers, charismatic leadership, political neutrality, nonsectarian spirituality, and loose organization above the local level. Both groups, moreover, share an institutional culture stemming from their "common ancestry in Anglo-American Protestant religious belief and practice."[7] That is, both groups are fundamentally evangelical in a specifically Protestant way. In an anthropological study, Paul Antze suggests:

> That AA's whole outlook owes a major debt to Christianity is obvious enough. Indeed, the group's emphasis on an experience of radical despair leading to a "spiritual awakening" (an experience that Martin Luther called *metanoia*) indicates that the operative model may be more narrowly a Protestant one. . . .
> AA's teachings draw their essential logic from Protestant theology of a very traditional kind. Once certain substitutions are made, in fact, there is a point-by-point homology between AA's dramatic model of the alcoholic's predicament and the venerable Protestant drama of sin and salvation.[8]

Although A.A. may not have derived directly from the Washington Society, it became one in spirit with this institutional forebear by reviving the *temperance narrative* and refashioning it into the *recovery narrative,* a genre just as essential to A.A.s as its generic predecessor had been to the Washingtonians. Both the temperance narrative and the recovery narrative, moreover, are types of the *spiritual autobiography,* in which, at least since colonial times in America, devout Protestants have recounted the pilgrim's progress of individual salvation. In a study of such narratives, Daniel B. Shea asserts that they are "primarily concerned with the question of grace: whether or not the individual has been accepted into divine life, an acceptance signified by psychological and moral changes which the autobiographer comes to discern in his past experience."[9]

The Big Book may be characterized as a collective spiritual autobiography that comprises individual recovery narratives. "Bill's Story," in particular, bridges the gap between the one and the many by making his singular experience representative. Wilson's account of his own life, as Edmund B. O'Reilly says, "has attained a certain canonical character in AA, and acts as an important reference point, both historically and structurally. There is an agreeable congruence between the story of Wilson's recovery from alcoholism and the story of AA's origin."[10] Insofar as it answers to a need in A.A. for an exemplary life narrative— by scanting those aspects of Wilson's experience that do not bear directly on the common good—"Bill's Story" may be said to be "generic"; that is, equivalent to and interchangeable with any other alcoholic's story, such as those included in the second part of the Big Book: its New Testament, so to speak. Wilson understood that the audience for any of the individual stories in *Alcoholics Anonymous* was not exclusively oneself, but also those to be won over by sober example.

The chief contemporary models for "Bill's Story" were not the temperance narratives produced by the Washingtonians—Wilson never read this arcane material—but rather the didactic spiritual autobiographies written by advocates of the Oxford Group during the period when Wilson himself was getting sober through the auspices of the Oxford Group. One such book, A. J. Russell's *For Sinners Only* (1932), appears both on the brief catalog of "books early AAs read" (as compiled by Nell Wing, Wilson's secretary), and also on Dr. Bob's required reading list. Bill Pittman has identified more than thirty other titles by Oxford Group members, in addition to the works of the Reverend Samuel Shoemaker and other leaders of the movement.[11] In fact, Harper and Brothers published a continuing and best-selling Oxford Group series throughout the 1930s.

Although it is commonly known that the Oxford Group was the immediate precursor of Alcoholics Anonymous, A.A. officials, including Wilson himself, have tended to minimize the debt. For example, Mel B.'s study of A.A.'s spiritual heritage remarks upon the squeamishness aroused by a 1978 centenary celebration of Frank Buchman, the charismatic and controversial founder of the Oxford Group. Buchman had a legitimate claim to the title of godfather to A.A. Indeed, Wilson himself acknowledged, after the man's death in 1961: "Now that Frank Buchman is gone and I realize more than ever what we owe to him, I wish I had sought him out in recent years to tell him of our appreciation" (*PIO,* 387). But A.A. was following Wilson's own lead when it declined in 1978 to join other progeny of Buchmanism in celebrating his paternal influence. As Bob P., then the general manager of A.A. World Services, put it with a bluntness bordering on tactlessness, "I think some of our members would say that we got out of bed with those people—why should we now get back in?"[12]

The Oxford Group, which flourished during the early decades of the twentieth century, was the modern counterpart to a traditional and recurrent type of Protestant evangelicism: "a good example of a reform religious movement with a pietistic tinge and an ardent missionary enthusiasm aiming to revive both the church and the world."[13] Oriented toward laypersons and loosely modeled on the apostolic Christian fellowship of the first century, the Oxford Group focused on creating "changed" lives: lives reoriented in response to conversion. Buchman himself had begun as a Lutheran minister, working with young men at a hospice he started in Philadelphia and later at such colleges as Penn State and Princeton. Having undergone a spiritual experience in 1905, Buchman became remarkably adept at inspiring such conversions in others—such as Sam Shoemaker, who would become Bill Wilson's Oxford Group mentor.

According to Walter Houston Clark, a historian of the movement, it defined its mission "in terms of changing people rather than in changing political situations, the social structure, or economic systems." Virulently anticommunist, Buchman attracted some liberals and even socialists to his cause; but it found an especially "warm spot in the hearts of many conservatives and those whose vested interests [lay] in the preservation of the *status quo*."[14] The typical member was both prosperous and prominent. Buchman nevertheless envisioned a radically transformative role for what he would later call "Moral Re-Armament." "The Oxford Group is a Christian revolution, whose concern is vital Christianity," he proclaimed in 1934, the same year Bill W. saw the light. "Its aim is a new social order under the dictatorship of the spirit of God making for better human relationships, for unselfish co-operation, for cleaner business, for cleaner politics, for the elimination of political, industrial, and racial antagonisms."[15] According to one English member of the movement, the Oxford Group drew together people "who, from every rank, profession, and trade, in many countries, have surrendered their lives to God and who are endeavouring to lead a spiritual quality of life under the guidance of the Holy Spirit." The Oxford Group, he continued, was not a religion; "it has no hierarchy, no temples, no endowments; its workers have no salaries, no plans but God's Plan; every country is their country, every man their brother."[16]

One of the spiritual techniques of the Oxford Group was "quiet time": daily meditation in which one sought divine guidance that would then be confirmed in conversation and consulation with other members. The Oxford Group also emphasized what it called the Four

Absolutes of Christ (Honesty, Purity, Unselfishness, Love), as well as the five Cs (Confidence, Confession, Conviction, Conversion, Continuance) that marked the path to a "changed" life. These stages recall those of Protestant "justification" in spiritual autobiographies of the seventeenth century and after.

Although the Oxford Group was never concerned with doctrinal niceties—or even with strictness of belief: "to act *as if* there were a God was sufficient; a genuine belief in God frequently followed the assumption through this pragmatic process"—it was nonetheless governed by an unwritten set of six tenets, which indubitably inspired the Twelve Steps of Alcoholics Anonymous. These were:

1. Men are sinners.
2. Men can be changed.
3. Confession is prerequisite to change.
4. The changed soul has direct access to God.
5. The Age of Miracles has returned (through changed lives, miraculous coincidences, etc.).
6. Those who have been changed must change others.[17]

It was under the sway of this last "step" that Bill W. received what would later have been known as a Twelfth-Step call from his boyhood friend, Edwin T. ("Ebby") T., late in November 1934, on or around Wilson's thirty-ninth birthday. The story of Ebby's crucial meeting with Bill, like the tale of the Mayflower lobby, has become one of the foundational legends of A.A. In most versions it begins with Ebby's own battle with the bottle, which was waged intermittently throughout his life.

Scion of a wealthy and political Albany family, Ebby T. summered at Manchester, Vermont, where he met young Bill Wilson in 1911. They attended Burr and Burton Academy together for a term, and they later became drinking buddies when, in 1929, Bill passed through Albany on his way to Vermont and looked Ebby up. Under the influence of an all-night binge, they decided to have some fun by renting a stunt plane for the last leg of Bill's trip. An airfield had recently been built at Manchester; when local citizens learned that a plane from Albany would be christening the new runway, many turned out, with the town band in tow, as a reception committee. Unfortunately for the decorum of the occasion, the intrepid flyers, including the pilot, tippled while airborne and arrived as drunk as skunks. When the welcoming delegation pressed forward, as Wilson laconically recalled, "It was up to Ebby and me to do something, but we could do absolutely nothing. We somehow slid out of the cockpit, fell to the ground, and there we lay, immobile" (*PIO*, 84).

Bill's drunken high jinks became less comical and more calamitous during his alcoholic deterioration. So did Ebby's. The two men, who hit the bars together whenever Ebby came to town, followed parallel tracks during the early 1930s. In New York in the fall of 1933, Bill was finally receiving medical treatment at the urgence of his brother-in-law, Dr. Leonard Strong, who along with Lois and Dorothy Wilson Strong never lost hope of a cure for Bill's drinking. Strong paid the tab for Wilson's admission to the Charles B. Towns Hospital on Central Park West, an expensive drying-out place. Over the next year, Wilson would check in four times.[18]

Wilson took great hope from his physician at Towns, Dr. William D. Silkworth, who had developed a theory (later shown to be scientifically untenable) that alcoholism was a physical "allergy" combined with a mental obsession. Bill leapt at the idea that his compulsion to drink and his failure to stop drinking were not merely the consequences of his own defective willpower, that "though certainly selfish and foolish, I had been seriously ill, bodily and mentally." It was a relief to learn "that in alcoholics the will is amazingly weakened when it comes to combating liquor, though it often remains strong in other respects. My incredible behavior in the face of a desperate desire to stop was explained" (*AA*, 7). Surely, self-knowledge was the answer! Mere insight, however, did not keep Wilson sober, and by his third relapse, Dr. Silkworth had concluded that his was a hopeless case. If Bill was to survive on any terms, the doctor told Lois, she had better lock him away in an insane asylum, where he would at least be safe from an otherwise inevitable course of self-destruction.

In Vermont, meanwhile, Ebby had come to the same narrow pass. Having shamed his family in Albany, he was living in exile at their summer home, where he continued to raise hell and eventually managed to land himself in jail. When, in August 1934, a judge in Manchester decided to commit Ebby to Brattleboro Asylum, he was spared incarceration only by the timely intervention of an old friend, Rowland H., a fellow alcoholic, who had found sobriety in religion after psychoanalysis with Carl Jung had failed to work.[19] Jung reportedly told Rowland that only a spiritual awakening could save him, and the young man earnestly sought such a conversion experience in the Oxford Group, first in England and then at Calvary Episcopal Church in New York, the hub of the American branch, where Sam Shoemaker presided.

Rowland took charge of Ebby and brought him to New York. Once he was surrounded with good influences at Calvary, Ebby was able to stay sober for a few months. Then, following the example of those who had rescued him, he resolved to call on Bill Wilson, about whose drinking problems he had heard. This was the celebrated visit during which Ebby tried to sell his skeptical friend on finding God as the royal road to sobriety. "I was aghast," Wilson recalled. "So that was it—last summer an alcoholic crackpot; now, I suspected, a little cracked about religion" (*AA*, 9).

Detailed accounts of the event appear both in the Big Book and in *Alcoholics Anonymous Comes of Age*. Visitors to Stepping Stones, the Wilsons' home in suburban New York, are encouraged to reanimate the scene in their own imaginations; for there in the modest (and, by modern standards, primitive) kitchen stands the chipped and worn white porcelain-topped table at which Bill and Ebby sat that very day in Brooklyn, with a pitcher of pineapple juice and a bottle of gin set between them. (By 1934, with Prohibition repealed, the gin, which Bill was squirreling all over the house, would no longer have been of the bathtub variety.) This small table is the only place at Stepping Stones, in fact, where tourists are permitted to sit down and let it all soak in. During my own first day there, it was while I was sitting at this table—as if before the A.A. altar—that I was allowed to handle two other precious relics: the Bible in which Bill inscribed his abject pledges of sobriety, and the first copy of *Alcoholics Anonymous*, which Bill inscribed to Lois.

The *mysterium tremendum* of the kitchen table arises from the miraculous moment it commemorates. For Ernest Kurtz, in his authoritative history, it was Bill's 1934 meeting with Ebby rather than his 1935 meeting with Dr. Bob that witnessed "the birth of the idea of Alcoholics Anonymous." It was there that Ebby planted the seed that Bill "eventually nurtured and cultivated into the core of the program and fellowship of Alcoholics Anonymous: 'In the kinship of common suffering, *one alcoholic had been talking to another.'''* Kurtz chooses, in fact, to open his book with an evocation of this event, while conceding that "such moments of origin are always difficult to pinpoint, and Alcoholics Anonymous itself cherishes the memory of a different 'founding moment'" (*NG*, 8).

Kurtz's emphasis faithfully adheres to that of the Big Book, where the Ebby incident occupies four of the sixteen pages of "Bill's Story," while the meeting with Dr. Bob covers only two pages in the last chapter of the first part, "A Vision for You." (The oblique account there does not even identify the parties involved as Wilson and Smith; Bill W. appears only as "one of our number" [*AA*, 153].) Kurtz is right to suppose, however, that Bill's meeting with Ebby has been eclipsed by his meeting with Dr. Bob. Wilson himself shifted the emphasis in *Alcoholics Anonymous Comes of Age*, and program lore has followed suit. The official "birthday" of A.A. is 10 June 1935, the date of Dr. Bob's last drink, a month or so after he met Bill.[20]

It seems clear in retrospect that A.A. has purposefully overlooked the Ebby visit as its "moment of origin" in the same way it has "forgotten" Frank Buchman and minimized its original affiliation with the Oxford Group. For various reasons it became expedient to place the "birth" of A.A. in Akron in 1935 rather than New York in 1934 or at some other place and time. It might be argued, for instance, that the idea of A.A. was born in Towns Hospital, when Wilson had the thought that "there were thousands of hopeless alcoholics who might be glad to have what had been so freely given me. Perhaps I could help some of them. They in turn might work with others" (*AA*, 14).

What is most problematic about Ebby's visit to Bill as a "founding moment," I suspect, is that it puts the matter of religion at the center of an institution whose long-term survival has largely depended on its finessing the relationship between the sacred and the secular through the intermediary concept of "spirituality." In the Big Book, although the Oxford Group is not explicitly named, Ebby and Bill clearly are seen discussing its attempts to reawaken first-century Christianity.

Wilson sardonically recalls his alcoholic skepticism. If Ebby wasn't drinking, then there would be all the more gin for himself, and it would outlast the preaching. But Ebby wasn't preaching. He was sharing his experience, strength, and hope in a manner, employed by Washingtonians and Oxford Groupers alike, that would later become integral to Alcoholics Anonymous. The old friends talked for hours. Bill relaxed into childhood memories of starchy Sunday sermons and old-time temperance pledges (he never signed one) and his own grandfather's wariness of established religion. Bill could believe in "a Spirit of the Universe, who knew neither time nor limitation. But that was as far as I had gone." His mind "snapped shut" at the idea of "a God personal to me, who was love, superhuman strength and direction" (*AA*, 10). As for Jesus Christ: a great man, to be sure, but one whose alleged followers had often betrayed his admirable, but impracticably demanding moral teachings. Under the influence of alcohol, moreover, Bill shared the jaundiced outlook of his jaded and war-weary literary contemporaries: "Judging from what I had seen in Europe and since, the power of God in human affairs was negligible, the Brotherhood of Man a grim jest. If there was a Devil, he seemed the Boss Universal, and he certainly had me" (*AA*, 11).

Despite Bill's resistance and (it may be supposed) his thickening intoxication, the unflappable Ebby carried on, shouting "great tidings," testifying "that God had done for him what he could not do for himself" (*AA*, 11). His very presence sober in Wilson's kitchen was no less than marvelous, and Bill had no choice but to take heed, for he knew that Ebby had succeeded where he himself had failed so miserably. Somehow his friend had become "much more than inwardly reorganized. He was on a different footing. His roots grasped a new soil" (*AA*, 11–12). Ebby offered Bill the key to the kingdom of belief: "*Why don't you choose your own conception of God?*" Nothing more was required of him, Bill realized, than "*being willing to believe in a Power greater than myself*" (*AA*, 12).

This "will to believe" in a God of one's own understanding recalls how William James, whom Wilson declared one of the founders of A.A., resolved his own youthful religious crisis. In 1870, spiritually perplexed by a French philosopher's discussion of free will versus determinism, James cleared his mental fog by seeing "no reason why his definition of Free Will—'the sustaining of a thought *because I choose to* when I might have other thoughts'—need be the definition of an illusion."[21] Free will, in other words, could be demonstrated through its very exercise; the enabling act of free will was to believe in free will itself and thus to prove its efficacy. Also implicit here was James's later pragmatic test of truth, which lies at the heart of A.A.'s down-to-earth

praxis. "The truth of an idea is not a stagnant property inherent in it,"
James wrote. "Truth *happens* to an idea. It *becomes* true, is *made* true
by events. Its verity *is* in fact an event, a process: the process namely
of its verifying itself, its veri-*fication*. Its validity is the process of its
vali-*dation*."[22] The same idea underlies A.A.'s notion (in the Twelve
Steps) of "God, *as we understood Him*," and of sobriety itself as a self-
verifying process. William J.'s story is much like Bill W.'s story insofar
as it is also "a tale of rebirth typical of Christian spiritual biography
that depends on three elements for its power to convince: the unique-
ness of the 'crisis,' an ensuing conversion to a new belief, and a marked
improvement in health proving its curative value."[23]

Before Wilson reached his own "crisis," however, he had first to dry
out. When Ebby paid him a return visit at 182 Clinton Street, he
brought along another member of the Oxford Group: Shep Cornell,
an upper-crust stockbroker, who had also accompanied Roland H. on
his mission to rescue Ebby. Wilson took a visceral dislike to Shep,
whose Ivy League airs and aggressive sales pitch annoyed him. Bill
pegged him as a socialite snob and dismissed him as a "pantywaist"
drinker, "a man who'd probably gone wild one night on too many
sherries at a Junior League cotillion" (*BW*, 211).[24]

Bill, the washed-up investment analyst once renowned for his
searching site inspections, decided to see for himself if the Oxford
Group might be a good investment. He would check out their operation, under Shoemaker's leadership, at one of the oldest rescue missions in New York City, at 246 East Twenty-third Street. Bill fit right
in with the usual mission clientele of destitute drunkards; by the time
he got there, he had visited several bars en route from the subway.
After arriving half-cocked and fully loaded, Wilson shot off his mouth
before the prayer service and then, slightly sobered on beans and
coffee, joined the shaking penitents on a ritual march to the amen
corner. There Bill earnestly testified, though he could not later recall
what he had said. "Ebby, who at first had been embarrassed to death,
told me with relief that I had done all right and had 'given my life to
God'" (*AACA*, 60).

Salvation did not take hold for a few more besotted days. After telling Lois he had found the answer, Bill also found the bottle and took
the hair of the dog for his hangover. This set him off on a three-day
blow during which he felt haunted by his experience at the mission.

On the morning of the third day, resolving to seek spiritual help, Wilson also recognized his need for human assistance. This meant another appeal to Dr. Silkworth. He determined to reenter Towns Hospital but this time to place himself humbly and unreservedly under God's care and direction. He was seeking a balm both for body and for soul: *the way out,* as the Big Book would tentatively be titled. So at 2:30 on the Tuesday afternoon of 11 December 1934, fortified by four beers cadged on credit, Bill returned to Towns—for the last time, as it happened.

Bill's willingness, under Ebby's tutelage, to seek guidance from a Higher Power led him to infuse pragmatism with spirituality and spirituality with pragmatism: "I was to test my thinking by the new God-consciousness within. Common sense would thus become uncommon sense" (*AA,* 13). "God-consciousness" was not, however, a term taken from James, but rather from the Oxford Group; it described the nature of personal revelation. Consider, for example, the definition in V. C. Kitchen's *I Was A Pagan* (1934), an Oxford Group testimonial, by a reformed drunkard, that Wilson likely read. "I am now, in other words," writes Kitchen, "receiving supernatural aid—not through a nonsensical Ouija Board nor any other spiritualistic 'instrument'—but through God-consciousness—through direct personal contact with the third environment—the spiritual environment I had so long been seeking."[25]

"At long last I saw, I felt, I believed," Wilson similarly asserts in "Bill's Story." "Scales of pride and prejudice fell from my eyes. A new world came into view" (*AA,* 12). He was alluding here to his conversion experience, which he did not fully disclose until the revised version of his story in *Alcoholics Anonymous Comes of Age.* In the Big Book he obliquely describes the "electric" effect of his surrender to "the Father of light who presides over us all." He felt peace, serenity, confidence, and a sense of victory. "I felt lifted up, as though the great clean wind of a mountain top blew through and through. God comes to most men gradually, but His impact on me was sudden and profound" (*AA,* 14).

Bill's imagery, especially the idea of a divinely expired wind surging through him, recalls Emerson's famous description in *Nature* (1836) of his own "spiritual experience": "Standing on the bare ground,—my head bathed by the blithe air and uplifted into infinite space,—all mean egotism vanishes. I become a transparent eyeball; I am nothing;

I see all; the currents of the Universal Being circulate through me; I am part or parcel of God."[26] In fact, Wilson stands in the great New England tradition that transmuted Calvinism first into Transcendentalism and then into Pragmatism. As Andrew and Thomas Delbanco demonstrate, Wilson has affinities not only to James and Emerson, but also to Jonathan Edwards, their philosophical forebear, whose complex doctrine of original sin—as a faculty by which the soul is rapt or repelled by sensible objects—uncannily resonates with the Big Book. Both Edwards and Wilson regard this faculty as inborn,

> and yet both insist that people are fully responsible for how they act on its inclinations. Edwards thought of this paradox as a war in the soul between the destructive desires that he called sin or self-love ("self-love run riot" is the Big Book's phrase) and the productive love that goes outward, asking no reward, to other people and, through them, to God.

If Alcoholics Anonymous was not exactly a religion, the Delbancos contend, it was at least "a 'church' in which rights were kept in steady balance with responsibilities through the mechanisms of free expression and requisite community service."[27]

Certainly, A.A. would never have existed if both Wilson and Smith had not, like Ebby, gotten religion in the Oxford Group. But although Bill W. embraced its explicitly Christian doctrines up to a point, he was not so much of a true believer as his cofounder, Dr. Bob. He never surrendered his Yankee skepticism about established religion and its institutional trappings. Furthermore, if A.A., with its precarious balance between secular and sacred missions, is to be considered any sort of "church," it can only be so within a loose definition of "religion," one as capacious as William James's.[28] "Were one asked to characterize the life of religion in the broadest and most general terms possible," James writes, "one might say that it consists of the belief that there is an unseen order, and that our supreme good lies in harmoniously adjusting ourselves thereto" (VRE, 53).

Bill's "Hot Flash"

"Things hot and vital to us to-day are cold to-morrow," says William James in *The Varieties of Religious Experience* (1902). The "hot place" in the mental field is the set of ideas to which a man is devoted and from which he works: *"the habitual centre of his personal energy."* The cold parts, located on the margins of consciousness, "leave us indifferent and passive in proportion to their coldness." Conversion consists of a sudden reversal of hot and cold: "To say that a man is 'converted' means, in these terms, that religious ideas, previously peripheral in his consciousness, now take a central place, and that religious aims form the habitual centre of his energy" (*VRE*, 195–96). Whether or not this passage prompted Bill Wilson to speak of his 1934 conversion as a "hot flash," he was deeply indebted to James's book for the conceptual framework by which to comprehend what had happened to him.

In *Alcoholics Anonymous Comes of Age*, Wilson gave a detailed rendering of his spiritual experience in Towns Hospital. Greeted upon his arrival by Dr. Silkworth, Bill was put to bed upstairs. He felt right at home, but once he dried out, he also felt extremely depressed, "still choking on the God Business" (*AACA*, 62). Ebby arrived bright and early one morning, and Bill dreaded that he had come to evangelize. But only at Bill's prompting did Ebby offer his "neat little formula" from the Oxford Group: "You admit you are licked; you get honest with yourself; you talk it out with somebody else; you make restitution to the people you have harmed; you try to give of yourself without stint, with no demand for reward; and you pray to whatever God you think there is, even as an experiment." This simple message only deepened Bill's depression, until he felt himself to be "at the very bottom of the pit" (AA, 62–63).

At this point, alone in his room, he cried out in despair, "If there is a God, let Him show Himself! I am ready to do anything, anything!" Lo and behold,

> Suddenly the room lit up with a great white light. I was caught up into an ecstasy which there are no words to describe. It seemed to me, in the mind's eye, that I was on a mountain and that a wind not of air but of spirit was blowing. And then it burst upon me that I was a free man. Slowly the ecstasy subsided. I lay on the bed, but now for a time I was in another world, a new world of consciousness. All about me and through me there was a wonderful feeling of Presence, and I thought to myself, "So this is the God of the preachers!" A great peace stole over me and I thought, "No matter how wrong things seem to be, they are still all right." (AACA, 63)

Gradually, Bill's native skepticism came to the fore. "You are hallucinating," he told himself. "You had better get the doctor." But Silkworth assured him, after cross-examination, that he was not crazy. There had evidently been "some basic psychological or spiritual event here," of the sort he had read about, which sometimes did "release people from alcoholism" (AACA, 63). After one look at Bill, Lois confirmed the doctor's opinion. "The minute I saw him at the hospital," she recalled, "I knew something overwhelming had happened. His eyes were filled with light. His whole being expressed hope and joy. From that moment on I shared his confidence in the future. I never doubted that at last he was free" (LR, 89).

Rational light on this mystical event came "the next day," when someone ("It was Ebby, I think") handed Bill a copy of The Varieties of Religious Experience, which he found to be "rather difficult reading" but nonetheless devoured "from cover to cover" (AACA, 64). In later years, Wilson would "frequently and avidly" recommend Varieties "to correspondents telling of difficulty with the A.A. program or concern over their 'spiritual experience'" (NG, 256 n. 52). But he himself seldom, if ever, revisited the book that once had touched him so profoundly. "I must confess that I have never since read William James to any extent," Bill W. wrote in 1965 to Robert J. Roth, a Jesuit who was preparing an article on "William James and Alcoholics Anonymous." Nor could Wilson recall in detail any particular part of *Varieties*. What he *did* remember was "that in general the experiences described, whatever their variety, did often arise out of conditions of complete hope-lessness—exactly my own just prior to the illumination."[1]

It's possible that Bill actually received *Varieties* from Dr. Silkworth, who had boned up on such matters, rather than Ebby, who had not—or possibly from Rowland.[2] Given the blurriness of the time sequence in various versions of the event, it's also possible that he read James's book *before* rather than *after* his "hot flash"—in which case it may have served to shape rather than merely to validate his experience. It is not surprising, in any case, that Bill W. should have had a shock of recognition in reading *Varieties:* the book brilliantly achieves the pragmatic accommodation Wilson himself sought between Christianity and modern science, spirit and mind, free will and determinism.

Whether or not Wilson read every last word of *Varieties,* his attention no doubt lingered over the stories, some quoted at length, of other drunkards' spiritual awakenings. Bill's experience resembled theirs especially in its benign generality: the God of drunkards turns out to be less dogmatically envisioned than the "God of the preachers." James cites, for instance, Samuel H. Hadley on the conversion he had while drying out at Jerry McAuley's Water Street Mission in 1882. Like Wilson's conversion, Hadley's exhibited what James called *photisms:* the "hallucinatory or pseudo-hallucinatory luminous phenomena" that frequently occur in such visions (*VRE*, 251):

> Never with mortal tongue can I describe that moment. Although up to that moment my soul had been filled with indescribable gloom, I felt the glorious brightness of the noonday sun shine into my heart. I felt I was a free man. Oh, the precious feeling of safety, of freedom, of resting on Jesus! I felt that Christ with all his brightness and power had come into my life; that, indeed, old things had passed away and all things had become new. (*VRE*, 203)

In remarking that there is "little doctrinal theology in such an experience, which starts with the absolute need of a higher helper, and ends with the sense that he has helped us," James might have been describing Wilson's own story. James refers also to the *Autobiography* of John B. Gough, a leading voice of the Washingtonian Movement, whose narrative seems so "purely ethical" and so devoid of specific beliefs that it is virtually "the conversion of an atheist—neither God nor Jesus being mentioned" (*VRE*, 203).[3]

Elsewhere in *Varieties*, James repeats an adage he has "heard quoted from some medical man": "The only radical remedy I know for dipsomania is religiomania" (*VRE*, 268 n. 1). This is the same advice that Carl Jung allegedly gave Rowland H. and that Ebby T. in turn passed on to Bill W.: that getting religion was the key to getting sober. Wilson's narrative goes on to summarize James's thoughts on spiritual experiences and to conclude: "Complete hopelessness and deflation at depth were almost always required to make the recipient ready. . . . *Deflation at depth*—yes, that was *it*" (*AACA*, 65).

Ernest Kurtz points out that whereas Wilson "seemed to attribute the phrase 'deflation at depth' to William James . . . neither this expression nor the bare word *deflation* appears anywhere" in *The Varieties of Religious Experience* (*NG*, 23). But the word, used in a context that closely matches Wilson's, *does* appear in one of the Oxford Group books he almost certainly read about the time of his conversion. In *I Was a Pagan* (1934), V. C. Kitchen, another recovered alcoholic, writes that his own spiritual growth, particularly his "sudden leap into God's light," seemed to result from a "process of breaking-down—of disorganization—of emptying out—a matter of *deflation in my own self-esteem* until self-approval and concern for the approval of others had shrunk to a point where I was willing to step entirely aside and give God a chance to shine" (my emphasis).[4]

Because, as Bill Pittman has found, *The Varieties of Religious Experience* was "the most often quoted book" in Oxford Group literature,[5] it would not be remarkable if Wilson conflated James's thinking with what he had learned from Ebby. Aside from Kitchen's book, Bill probably read other Oxford Group tracts at this time, and he later likely encountered *The Big Bender* (1938), Charles Clapp's confession of his own release from the bondage of self and of alcohol.[6] A highly successful bond salesman, whose parents lived in the same Westchester suburb, Bedford Hills, where the Wilsons would eventually settle, Clapp had followed a path very similar to Wilson's during the 1920s. Clapp too sank heavily into debt after the stock market crash and alienated his wife and friends with his drinking. Clapp was also introduced to the Oxford Group in the early 1930s, and he emulated the same member, Shep Cornell, who had tried to win over Wilson. The agent of Clapp's conversion, moreover, was Sam Shoemaker, who would have a similarly catalytic effect on Wilson.

Clapp recalls how he made two appointments one March day in 1933. He agreed to meet with Shoemaker in his apartment; but lest he "become too involved with the spiritual, and completely forget myself in a wave of evangelical salesmanship," he provided for his carnal needs as well, by arranging an adulterous dinner date. In a three-hour session the men covered "every angle of the Group and what it stood for, as well as some theology, psychology, sexology, pathology, horse-racing, etc." (Clapp was a polo aficionado.) But Shoemaker's main topic was his "own failures and defeats, what he had done about them, relating them to some of the things I told him of myself." Clapp was impressed by such candor, but he was not sure, after all, "that there was a God." Shoemaker challenged him to find out. "Possibly, at some later time," Clapp parried. "I did not want to start anything with that dinner date waiting for me. I felt there would be plenty of time for me to go in for this sort of life. After I reached fifty, then I would not mind slowing up a bit." As for his drinking, Clapp assured Shoemaker that "liquor was no real problem; I could stop at any time."

Anxious to escape, Clapp dodged Shoemaker's suggestion of a parting prayer that God would "reveal Himself to me and show me what He wanted me to do with my life." Clapp had other plans. But so, apparently, did God. In a taxi, thinking over what he had just heard, Clapp suddenly saw the street lights dim:

> The most overwhelmingly powerful feeling gripped me, something inside me said, "You must surrender your life to Me!" Gradually the lights returned to their natural brightness, the gripping feeling left, and I was sitting bolt upright, tingling all over.

Clapp soon ditched his dinner date and flew back to Shoemaker for further guidance. Sam recalled for him the prototypical conversion of Saint Paul on the road to Damascus and told of comparable modern-day marvels. Clapp now dropped to his knees and "prayed out loud for the first time in my life, simply asking God to take my life and run

it; I also thanked Him for revealing Himself to me, after I had so definitely turned my back on Him."[7]

Here, as in Hadley's and Wilson's narratives, God is almost entirely
uncharacterized; conversion has more to do with a new outlook on
life than with any specific idea of divinity. In this way, as James
implied, the spiritual awakenings of drunkards, whether within or
without sectarian religion, are characteristically down-to-earth and
pragmatic.

These are the very qualities, as Kevin McCarron argues from a
strictly Christian perspective, that serve to distinguish A.A.'s flexible
idea of "spirituality" from the doctrinal rigor of true religion. Whereas
A.A.'s emphasis on public disclosure links it to a European Protestant
tradition, says McCarron, the program's pragmatism makes it characteristically American:

> AA is not interested in theological speculation; it is interested in the
> continuous sobriety of the alcoholic. To AA members, sobriety is God.
> To engage in debates about the precise ontological status of the individ-
> ual's "Higher Power" would be pointless, even prejudicial to the indi-
> vidual's sobriety.

Beginning with Bill W.'s exemplary story, the nature of spiritual experience in A.A. recovery narratives tends to be strikingly and expediently
vague—precisely because, McCarron laments, the word "spiritual" itself has been drained of all theological content and reduced to "an
inchoate term of approbation without any determinable referent."
Thus despite its heritage of Protestant belief, A.A. has subtly adapted
the rhetoric of Christianity to its own deformingly modern purposes.
It thereby reflects "the growing tendency within Western democracies
to substitute a secular humanism for a transcendent God." In fact,
McCarron sententiously avers, "God is dead within the recovery narrative."[8]

Maybe so. But by stressing the supposed vacuity of A.A.'s secularized "spirituality," McCarron arbitrarily denies any claim to religious
authenticity in alcoholic conversion narratives. His extreme position
echoes the sort of objections James had anticipated from religionists
to *The Varieties of Religious Experience*. Carefully distinguishing between
an "existential" and a "spiritual" judgment—the one concerned with

the "constitution, origin, and history" of something, the other with its "importance, meaning, or significance"—James proposed to concern himself primarily with the former (*VRE*, 4). That way he would forestall the predictable complaints of true believers about his scientific approach to religious phenomena. "When I handle them biologically and psychologically as if they were mere curious facts of individual history, some of you may think it a degradation of so sublime a subject, and may even suspect me, until my purpose gets more fully expressed, of deliberately seeking to discredit the religious side of life" (*VRE*, 6). But James's aim was to enlarge, not to shrink, the confines of religion and to entertain a fuller range of explanations for conversion experiences.

In that spirit, then, let's reexamine Wilson's "hot flash," first biologically and then psychologically.

In "Bill's Story," he mentions the medical regimen during his first admission to the hospital: "Under the so-called belladonna treatment my brain cleared. Hydrotherapy and mild exercise helped much" (*AA*, 7). There's no reason to suppose that his case was handled any differently during his subsequent admissions. Taking this hint from the Big Book, Bill Pittman has delved into the "belladonna treatment," which was as much a specialty of the house at Charles B. Town's establishment as Dr. Leslie E. Keeley's magic bullet (bichloride of gold) had been at his inebriate clinics during the 1890s.[9]

As described in the medical literature between 1909 and 1912, the Towns remedy consisted of hourly doses of a mixture of belladonna, hyoscyamus, and zanthoxylum, taken along with a powerful cathartic mixture and castor oil. Belladonna (a.k.a. deadly nightshade) is a hallucinogenic agent; hyoscyamus, (a.k.a. henbane or hog's bean) sedates the central nervous system; zanthoxylum eases gastrointestinal discomfort. These potent drugs were administered only after patients had been weaned off alcohol with sedatives, including chloral hydrate, paraldehyde, and a pinch of morphine. The same drug cocktail was administered to drug addicts at Towns Hospital, but alcoholic patients were monitored more closely because they were more susceptible to belladonna delirium.

According to Dr. Alexander Lambert, Towns's partner in the belladonna cure,

The amount necessary to give is judged by the physiologic action of the belladonna it contains. When the face becomes flushed, the throat dry, and the pupils of the eyes dilated, you must cut down your mixture or cease giving it altogether, until these symptoms pass. You must, however, push this mixture until these symptoms appear, or you will not obtain a clear cut cessation of the desire for the narcotic.

Such "belladonna intoxication," Pittman adds, is "apt to be confined to one or two ideas on which the patient is very insistent."[10] After detoxification was complete, patients received "recuperative treatment," which consisted of "combinations of specialized diets, exercise, massage, hydrotherapy, and 'electrical baths.'" The average course of treatment at Towns Hospital was "four or five days for alcoholism or as long as eight to fourteen days for various drug habits."[11] Bill's final stay of seven days, it seems, was slightly longer than usual.

Having arrived at Towns in a mildly intoxicated state, Wilson was sedated at first and then, likely, given the belladonna specific. His spiritual awakening occurred either his second or third night in the hospital. Cautiously and controversially, Pittman concludes: "Considering his alcohol and chloral hydrate use upon entering Towns and adding this to the hypnotic drugs he received during the first few day [sic] of his stay, there is the possibility that his 'hot flash' may have been delusions and hallucinations characteristic of momentary alcoholic toxic psychosis."[12] Bill himself, after all, immediately suspected he was "hallucinating," even though he was "free of what little sedative they gave me" (AACA, 62). Only later, with Dr. Silkworth's paternal encouragement, did he begin to characterize his experience as "spiritual." Was he right the first time? Maybe it was a drug-induced hallucination.

Such questioning of the "hot flash" is liable to make some A.A.s very hot under the collar. So let me invoke James here, in order to mitigate any impression that an "existential" approach to Bill W.'s conversion experience is necessarily "a degradation of so sublime a subject," an instance of "deliberately seeking to discredit the religious side of life." As James pragmatically remarks, in regard to a 1900 study of persons predisposed to such visions: "Does this temperamental origin diminish the significance of the sudden conversion when it has occurred? Not in the least, as Professor Coe well says; for 'the ultimate test of religious values is nothing psychological, nothing definable in terms of *how it happens,* but something ethical, definable only in terms of *what is attained*'" (*VRE,* 241).

Following James, A.A. has taken great pains to assure its members that Bill W.'s "hot flash" does not set the standard of "spiritual awakening" that is seemingly mandated by the Twelfth Step. ("Having had a spiritual awakening as the result of these steps," etc.; Wilson's original wording, in his draft of the Big Book, was "spiritual experience.") In an appendix to the Big Book, starting with the second edition in 1955, Wilson attempted to correct a common but mistaken impression that such "personality changes, or religious experiences, must be in the nature of sudden and spectacular upheavals." On the contrary, he asserted, although some early A.A. members may have attained "an immediate and overwhelming 'God-consciousness' followed at once by a vast change in feeling and outlook," this degree of upheaval is *not* prerequisite to recovery from alcoholism. Most members' experiences, indeed, are "what the psychologist William James calls the 'educational variety' because they develop slowly over a period of time" (*AA,* 569).

Two years later, in *Alcoholics Anonymous Comes of Age,* a cautionary footnote, appended to Bill's "hot flash" account, reiterated that spiritual experiences are ordinarily "gradual and may take place over periods of months or even years." Bill and others who had the "sudden" variety "see no great difference so far as the practical result is concerned between their quick illumination and the slower, more typical kinds of spiritual awakening" (*AACA,* 63 n). Unlike the Big Book appendix, this footnote does not mention William James, but it borrows his distinction between "sudden" and "gradual" conversion experiences as well as his conclusion that the form of a "regenerative change" has "no general spiritual significance, but only a psychological significance" (*VRE,* 240).

From a psychological perspective, George A. Coe, an authority cited by James, found that those persons who had undergone such "striking" transformations were relatively passive and self-suggestive subjects in "possession of an active subliminal self": a "hypnotic sensibility" that is open to "hypnagogic hallucinations, odd impulses, religious dreams about the time of their conversion" (*VRE,* 240).

The idea of a "subliminal self" reflects the influence on American

psychology of European theories, most often associated with psychoanalysis, that were articulating a new model of mind at the fin de
siècle. As James remarked in *Varieties:*

> In the wonderful explorations by Binet, Janet, Breuer, Freud, Mason,
> Prince, and others, of the subliminal consciousness of patients with
> hysteria, we have revealed to us whole systems of underground life, in
> the shape of memories of a painful sort which lead a parasitic existence,
> buried outside the primary fields of consciousness, and making ir-
> ruptions thereinto with hallucinations, pains, convulsions, paralyses of
> feeling and of motion, and the whole procession of symptoms of hys-
> teric disease of body and of mind. (*VRE,* 234–35)

These clinical findings, which "sound like fairy-tales when one first
reads them," throw "a wholly new light upon our natural constitution"
and inevitably invite further study of the possible relationship between
a wide range of mental phenomena and the subject's "subconscious
life." Henceforth, James argues, "wherever we meet with a phenomenon of automatism," we are bound first to consider "whether it be
not an explosion, into the fields of ordinary consciousness, of ideas
elaborated outside of those fields in subliminal regions of the mind"
(*VRE,* 235).[13]

By the time Bill W. read *The Varieties of Religious Experience,* such
ideas had long since predominated the discipline of psychology;
through popularization in the mass media, they had also become
"common sense." So although Wilson did not become personally involved with psychoanalysis until the late 1940s, when he went to a
Freudian and then to a Jungian analyst for treatment of his depression,
he surely had some notion in 1934 that his "hot flash" could have been
an eruption from his "subliminal regions."

There is no need, however, to go beyond *Varieties* for a psychological interpretation of Wilson's spiritual experience. In the chapter on
"Saintliness," James considers instances of radical reformation by those
in thrall to "lower temptations" such as alcohol. He refers again to the
Hadley case and to those of other reformed drunkards as proof of
how strong addictions have been "completely annulled, apart from
transient emotion and as if by alteration of the man's habitual nature"
(*VRE,* 268). Such a "rapid abolition of ancient impulses and propensit-
ies," says James, "reminds us so strongly of what has been observed as

the result of hypnotic suggestion that it is difficult not to believe that subliminal influences play the decisive part in these abrupt changes of heart, just as they do in hypnotism" (*VRE*, 269–70).

In *Asylum* (1935), William Seabrook's account of his recovery from alcoholism (temporary, as it turned out), he viewed his own such change of heart skeptically. Seabrook recalls arriving at a strange but pleasant state of mind after three months of sobriety in the mental hospital, a curious state he describes as being "drunk on sobriety":

> I began to find myself interiorly illumined with a sort of mystical, if not maudlin, exaltation strangely like that which comes sometimes from prolonged drinking when the whiskey is good and one drinks a lot of it without becoming violent or sick. . . . It was as if a veil, or scum, or film had been stripped from all things visual and auditory, or as if the world had been suddenly diffused with a soft, unearthly, revealing light.[14]

Seabrook felt suffused by an incredible sense of safety and well-being; it was as if, he recognized, he had undergone a religious conversion despite his nonbelief:

> I suddenly realized that in the factual history of my actual clinical case there had been a strong parallel, a striking analogy at any rate, with the mystical process of salvation as doctrinally outlined by the Christian church. At a given moment, I had "repented" in considerable fear and terror. I had known I was "lost" and wanted to be "saved." I had known that my own strength, my own will, could no longer save me. At the least, I had begged, screamed, pleaded to be "saved." I had been willing to "abase" myself, to relinquish myself, my life, my will, my body into hands stronger than my own. I was through, and I knew it, so far as any effort to save myself was concerned. I was stripped down, naked, to one thing only, which was the one and only thing the Church Fathers doctrinally recommend, *the desire for salvation.*

As a staunch atheist, Seabrook interprets his experience not as religious, but rather as purely psychological; not as evidence of any heavenly visitation, but rather as a curious mental phenomenon—as "what happens to a drunkard who seeks serious, modern, scientific, medical-psychiatric aid to be cured," as part of "what any man who has been a hard drinker for years must go through to come out of it."[15]

Like Seabrook's "conversion," Bill W.'s "hot flash" might be attributed to any number of "subliminal" predispositions, including the seed of religious belief that had been planted by Ebby. Wilson was ripe, one might say, to drop into the hands of the Oxford Group. Even if we take the "hot flash" as a sign of divine intervention, we still might agree with James that "if the grace of God miraculously operates, it probably operates through the subliminal door." We might also agree that because "just *how* anything operates in this region is still unexplained," it is prudent "to say good-by to the *process* of transformation altogether,—leaving it, if you like, a good deal of a psychological or theological mystery,—and to turn our attention to the fruits of the religious condition, no matter in what way they may have been produced" (*VRE*, 270).

After his initial bewilderment, Wilson never questioned the supernatural source of his conversion. In a 1956 letter to Mel B., he asserted: "With me, the original experience was so prodigious, the preview of destiny so intense, that I have never had any difficulty with doubts since that time. Even at my worst, and that has often been damn bad, the sense of the presence of God has never deserted me."[16] Two years later, Bill told Marjorie W.: "What I really meant was this: I was catapulted into a spiritual experience, which gave me the capability of feeling the presence of God, His love, and His omnipotence. And, most of all, His personal availability to me" (*NG*, 255 n. 41).

Wilson lost no time acting upon his new state of grace. Immediately after his release from Towns Hospital, he and Lois began to attend Oxford Group meetings at the Calvary Episcopal Church annex, dubbed the "Spiritual Power House," which also served as Sam Shoemaker's residence and the American headquarters of the movement. Wilson accepted personal guidance from Shoemaker, who became a lifelong friend and confidant. Working closely with drunkards was something that Shoemaker emphasized, although some Oxford Group colleagues, weary of their failure to change the lives of alcoholics, thought the practice misguided. With Silkworth's compliance, Wilson met with patients at Towns Hospital. He also proselytized at Calvary's mission outpost on the lower East Side, which provided two hots and a flop on any given day to more than fifty homeless men, many of whom were chronic alcoholics.[17] Ebby, for one, was staying at Calvary Mission when he made his first contact with Bill in November 1934.

Wilson "started out for drunks," he said, "on jet propulsion," cocksure he could "fix up all the drunks in the world, even though the batting average on them had been virtually nil for the last 5,000 years" (*AACA*, 64). Sometime during 1935—sources differ about whether it was before or after Wilson's trip to Akron in May—Bill went one better than Shoemaker's example of housing drunkards by inviting them into his own home. Ebby became a semipermanent guest. Others came and went in drunken droves. Bill was frustrated, but he carried on.

Meanwhile Wilson joined an Oxford Group team of six, which met in Quaker-style meetings and listened for divine direction. As Lois recalled, the others on Bill's team "would get guidance for him to work with such and such a person in order to 'bring him to God.' Bill usually had different guidance and felt no identity with the person they selected. He became a bit annoyed at being told what to do" (*LR*, 93–94).[18] Here, then, are the origins of Wilson's gradual alienation from the Oxford Group. In their view, Bill was not getting results; he was not repaying either their spiritual investment in him or his own spiritual debt; instead he was wasting his time with the hopelessly unregenerate. "Naturally the Oxford Groupers became very cool indeed toward my drunk-fixing" (*AACA*, 65). Wilson resisted such "guidance," however. He believed so single-mindedly in his special mission to alcoholics that he was soon diverting them from the Oxford Group mainstream into what might be considered a prototypical A.A. meeting.

Bill had discovered that several reformed alcoholics, including Rowland and Ebby, regularly gathered at Stewart's Cafeteria, around the corner from the Twenty-third Street Mission, and carried on for hours over cigarettes and coffee. As Robert Thomsen describes it, Wilson felt a special communion with this gang; he "knew immediately and instinctively that these were his people. He could say anything to them, they anything to him, and it would be all right" (*BW*, 230). In fact, the group manifested Wilson's vision of "a chain reaction among alcoholics, one carrying this message and these principles to the next" (*AACA*, 64). If the meetings at Stewart's Cafeteria were sometimes bull sessions, they also addressed spiritual concerns that sprang from religious fervor.

This combination of the sacred and the profane, the spiritual and the pragmatic—with both elements tempered by the tension of their counterpoise—was the conceptual center of Alcoholics Anonymous. All that was needed now for A.A. to precipitate out of the Oxford

Group solution was for Wilson to revise his sales pitch. Having tried and failed to sway alcoholics with a religious message, one with heavy-handed emphasis on the Oxford Group's idea of conversion, Bill took some more advice from Silkworth. "For God's sake stop preaching," the doctor implored. "You're scaring the poor drunks half crazy. They want to get sober, but you're telling them they can only do it as you did, by some special hot flash." Bill was advised to save all that stuff for later, as drunks were naturally averse to religion, and instead to put over Silkworth's disease theory: "Tell about the obsession and the physical sensitivity they are developing that will condemn them to go mad or die. Pour it on. Say it's lethal as cancer" (BW, 233–34).[19]

Throughout the winter of 1935, as Bill pursued his full-time work with other alcoholics, Lois brought home the bacon from her job at Loeser's department store, where she had moved from Macy's in 1934, while Bill was still drinking, in order to be closer to home and what-ever emergencies might arise there. As Wilson recalled, somewhat sheepishly, "folks were beginning to say, 'Is this fellow Bill going to be a missionary for life? Why doesn't he go to work?'" (AACA, 65). Of course, he had never labored any harder than he did now trying to get drunks sober. But Wilson himself could not easily have imagined this calling to be a "real" job. In his 1954 address in Syracuse, New York, where the narrative for Alcoholics Anonymous Comes of Age was field-tested, he put even more stress on the pathetic "unmanliness" of his situation: "About this time, people began to say 'This fellow ought to quit being a missionary and go to work. His wife is still in that depart-ment store.'" So "like Micawber," the amiably hapless ne'er-do-well in Dicken's David Copperfield, he "began to sit around on benches in customer's rooms over on Wall Street . . . hoping that something would turn up."[20]

"That Bill felt demeaned by his wife working is understandable," asserts Ernest Kurtz. But he chides Wilson's biographers, especially Thomsen, for placing "misguided emphasis" on the idea that Lois "had to work." She had held jobs quite voluntarily, after all, since the earliest days of the marriage. At both department stores, moreover, she had pursued her plan of becoming a freelance interior decorator, a career she found to be "creative and fulfilling"—although she never had much occasion to practice it except on her own home in West-chester (NG, 258 n. 58).

But Kurtz largely misses the point: it's not whether Lois took her own work seriously or, for that matter, whether Bill took it seriously, but how Bill's attitude toward *his* "joblessness" was conditioned by the conventional division of gender roles. As Lori E. Rotskoff points out, "In keeping with dominant attitudes at the time, Wilson believed that a husband was supposed to support his wife; for him, the baneful effects of alcoholism were intertwined with the shame of economic dependence." Central to A.A.'s ideology, Rotskoff shows, was a model of "sober manhood" meant to reinstate recovered alcoholics in "the self-reliant, respectable breadwinner role." Throughout the Big Book are examples of formerly drunk and irresponsible men who have re-claimed "the familial status and privileges that came with breadwinning." When such stories itemize the material gains of sobriety, they mention "things like home mortgages, furniture, and the monthly bills of workaday life."[21]

Perhaps the best evidence of Bill W.'s gendered shame and insecurity is the term he (but not Lois) routinely used as shorthand for his conversion experience: "hot flash." The usual understanding is that Wilson's sardonic sense of humor, coupled with his desire not to turn off drunks with anything that smacked of religion, led him to speak of his spiritual awakening in a mildly deprecatory fashion—as a kind of in-joke among A.A. men who might otherwise have had to wonder about another man's talking openly about that sort of thing. The joke (such as it is) has decidedly misogynist overtones. "Hot flash," since its coinage around 1910, has referred to an exclusively female experience during menopause. Real men, unless they are rhetorically in drag, don't have hot flashes; and the ones who claim they do may not be real men.

That a "hot flash" can be an exasperating and embarrassing phenomenon is attested by *Sister Gin* (1975), June Arnold's feminist novel, centered on a lesbian alcoholic journalist, which is probably the first American book to celebrate the vicissitudes of menopause. When Su McCulvey has one of her many hot flashes, during dinner with her lover and her lover's mother, she complains:

> I don't mind flashing when I'm alone and can relax into it as if it were a hot bath; it makes you feel a little faint but not at all unpleasant, really. It's when the flash comes in the middle of a conversation that it is so distracting. I simply can't remember what anyone is talking about until the flash is over.[22]

But hot flashes have a positive side as well. Throughout the novel they are subtly related to Su's obstreperous subliminal alter ego, Sister Gin, who sometimes usurps Su's consciousness and compels her to write book reviews that are too honest to be politic. Sister Gin, the agent of Su's liberation from the censorial inhibitions she has internalized, is more like Sister Djinn (a pun never spelled out in the novel): a genie in the bottle of the mind whose marvelous powers mimic those of alcohol. And although Arnold, who was herself alcoholic, takes account of the damage done by drinking to Su and her lover Bettina, she also celebrates the ancient linking of spirits to inspiration.

Mamie Carter, an elegant octogenarian with whom Su has a passionate affair, explicates her delightfully dotty philosophy of alcohol:

> "Did you ever think of all the people who never drink enough?" Mamie Carter leaned toward Bettina like a conspirator, eyes agleam. "Not that they don't have the opportunity, either. They just never take it. Year after year, they go on drinking too little. Year by year. Never enough." . . .
>
> "It's a fact," Mamie Carter said. "Some people never do understand how important drinking is. There's the brain, crowded with thousands of unused cells and no space between. Every logician knows that growth is greatest when there is greatest space, that each incident which destroys cells creates a proportionate increase in the growth rate of those adjoining. . . . It is the martini, the lowly much-maligned martini itself that kills the idle bystanders so the idea-cells can have room to grow."[23]

Bill Wilson could not, of course, have read *Sister Gin*, but he did read *The Varieties of Religious Experience*, where James, like Arnold, uses the imagery of heat to portray "drunken consciousness" as "one bit of the mystic consciousness." "Sobriety diminishes, discriminates, and says no," says James; "drunkenness expands, unites, and says yes. It is in fact the great exciter of the *Yes* function in man [and woman!]. It brings its votary from the chill periphery of things to the radiant core. It makes him for the moment one with truth. Not through mere perversity do men run after it" (*VRE*, 387). Bill Wilson's cross-gendered hot flash perversely marked the displacement of gin by djinn in the hot place at "the habitual centre of his energy."

Bill W. Meets Dr. Bob

S I X

In *Liquor, The Servant of Man* (1939), published the same year as the Big Book but aimed at the "average" rather than the "problem" drinker, the following epigram is cited: "the first couple of drinks might make a man democratic but . . . at the bottom of every glass thereafter lie aloofness and superiority."[1] One of the proudest traditions in Alcoholics Anonymous is its openness to all comers, its ardently democratic ethos. What the original A.A.s quickly discovered, however, was that aloofness and superiority could result not only from drunkenness, but also from sobriety. It was the subtle elitism of the Oxford Group that made its continuing association with alcoholics impossible. The story of early A.A. is largely about its institutional and philosophical disentanglement from the Oxford Group, a development that was closely related to the emergent rivalry between A.A.'s eastern and midwestern branches. When Bill W. first met Dr. Bob, it may have been the Oxford Group that brought them together, but it was A.A. that kept them together.

What drew Wilson midwestward in May 1935 was an opportunity to recoup professionally and financially. "I insinuated myself," he recalled, "into a proxy row that involved control of a little machine tool company in Akron, Ohio" (*AACA*, 65). The National Rubber Machinery Company, which manufactured tire-making equipment, was weathering the Depression, but barely. There was so much internal

dissension that the firm was vulnerable to invasion by outside speculators. Wilson's New York associates at Beer (!) and Company must
surely have valued his shrewdness, for he had no other assets to pool
with theirs. They also gave him cause to think he might take charge
of National Rubber Machinery if their bid were successful. The "proxy
fight," as it is generally known in A.A. literature, is not described there
in any detail. It seems incidental to the story of Bill W. and Dr. Bob,
and it involves potentially boring stuff about business maneuvering.
This row typifies the predatory operations of capitalism; the "proxy
fight" would later have been called a "hostile takeover." The newly
sober Wilson had reverted to his old ways insofar as he was impelled
once again by vaunting ambition and barely sublimated aggression.

The proxy fight turned out to be, however, the end of his business
career as such. Although Wilson was afterward to work now and then
as an stock analyst, he never fully reentered the corporate world, although his experience there had an enormous impact on his management of Alcoholics Anonymous. As he wrote in 1960 to Elise Shaw,
wife of his old Wall Street friend:

> It is both amazing and comforting that this experience of mine with
> Frank in Wall Street has had a great deal to do with the present success
> of A.A. It was the training I then received in large affairs and in the
> constant effort to foresee and to evaluate the future that has since
> counted for so much. Without such an invaluable experience, I would
> have made a great many grievous errors. By no stretch of the imagina-
> tion could I have integrated the business and policy side of our A.A.
> affairs with its spiritual objective. (*PIO,* 175)

Wilson's 1935 journey to Akron had one overriding purpose: to sal-
vage his career. "Success in the proxy fight could restore his standing
on Wall Street. Sobriety and success could mean a new, comfortable
life for the Wilsons; Lois could leave the department store forever"
(*PIO,* 134). In other words, Bill also had a chance to repair his damaged
sense of manhood, not only by liberating his wife from her shameful
(to him) employment, but also by underwriting the conspicuous consumption to which they had once been accustomed. Such high living
would signify his renewed "success." "Think of it, darling," Bill wrote
to Lois during the summer of 1935, while the outcome in Akron was
still pending:

the opportunity to be president of this company and have some real income to pay bills with, a new life, new people, new scenes. No more Loeser's—a chance to travel, to be somebody; to have you rested at last after your long wait for me to get somewhere. All these things are at stake. Is it not worth the worry, dear heart? I have never tried to do my best before, but I have this time, and I shall not have regrets if I lose. (*PIO,* 146)

Bill had no intention of losing. The campaign went well at first. He and his partners amassed a significant block of proxy votes in their bid to seize power at the annual stockholders' meeting. A group of rival New York investors, however, cleverly formed an alliance with National Rubber Machinery's management; and together they fended off Beer and Company and, later in the summer, won the showdown vote. Bill's colleagues suspected chicanery and vowed to fight it out in court, but he could ill afford to await any settlement, even a favorable one, in the indefinite future. Stranded in Akron with little money and no prospects, he was in need of immediate relief, both economic and emotional.

The moment of truth in the Mayflower lobby thus came at an unpropitious time, when "Bill faced a solitary weekend in a strange city where he had just sustained a colossal disappointment. He had time on his hands and bitterness in his heart; fate had suddenly turned against him" (*PIO,* 135). That he did not drink under these trying circumstances is itself remarkable. What seems truly miraculous—and so A.A. literature has portrayed it—is the chain of events that led Bill W. to Dr. Bob, as if their blessed conjunction were foreordained by a Higher Power.

Consider, for example, the first link in this chain: Bill W.'s call to the Reverend Walter F. Tunks, whose name he singled out, apparently "quite at random," from an inclusive church directory in the Mayflower lobby:

> He had no conscious reason for picking Tunks's name; it may have been because his favorite Vermont expression was 'taking a tunk,' which meant 'taking a walk.' Or perhaps he picked out Tunks because the minister was an Episcopalian like Sam Shoemaker. Lois thought it was because Bill liked funny names. Whatever Bill's reason, he unwittingly picked the strongest Oxford Grouper among all of Akron's clergymen. (*PIO,* 136)

Because of Tunks's Oxford Group affiliation, he was familiar with reformed drunkards, and he was unreservedly receptive to Wilson's seemingly bizarre request that he needed help making contact with another alcoholic. When Tunks supplied him with ten leads, Wilson called them all, without success; but one person directed him to Henrietta Seiberling, whose name, as Bill recognized, placed her in the family that had founded Goodyear. Mrs. Seiberling, the divorcing daughter-in-law rather than the wife of the rubber magnate, was an active member of the Oxford Group; and she had lately been praying for guidance on behalf of Robert Smith, a surgeon who had recently confessed his drinking problem to other Groupers. Although Henrietta was separated from her husband and living alone with her children, she did not hesitate to invite a complete stranger—no less "a rum hound from New York," as Bill flippantly called himself (*PIO*, 137)—into her home.

Wilson also told her, however, that he was "from the Oxford Group," and when the role of the Oxford Group is taken fully into account, the meeting of Bill and Bob seems less than entirely serendipitous. As Mel B. suggests, in his study of early A.A., histories of the program have always "focused on the immediate events" that put the founders in touch with each other.

> In reviewing this fortunate meeting, however, little attention has been paid to steps that put everything in place. How was it that Henrietta Seiberling happened to be a member of the Oxford Group? What brought the Group to Akron in the first place? Why did Mrs. Seiberling respond so quickly to the idea of introducing Bill to another alcoholic? What had made the Oxford Group such a strong force in Akron compared with other cities? And how did it happen that it was the Akron Oxford Group that was known from the start as a fellowship that could help alcoholics?[2]

These are excellent questions. Mel B.'s answers may be summarized as follows. Not only was the Oxford Group exceptionally well established in Akron, where it had been a presence since 1924, it was also renowned for its "special task of helping alcoholics." This zeal, which set Akron Groupers notably apart from their peers at Calvary Church, arose from a local situation: the 1931 conversion of Russell ("Bud") Firestone, scion of tire tycoon Harvey Firestone. Young Firestone was a notorious sot whose drinking had exasperated and mortified his prominent family. When Bud got sober through the ministrations of the Oxford Group, it became known in Akron "as a society with special expertise in helping drunks." So grateful was Harvey Firestone for his son's deliverance that he sponsored a huge festival for the Oxford Group in January 1933. Frank Buchman himself appeared, with an entourage of twenty-nine trusted lieutenants. (Walter Tunks was one of the dignitaries who met Buchman at the train station.) "An exciting, spectacular affair," this Oxford Group conference grabbed local headlines; and from its headquarters at the Mayflower Hotel, it fanned out "to churches and other places throughout the city," including even the tire factories.[3]

The magnitude of the event far exceeded the small-group meetings (the so-called house parties) that had been more typical of Oxford Group conclaves. Mel B. suggests that this jamboree was a bellwether of the Oxford Group's evolution into Moral Re-Armament, with its expansive public mission. The event also exhibited Buchman's growing emphasis on the "key person" strategy for building membership. He had believed from the start of his career that wholesale reform was more effectively accomplished from the top down: capture the leaders, who lend their visibility and respectability to the cause, and ordinary people will come along. Buchman made certain that the cream of Akron society figured prominently among what one Akron paper called "dinner jacket revivalists" (*PIO*, 141). The main event of the conference was Bud Firestone's personal witness to the spiritual prowess of the Oxford Group.

Mel B. notes that although Anne Smith attended the festivities in 1933, her husband did not. Firestone's amazing grace, however, could not have escaped Dr. Smith's notice, and it must have given him hope for his own recovery. He came into the Oxford Group soon afterward. As a prominent physician, he would have offered another opportunity for Akron Groupers to practice the "key person" strategy.

Given this historical context, it becomes clearer why Bill Wilson was so warmly received in 1935. The ground had been very well prepared for his seemingly fortuitous arrival. It is plausible to suppose that Bill was equally primed for what happened. His trip in May was actually his *second* journey to Akron; he had accompanied his partners a month earlier on a reconnaissance tour of the National Rubber Machinery Company. Aside from the business at hand, the two things foremost in Wilson's mind at the time were his work with alcoholics in the Oxford Group and his own reputation for drinking, rumors of which his foes were ruthlessly spreading as they tried to sway stockholders. On this April trip, did Wilson ever become aware of the Akron Oxford Group and its local reputation for healing alcoholics? Did he hear any gossip, for instance, about Bud Firestone, the catalyst of whose conversion had been his own mentor, Sam Shoemaker? Might Tunks's name have been dropped by Shoemaker or someone else in New York who had attended the Akron rally in 1933? Perhaps it wasn't "quite at random" that Bill plucked Tunks's name from the church directory. At the very least, he might naturally have supposed that the Oxford Group in Akron would be, as it was in New York, closely affiliated with an Episcopal church.

The magical aura that surrounds Bill W.'s meeting with Dr. Bob seems to exceed the grasp of any purely rational explanation. "There were just too many coincidences," Henrietta Seiberling observed.[4] Or, as Carl Jung might have said, the uncanny concatenation of circumstances surrounding the seemingly fated meeting of Wilson and Smith exemplified *synchronicity,* Jung's term for "a *meaningful coincidence* of two or more events, where something other than the probability of chance is involved."[5] Nonetheless, what matters is not *how* Bill came to find Bob but *why* they hit it off so well.

Perhaps the most improbable, yet indispensable, coincidence at the embryonic stage of A.A.'s development was that both its founders were Vermonters as well as alcoholics, and thus that they voiced their common experience in the same regionally inflected language. Smith, by all accounts, was severely formal and reserved: not at all the sort of man to bare his soul to a fast-talking stranger nearly young enough to be his son. For more than two years, in fact, despite the encouragement of the Oxford Group, to which his weakness for alcohol was already common knowledge, Smith could never thaw himself out far enough to divulge his inner torment. Finally, with exquisite sensitivity to his pride, the Groupers managed to wring an admission from Bob just weeks before Bill's arrival, and only then by priming him with comparable revelations of their own. "Well," said Smith, "you good people have all shared things that I am sure were very costly to you, and I am going to tell you something which may cost me my profession. I am a silent drinker, and I can't stop."[6]

Mel B. points out that Smith's actual words may have been, "I am a *secret* drinker."[7] But *silent* speaks more directly to his Yankee taciturnity, which Bill knew instinctively how to penetrate once they sat down together in the small library of Henrietta Seiberling's cozy gatehouse home. He would just go on a bit about his own case, until the other man "got a good identification with me, until he began to say, 'Yes, that's me, I'm like that'" (*AACA*, 68). Whereas Smith had planned to humor his friend Henrietta's whim by politely spending fifteen minutes with her guest from New York, the two men talked for five or six hours (depending on whether or not they ate dinner first).

Or rather, we may safely assume, Bill did most of the talking. "Whatever Bill said," write the anonymous authors of Dr. Bob's official A.A. biography, "he must have thrown in everything he ever knew or guessed about alcoholism, and told the long version of his story to boot" (*DB*, 68–69). The only accounts we have of what transpired during that epical conversation are Wilson's, and he wrote surprisingly little about what was said: merely that he had remembered Silkworth's advice and dampened "the fireworks of religious experience" (*AACA*, 68) while he "bore down heavily on the medical hopelessness of Dr. Bob's case, freely using Dr. Silkworth's words describing the alcoholic's dilemma, the 'obsession plus allergy' theme." Bill believed it was this "bad news" about "those twin ogres of madness and death" that "hit him hard" and "triggered him into a new life" (*AACA*, 69–70).

Bill also claimed that Bob "talked to me about himself as he had never talked before" (*AACA*, 68), that their talk was "a completely *mutual* thing" (*AACA*, 70). Bill, who knew he needed this other drunk as much as Bob needed him, thought he had found in this mutuality "the final missing link" in the evolution of Alcoholics Anonymous: *"This was it.* And this mutual give-and-take is at the very heart of all of A.A.'s Twelfth-Step work today" (*AACA*, 70). However, it is at least doubtful that, as Robert Thomsen has it, "Soon Dr. Bob had opened up and was speaking as frankly, as unashamedly, as Bill" (*BW*, 238). More likely, as he had done with his Oxford Group colleagues, Smith repaid Wilson's voluble sharing of intimacies with a relatively succinct reckoning of his own.

Like the canonical gospels of the New Testament, the foundational narratives of Alcoholics Anonymous show the superimposition of later doctrinal imperatives on the original story. What happened in 1935 has been subtly overlaid in the retelling, for purposes of pointing a lesson about A.A. fundamentals. It is amusing, and perhaps instructive, to juxtapose Bill's elaborate account to Bob's characteristically clipped version, the gaping holes in which are comically expansive: "We entered her house at exactly five o'clock and it was eleven fifteen when we left. I had a couple of shorter talks with this man afterward, and stopped drinking abruptly" (AA, 179). Keep it simple!

Although Bill W. always stressed *what* he had told Dr. Bob, Smith himself stressed *who* the teller was. There was very little news for Bob in Bill's presentation; Bob had already read up about alcoholism and the spiritual approach to curing it. As Dr. Bob's biographers put it, with hyperbolic humor, "If William James, Carl Jung, and Dr. Silkworth, along with Frank Buchman and all the members of the Oxford Group, had been doing the talking, it would have been just another lecture" (DB, 69). The visitor's message about Silkworth's theory was "undoubtedly helpful," Bob dryly said, but Bill's authority derived from his own life, not from any book-learning. Smith underscored the point: *"Of far more importance was the fact that he was the first living human with whom I had ever talked, who knew what he was talking about in regard to alcoholism from actual experience. In other words, he talked my language"* (AA, 180). And, as I have suggested, that language was Vermontese.

But did they have dinner? Bill's story says that while food was provided, Bob, who had the shakes and one of the worst hangovers of his life, could not eat. Bob's story suggests it was his fifteen-minute limit that obviated dining. Ernest Kurtz convincingly argues that a hostess of Henrietta Seiberling's social caliber could never imaginably have invited guests for five o'clock on a Sunday afternoon without intending to serve them a meal. But did they actually eat?

The point, as Kurtz suggests, is that A.A.'s official narratives have focused so tightly on "the *immediacy* of identification between Bill and Bob," that they have skipped dinner, so to speak. Kurtz conjectures that Bill, whose immediate reaction to Bob was that he badly needed a drink, may have noted Bob's "discomfort at facing in his condition a fully laden table" and suggested, even before they sat down, that they ought better retire for a private talk (NG, 260 n. 66).

Building upon his own speculation, Kurtz then suggests that Bill's (hypothetical) breach of manners—the rudeness of his supposedly proposing to pass up dinner—"fits well with" Henrietta Seiberling's first impression of Wilson's loutish "deficiencies in 'class'" (*NG*, 260 n. 66). According to her later and highly unflattering recollections, Bill had shown up that day in uncouth clothing, and he had stood hunched over instead of fully erect. "He laughed too loudly," she said, "and showed too many teeth even when talking. He had this mannerism of rubbing his hands together and a simpering smile—a regular Uriah Heep." For Kurtz, the snobbery of Mrs. Seiberling's reaction to the vulgar "rum hound from New York" helps to explain "some of the tensions which over the years marked the relationship between the Oxford Group and Alcoholics Anonymous as it came into being" (*NG*, 259 n. 64).

These class tensions arose from one fundamental difference. Whereas A.A. promised alcoholics, many of whom had lost caste through their drinking, the recovery (or attainment) of middle-class respectability; the Oxford Group assured its members of an even more elite status. That is, although both organizations implicitly promoted upward class mobility, A.A. was demographically centered on the cusp of the lower and middle classes, while the Oxford Group was positioned on the threshold of the middle and upper classes.

Frank Buchman himself was attracted to the wealthy and worldly, the movers and shakers, and many of his followers were not only socially upscale, but also acutely class conscious. Such people, both in Akron and New York, were discomfited by the burgeoning presence of alcoholics in their midst. Their own prestige was threatened when people insolently "began calling the Oxford Group an 'upper-class Salvation Army.'"[8] Some Akron Groupers went so far as to propose "that the alcoholics be screened so that only the most socially acceptable would be allowed in" (*DB*, 158). Even with "acceptable" alcoholics, however, the "key person" strategy involved risk. In fact, it backfired in Bud Firestone's case: "When the rubber baron's son (whose 'change' had, incidentally, been very highly publicized) took a dive back into the bottle, many church people became rather patronizing toward the Oxford Group" (*DB*, 159).

Aside from class tensions, A.A. and the Oxford Group came to be divided by proprietary disputes about exactly when A.A. was founded

and who was ultimately responsible for its success. Henrietta Seiberling, for instance, always counted herself, along with Anne Smith, Bob,
and Bill, as one of the *four* cofounders (*NG*, 264–65 n. 15).[9] From her
perspective, shared by many in the Akron group, the true origin of
A.A. lay not in any events in faraway New York (Ebby's visit to Bill W.,
Bill's "hot flash"), or even in Wilson's crisis in the Mayflower lobby,
but rather in the Oxford Group's prior conversion of Doctor Smith,
who was thus prepared to meet Wilson on at least equal terms. It
was once remarked to T. Henry Williams, in whose home the Akron
Groupers met for years, that he must know a lot about A.A. Yes, he
replied, it had started right in his living room; and he proudly pointed
to the place on the carpet where Bob had first hit his knees in surrender.

In this version of things, Wilson comes across as an interloper, who,
far from saving Dr. Bob single-handedly, merely assisted Smith's Akron
friends in a process of recovery they had already initiated. Throughout
the summer of 1935, furthermore, when Bill stayed for three months
with the Smiths and began working with Bob to dragoon other alcoholics into sobriety, the Oxford Group remained the spiritual center
of their lives—"the only conceptual home Wilson and Smith had"
(*NG*, 39)—to which any and all of their success might fairly have
been attributed.

Whatever the justice of these claims, on which official A.A. literature is generally mute, the major causes of the break were religious
and philosophical disagreements. Bill W. tactfully summarized the
points at issue in *Alcoholics Anonymous Comes of Age*. First, he said, the
Buchmanite mission "to save the whole world" conflicted with A.A.'s
singleness of purpose: saving alcoholics. Moreover, certain of the Oxford Group's "ideas and attitudes could not be sold to alcoholics," who
resisted "pressure in any form" and would not abide "the rather aggressive evangelism." As for "the principle of 'team guidance' for their
own personal lives," that was simply "too authoritarian." And the Oxford Group absolutes were much too rigorous for drunks who "simply
did not want to get 'too good too soon.'" Finally, whereas the Oxford
Group "depended very much upon the use of prominent names," such
publicity clashed with the evolving principle of anonymity as nothing
less than the spiritual foundation of all A.A. traditions (*AACA*, 74–75).[10]

What went unsaid in *Alcoholics Anonymous Comes of Age* was the

most delicate problem of all: how to allow for Catholic membership
in a decidedly Protestant organization, which the Roman Church
might well have deemed heretical in its teachings and therefore inter-
dicted for the faithful. Wilson was certainly aware of this potentially
disastrous difficulty, and he strove to placate Catholic authorities even
as he distanced himself from the Oxford Group. The religious issue
did not come to a climax, however, until the secession of the largely
Catholic Cleveland meeting from the Akron chapter in 1939. At that
time, as Kurtz remarks, "A.A. in New York City had but one Catholic
member, and he very recent, while Akron A.A.—still meeting side
by side with if not within the Oxford Group—acknowledged none"
(*NG*, 52).[11]

Catholics are now so abundant in A.A. that it is hard to imagine
it without them. But the Program manifests a discernible difference
between what might be called its "Protestant" and its "Catholic" styles
of fellowship and spirituality. Simply put, this has to do with the relative emphasis members place, respectively, on A.A. "scripture," especially the Big Book, and on A.A. meetings as a "mystical body" of
recovering alcoholics.

Another unstated source of friction with the Oxford Group was that
Frank Buchman had become a political liability. In a notorious 1936
interview, which received widely negative press coverage, Buchman
offered words of praise for Adolf Hitler as a bulwark of anticommun-
ism. Clearly, what Buchman had in mind was a "key person" coup:
converting the Fuehrer into a Grouper.

> Of course I don't condone everything the Nazis do. Anti-semitism?
> Bad, naturally. I suppose Hitler sees a Karl Marx in every Jew.
>
> But think what it would mean to the world if Hitler surrendered to
> the control of God. Or Mussolini. Or any dictator. Through such a
> man, God could control a nation overnight and solve every last bewil-
> dering problem . . . .
>
> Human problems aren't economic. They're moral and they can't be
> solved by immoral measures. They could be solved within a God-
> controlled democracy, or perhaps I should say a theocracy, and they
> could be solved through a God-controlled Fascist dictatorship.[12]

Buchman was overreaching foolishly here. The authoritative history
of the Oxford Group finds, however, "no evidence that the movement

as a whole," particularly after the outbreak of war, was harboring Nazi sympathizers. But its leader could never shed the stigma of his controversial remarks.[13]

The less than amicable parting between A.A. and the Oxford Group came in stages. After Wilson's return to New York in August 1935, Bill and Lois adopted the practice, initiated by Bob and Anne Smith the preceding summer, of opening their home to struggling alcoholics, some of them from the Calvary mission. Not surprisingly, the Wilsons' generosity of spirit soon exhausted their mental and material reserves; and when their extraordinary efforts seemed to yield no lasting success—all the drunks got drunk again—Bill and Lois switched to a less demanding approach. They hosted an open house every Tuesday evening. As the Wilsons' personal lives became more and more inextricably bound with those of alcoholics, in a way that created intense mutual loyalty, their own ties to the Oxford Group were attenuating.

Some Groupers at Calvary Church resented the separatist ramifications of the Wilsons' work: the weekly meetings at their Brooklyn home; the refusal of alcoholics Bill had enlisted to concern themselves with the larger goals of the Group, including the recruitment of "key persons." Whatever Sam Shoemaker may have thought, he kept his own counsel on the matter while he tacitly allowed his assistant to edge the alcoholics out of the Oxford Group—first by forbidding them to attend meetings at 182 Clinton Street, and then by smearing the Wilsons as "not really maximum" (that is, less than sufficiently committed to the cause).

Lois, who had never had much use for the Oxford Group and who was going along for Bill's sake, felt the sting of rejection more deeply than Bill. But, as Kurtz remarks, the privileged daughter of Dr. Clark Burnham, who might have been expected to feel "more comfortable among the habitués of Calvary Church than among the denizens of Stewart's cafeteria," did not "for whatever reasons of background and temperament" ever gravitate toward the religious swells, and she never ceased prompting her husband in the other direction (*NG*, 25). Bill and Lois nonetheless persisted with the Oxford Group until the summer of 1937, when they stopped attending meetings at Calvary as well as "house parties" elsewhere. By then, the as-yet-nameless bunch of drunks in New York was cohesive enough to sustain its autonomy.

In Ohio, however, the process of separation was much more protracted, in part because the Oxford Group there had always been more receptive than the Calvary people to the "alcoholic squad" (as it was known in Akron). Bob Smith and those he mentored wished also not to hurt T. Henry and Clarace Williams, who had shared their lives and home so generously and so long. The precipitating crisis was the founding in May 1939 of a separate group of drunks in Cleveland: the first, in fact, to adopt the title of the recently published Big Book and go by the name of Alcoholics Anonymous. Akron finally went along in December, amid much acrimony with Henrietta Seiberling. "Have definitely shaken off the shackles of the Oxford Group," Dr. Bob wrote to Bill W. on 2 January 1940, "and are meeting at my house for the time being" (DB, 218).

As Lois Wilson recalled the late 1930s, she really had to "wonder *what* we lived on" (LR, 105). There were small rent payments from the sisters who shared a top-floor room at 182 Clinton Street; there were modest earnings from Lois's self-employment as an interior decorator—she had quit Loeser's in March 1936 to satisfy Bill's wish that "I 'get out of that damned department store'"—(LR, 104); there were intermittent commissions from Bill's odd jobs on Wall Street.

Wilson's best opportunity had come from an unexpected direction. Late in 1935 Charles Towns, who was cognizant of Bill's knack with alcoholic patients and eager to improve the balance sheet at the hospital, offered him a full-time position as a lay counselor. "He was prepared to give him an office, a very decent drawing account, plus a healthy slice of the profits." As Thomsen imagines this scene, Bill's ego was swelling by the minute as Towns flattered him that "in no time at all he'd be the most renowned and successful therapist in New York, the number-one man" (BW, 258).

Although Bill was understandably enthusiastic about the offer, Lois was not; and the Tuesday night group yanked him down to earth by unanimously rejecting the idea, on the grounds that their movement would be destroyed if it were ever to become professionalized. Reluctantly, under additional pressure from Dr. Bob, Wilson understood "that this work could be done for love only, never for money." '*Pass It On*' adds that by portraying himself "as the impulsive, self-seeking opportunist who might have wrecked the fledgling movement had it not been for the wise and timely advice of others," Bill W. used this incident, rhetorically at his own expense, as a moral exemplum about the power of what A.A. would later call its "group conscience" (*PIO*, 177).

Now that Wilson was perceptibly sober, some of his old colleagues trusted him again to handle stock investigations, and he traveled throughout the Midwest. An Oxford Group contact also hired Bill to collect proxies on behalf of an investment consortium in Pennsylvania. Clayton Quaw, of Quaw and Foley, threw business his way and put him on the boards of the Fisk Tire Company in Boston and the Pierce Governor Company in Anderson, Indiana. But when the lingering economic depression forced Quaw to lay him off late in 1937, Wilson gave up on Wall Street. Instead he pursued small business ideas with Hank P., one of the alcoholics he had rescued in Towns Hospital. Working out of Hank's office in Newark, New Jersey, Bill dreamed up various and sundry business deals, all losing propositions. Their later partnership in the Big Book was to be no more profitable at first, although it proved to be a financial bonanza in the long run.

The genesis of the Big Book dates to November 1937, when Bill returned to Akron on a business trip and compared notes with Dr. Bob and the others on the present state and future possibilities of their movement. Despite many failures, including an alcoholic suicide in Wilson's own house, the founders could count forty formerly hopeless cases, half of them with a year's sobriety or more. Where to go from here? As Thomsen says, "Bill had a thousand ideas. The stalled motor of his imagination had started to turn again; the old power drive was coming back, full force" (*BW*, 267–68). He laid out for Dr. Bob a breathtakingly ambitious program, a quantum leap beyond anything he could have hoped to achieve at Towns Hospital. This was no longer just about his own career, but rather the perpetuation of what had saved their lives and those of the forty others.

First, Bill proposed, paid missionaries would be selected from the two extant groups, and they would spread the word as the Johnny Appleseeds of sobriety. Then there would need to be books and pamphlets to publicize their inevitable success. Then, once the public was clamoring for the miracle cure for alcoholism, there would be demand for a vast network of well-staffed alcoholic hospitals and/or sanitaria, the enormous costs of which would be covered by massive fundraising, especially among the American plutocracy.

Dr. Bob liked the idea of a book, in which their own experience would be set down for the encouragement of still suffering alcoholics, but he was cool toward the rest of Bill's program. Smith nonetheless agreed to back Wilson when he addressed the Akron chapter, which tried to overrule their visionary leader. But with Dr. Bob's support behind Bill W.'s strenuous arguments, the cofounders prevailed by a narrow majority. Wilson returned home with a mandate, however weak, to pursue his dreams.

The New York group needed less convincing. "Most of them soon fell in with my grandiose notions," Bill W. recalled. "It was felt that raising money for such a noble enterprise should present no difficulties at all." Why, they assured each other, "this is probably one of the greatest medical and spiritual developments of all time. Certainly the rich will help us. How could they do anything else?" (*AACA*, 146). But the capital campaign was an utter failure, despite the tantalizing hope of funding from the Rockefellers, who although they provided some modest financial relief for the cofounders, ultimately concluded that A.A. was better served by becoming financially autonomous.

Smith and Wilson scrapped the "grandiose notions" and returned to the project on which they had agreed most heartily: publication of a book. In writing *Alcoholics Anonymous,* which consolidated A.A.'s identity, Bill Wilson's life story became effectively fused with the subsequent history of A.A. If Bill W. thereafter led a life at all apart from A.A., it ceased to matter; he had become synonymous with the American institution he was building.

Although there is no doubt of Dr. Bob's immense and continuing influence in and around Akron, he never gained the national standing and visibility of Bill W. Of course, Wilson survived Smith by more than twenty years. Nonetheless, his greater fame was not simply the result of his longevity, but rather of his penchant for self-promotion and the force of his enormous talents as a leader and also as a writer. Wilson's leadership, indeed, was most fully expressed in his authorship. That writing became central to Wilson's vocation has not been sufficiently recognized in A.A. literature—perhaps because so much of it was written by Bill W. himself!

PART THREE

What We Are Like Now

Writing the Big Book

SEVEN

With a touch of hype, perhaps, Nan Robertson calls *Alcoholics Anonymous* "one of the greatest publishing successes of all time," having sold five million copies by 1985, the year of A.A.'s fiftieth anniversary.[1] The Wilsons' share of the royalties put them on easy street by the 1960s and made Lois rich after Bill died in 1971. In 1986, two years before her own death, she received nearly a million dollars from the sales of his books. None of this bounty could be returned to A.A. directly. It would have violated the Seventh Tradition: "Every A.A. group ought to be fully self-supporting, declining outside contributions," even from the cofounder's wife. But Lois donated much of her income to the Stepping Stones Foundation for research on alcoholism.

Ironically, Wilson's turnabout from a floundering business career led to his becoming not only a Number One man—in effect, the CEO of his own corporation—but also the manly provider he always wished to be. Although Wilson's new vocation as a writer issued from his verbal facility, the peculiar discipline of writing itself was dauntingly unfamiliar at first. Nell Wing, Wilson's loyal longtime secretary, recalls him as "a dedicated, tireless talker" who would often harangue his guests at Stepping Stones with protracted monologues. "Not many people interrupted him once he got started."[2] But this man who was never at a loss for words nonetheless struggled in writing the Big Book.

What became *Alcoholics Anonymous* was begun during the spring of 1938, while other fundraising initiatives were in progress.³ In short order Wilson drafted the two opening chapters: "Bill's Story" and "There Is a Solution." His method of composition was to make extensive notes to himself and then bring them to the Newark office of Honor Dealers, Bill's business venture with Hank P. (They were trying to organize northern New Jersey's gasoline dealers into a buyers' co-operative.) Wilson would extemporize from his notes, giving dictation to Ruth Hock, recently hired as the company's secretary and sole employee. She later recalled how Bill W. had stood behind her as she typed up his words, stopping after each section to "look back over the typed pages while his thoughts were still working in that vein" (PIO, 193). In another account, Hock remembered Bill's chain-smoking and his pacing back and forth as he expounded his ideas: "At various intervals he would include his philosophizing off the subject using lengthy, flowery metaphors that would later be edited out."⁴ The first two chapters were revised in consultation with the New York group and then multilithed for limited circulation to prospective financial backers. (In this format only, "Bill's Story" came after, rather than before, "There Is a Solution.")

On a tip from one of the recently installed (and nonalcoholic) trustees of the Alcoholic Foundation, a newly formed trust for the still nameless bunch of drunks, Wilson approached Eugene Exman, editor of religious books at Harper and Brothers. Exman, who had built Harper's list of Oxford Group titles, scanned Wilson's partial typescript during the summer of 1938 and immediately offered him a contract, along with a generous advance of $1,500 (worth ten times more in 1990s dollars). The trustees were as thrilled as Wilson himself at this promising development, but Hank persuaded Bill that it made better business sense for the alcoholics to put out their book by themselves; and Exman unexpectedly agreed, on the grounds "that a society like ours ought to control and publish its own literature" (AACA, 155).

Although the enterprise was never legally incorporated, Hank prepared a prospectus and some homemade stock certificates for Works Publishing Company, Inc., a name derived from Anne Smith's favorite biblical quotation ("Faith without works is dead") and/or a favorite slogan of the fellowship ("It works!"). Vast earnings were projected; Hank figured potential profits on sales up to a million copies! For their joint efforts, Hank and Bill each planned to take one-third (two hun-

dred shares) of the new company and to offer the remaining two hundred shares at $25 each. Bill would placate the trustees, dismayed at
the self-publishing plan, by giving his author's royalties to the Alcoholic Foundation. It was expected that the New York group, which
had encouraged the project, would snap up the stock, but they unanimously declined to finance an unfinished book. Eventually the two
hundred shares were sold, and a loan was obtained from Charles
Towns: enough to keep Bill afloat while he completed the typescript.[5]

Uncertain exactly where the book was going, Wilson dictated
rough drafts of chapters from a list of possible headings. Throughout
the fall of 1938, as each new one was finished, it was read to the New
York group and also sent to Akron for vetting by Dr. Bob and his associates there. Although no serious objections were forthcoming from
Ohio, the unrulier New York group engaged in heated arguments over
everything—"the chapters got a real mauling" (*AACA*, 159)—and Ruth
Hock typed revision after revision.

Wilson now reached the crucial point of drafting the fifth chapter,
the "backbone of the book," in which "we would have to tell how our
program for recovery from alcoholism really worked" (*AACA*, 159).
Exhausted by the wrangling over the first four chapters and doubtful
of his capacity to finish the job, Wilson retired to bed one night with
a pencil and a scratch pad. He thought about the six tenets of the
Oxford Group. (That is, the alcoholic squad's paraphrase of the basic
principles of the Oxford Group, which had never actually formalized
them as "steps.") Bill was promptly inspired to write:

> I set out to draft more than six steps; how many more I did not know.
> I relaxed and asked for guidance. With a speed that was astonishing,
> considering my jangling emotions, I completed the first draft. It took
> perhaps half an hour. The words kept right on coming. When I reached
> a stopping point, I numbered the new steps. They added up to twelve.
> Somehow this number seemed significant. Without any special rhyme
> or reason I connected them with the twelve apostles. Feeling greatly
> relieved now, I commenced to reread the draft. (*AACA*, 161)

There's a legendary air to this tale of quasi-automatic writing, which
recalls Sherwood Anderson's fabulous account of the creation of
Winesburg, Ohio (1919): "I was there naked in the bed and I sprang up.
I went to my typewriter and began to write. . . . I wrote it [the first
story], as I wrote them all, complete in the one sitting. I do not think

I afterwards changed a word of it."[6] In Anderson's case, the last claim is demonstrably false; the extant manuscript (written in pencil rather than typed!) shows many changes in wording. Wilson's original draft of the Twelve Steps does not survive, although an "approximate reconstruction" has been proffered (*PIO*, 198–99).

The original Twelve Steps, whatever their exact wording may have been, were undoubtedly closer in spirit to the Oxford Group than the secularized version that emerged from the debates of the New York drunks. Wilson later identified three conflicting factions. The conservatives wanted a book that was "Christian in the doctrinal sense of the word" and that said so in no uncertain (biblical) terms. The liberals, the largest contingent (nearly a majority), could live with "God," but they were "dead set against any other theological proposition." A small but vociferous radical wing of atheists and agnostics pressed for "a *psychological* book which would lure the alcoholic in. Once in, the prospect could take God or leave Him alone as he wished" (*AACA*, 162–63). Caught in the middle, but temperamentally aligned with the liberals, Wilson finally demanded the prerogative of settling all disputes by his own best judgment. The result, as in many documents produced by discordant committees, was a purposeful vagueness around major points of contention.

As Wilson worked out the conceptual part of the book, a section of case histories was being assembled, mainly in Akron, where the larger numbers allowed for a broader range of experiences to be told. Even so, as Kurtz notes, the homogeneity of the membership—middle-aged, middle-class, white Anglo-Saxon Protestant males—made it difficult to present much diversity in the narratives, which were artfully edited so as "to accent different phases of the drinkers' common experience" (*NG*, 73). Thus the "almost perfectly typical" story of "A.A. Number Three"—Bill D., the Akron lawyer who was the first man to be successfully sobered up by Bill W. and Dr. Bob—was left out of *Alcoholics Anonymous*. "His 'credentials,' in fact the usual ones for 'getting the program' in these early years, were apparently too blatant," Kurtz explains: "highly respectable upper middle-class background, above average education, intensive youthful religious training which had since been rejected, and former social prominence recently nullified by such behavior as his assault on two nurses [at the hospital where the cofounders first approached him]" (*NG*, 74).

Many of the sixteen narratives from Ohio were ghostwritten by Jim S., a former newspaperman; Dr. Bob, however, provided his own story, "The Doctor's Nightmare," which was given the place of pride at the head of the section. The New Yorkers produced twelve stories, most of which required revision by Bill and Hank, whose editorial labors often were resented.[7] Before finally going to press, the book cleared two additional obstacles.

The first concerned the title. Wilson himself preferred "Alcoholics Anonymous," a term, in bantering use during 1938,[8] that seemed to combine the disreputable and the genteel with an overtone of sardonic self-parody. The book's title-*noir* (so to speak), which now sounds as stylistically dated as its prose, still faintly resonates with the association between drinking and criminality that took hold during Prohibition—as if it named so luridly incongruous an outfit as "Murder, Incorporated." For lack of spiritual tone, "Alcoholics Anonymous" was strenuously resisted, especially in Akron. Of many suggested alternatives, the most popular became "The Way Out," until it was determined that two dozen books with that title were already listed at the Library of Congress. As Kurtz remarks, "the search for a happy euphemism had led the non-drinking alcoholics to refer to themselves in writing as 'The One Hundred Men Corporation'" (*NG*, 74). But "One Hundred Men" was too cryptic for a book title, and it excluded Florence R., the lone female member (who did not sustain her sobriety). "Alcoholics Anonymous" won out by default; the subtitle nonetheless remained "The Story of How More Than One Hundred *Men* Have Recovered From Alcoholism" (my emphasis).

Wilson, who had hoped to receive writerly credit, at least as "Bill W.," later confessed to "a shameless piece of egotism": having proposed that a suitable subtitle for "The Way Out" would be "The B. W. Movement" (*AACA*, 165–66). In the end no author was named, even by initials, on the title page. Wilson was responsible for "at least ten of the opening chapters"; Hank P. may have written "To Employers" (*PIO*, 200). Bill originally thought, as he told Bob, "that Anne [Smith] should do the one portraying the wife" (*DB*, 152). When she demurred, Bill did it himself, much to the chagrin of Lois, who reasonably supposed she was better qualified than her husband on this score. In fact, Lois had hoped Bill would ask her to write not only "To Wives," but also the following chapter, "The Family Afterward." But when she "shyly suggested this, he said no; he thought the book, except for the stories, should all be written in the same style" (*LR*, 114).[9]

Obviously, Bill's excuse to Lois makes no sense, given his first offering the assignment to Anne Smith. Lois, who kept her disappointment to herself, later recalled: "I have never known why he didn't want me to write about the wives, and it hurt me at first; but our lives were so full that I didn't have time to think about it much" (*LR*, 114). It may be that Wilson himself was feeling so insecure in his new authorial role that he shied from creating a potential rivalry with his wife. Or, perhaps, he was nervous about what she might say!

When everything was finally ready in January 1939, an experienced journalist at Columbia University, Tom Uzzell, performed a feat of surgical copyediting by cutting a third to a half of the bloated typescript and pruning the remainder.[10] Uzzell also voted for "Alcoholics Anonymous": "it described the fellowship, and it was catchy" (*PIO*, 204). Four hundred multilith copies of the book were run off and sent to experts in the alcoholism field, lest any glaring errors get into print undetected. One physician's response to this advance issue led to the addition of "The Doctor's Opinion" by Wilson's friend at Towns Hospital, Dr. Silkworth. The idea was to lend the book more medical credibility. Another respondent suggested the deletion of all forms of rhetorical coercion (in the manner of the Oxford Group): "to put our Fellowship on a 'we ought' basis instead of a 'you must' basis" (*PIO*, 204).

A second last-minute brouhaha concerned the final form of the Twelve Steps, which Wilson had adamantly refused to alter since his original inspiration. He was finally convinced, however, that the wording, redolent of the Oxford Group, would "scare off alcoholics by the thousands" (*AACA*, 167), and so he agreed to tone down their religiosity:

> In Step Two we decided to describe God as a "Power greater than ourselves." In Steps Three and Eleven we inserted the words "God *as we understood Him*." From Step Seven we deleted the expression "on our knees." And, as a lead-in sentence to all the steps we wrote these words: "Here are the steps we took which are suggested as a Program of Recovery." A.A.'s Twelve Steps were to be *suggestions* only. . . .
>
> God was certainly there in our Steps, but He was now expressed in terms that anybody—*anybody at all*—could accept and try. (*AACA*, 167)

Although this account is generally accurate, it is imprecise about details and misleading about chronology. The problem is that Bill W.

conflates into a single and comprehensive act of revision what was actually a series of partial changes made at different stages in the evolution of *Alcoholics Anonymous*. For example, the phrase "God *as we understood Him*," which was not present in Wilson's typescript, appeared in Step Three in the multilith edition, but *not* in Step Eleven until the book itself. The revision of the Twelve Steps is most easily seen by italicizing all the modifications made between the multilith text and the 1939 first edition:[11]

Step Three: Made a decision to turn our will and our lives over the care *and direction* [deleted] of God as we understood Him.

Step Six: Were entirely *willing that* [changed to *ready to have*] God remove all these defects of character.

Step Seven: Humbly, *on our knees,* [deleted] asked Him to remove our shortcomings—*holding nothing back* [deleted].

Step Eleven: Sought through prayer and meditation to improve our *conscious* [added] contact with God *as we understood Him* [added], praying only for knowledge of His will for us and the power to carry that out.

Step Twelve: Having had a spiritual *experience* [later changed to *awakening*] as the result of *this course of action* [changed to *these steps*], we tried to carry this message to *others, especially alcoholics* [changed to *other alcoholics*], and to practice these principles in all our affairs.

The Twelve Steps did not assume their definitive form until the final stages of book production. And in one particular—the shift from "spiritual experience" to "spiritual awakening" in Step Twelve—a major change was not made until years later.

Not surprisingly, the typescript Bill and Hank delivered to Edward Blackwell at Cornwall Press, a job printer, was far from clean setting copy; it "had been revised and changed so much that it was almost unreadable" (*PIO*, 205). But Hank talked the plant manager into waiving his professional objections. *Alcoholics Anonymous* finally appeared in April 1939. There were insufficient funds to cover production costs; so the first printing was scaled down to about five thousand copies,[12] and Cornwall Press obligingly agreed to defer full payment.[13] The price was set rather high at $3.50 (equivalent to $35 now), and so the book was deliberately bulked up, with the heaviest available paper stock and with generous leading of the type, to lend it an appearance of amplitude and thus "to convince the alcoholic purchaser that he was indeed getting his money's worth!" (*AACA,* 170). Hence the sobriquet, the "Big Book."

The book *is* truly big. It runs a little more than four hundred pages. Its panels measure six by nine-and-a-quarter inches. It's a full two inches thick: the same, by comparison, as my copy of *Merriam Webster's Collegiate Dictionary,* which contains nearly sixteen hundred pages (on Bible-leaf paper) and weighs in at more than three pounds. *Alcoholics Anonymous* is a relatively svelte two pounds.[14] The first printing is strikingly turned out in cardinal red cloth (all later printings were in blue cloth, except for the third printing, in green), with large gilt lettering in an art deco style that carries over to the "circus" dust jacket (as it is known in the book trade). The streamlined design of this wrapper features a bold and eyecatching composition of lines, rectangles, and circles in red, black, yellow, and white. The printed rear panel bears sample passages from the book; the flaps offer more excerpts. That ordering information appears in every possible place on the jacket (rear panel *and* both flaps) suggests how anxiously its authors wished the book to catch on.

It didn't. Stacks of unsold copies collected dust in Cornwall's warehouse until some fortuitous publicity, including a 1941 article in the *Saturday Evening Post,* aroused some public interest. But that's all part of A.A. history. What matters here (and what probably mattered to Bill W., the neophyte author) were the reviews.

Harry Emerson Fosdick, who had read the multilith edition, was known to be sympathetic; but his puff review appeared only in an obscure temperance publication, after it had been declined by the *New York Herald Tribune.* In the *New York Times* (25 June 1939), Percy Hutchison archly looked past the "risible" title of the book to its sober-sided content: "more soundly based psychologically than any other treatment of the subject I have ever come upon" (*PIO,* 223). But the unsigned review in the *Journal of the American Medical Association* (October 1939) superciliously dismissed *Alcoholics Anonymous* as "a curious combination of organizing propaganda and religious exhortation . . . the book has no scientific merit or interest" (*NG,* 92 n).

By far the harshest review appeared in the *Journal of Nervous and Mental Diseases* (September 1940). After mocking "this big, big book, *i.e.* big in words" as "a rambling sort of camp-meeting confession of experiences" told by God-bitten drunkards under the sway of "the 'big brothers of the spirit,'" the reviewer opined that *Alcoholics Anonymous* contains "hardly a word" about "the inner meaning of alcoholism." For this reader such "inner meaning" was not spiritual but psychological, and he denigrated alcoholics themselves with a contemptuous Freudian flourish: "Inasmuch as the alcoholic, speaking generally, lives in a wishfulfilling infantile regression to the omnipotency delusional state, perhaps he is best handled for the time being at least by regressive mass psychological methods, in which, as is realized, religious fervors belong, hence the religious trend of the book." After all, however, the quaint methods of a Billy Sunday have been superseded in this scientific age by those of such psychiatrists as Auguste Forel and Eugen Bleuler (*NG*, 92 n).

It is ironic that the reviewer, for the purpose of impugning *Alcoholics Anonymous,* should have alluded here to the Bürgholzli Clinic in Zurich, the seat of European psychiatry: the leadership of this renowned institution led patrilineally, mentor to mentored, from Forel through Bleuler to Carl Jung, whom Wilson credited with putting recovery from alcoholism on a spiritual as well as a psychological basis. As Kurtz observes, one of A.A.'s major contributions was to serve as "a bridge-builder between ancient religious insight and modern psychological understanding," in large part by translating traditional religious terminology into a psychological plain style accessible to garden-variety drunks. One subtle advantage of A.A.'s not revising the first part of the Big Book, in fact, has been that "by this freezing of vocabulary—no matter how time-bound or imprecise later critics may find it—all members of Alcoholics Anonymous were enabled to communicate with each other across lines of time, social class, and educational background" (*NG*, 193).

Aside from vernacular diction, Wilson's writing is characterized, as Robertson notes, by the use of "simple declarative sentences" and "some outdated slang," as well as "a boosterish tone of onward and upward with George Follansbee Babbitt."[15] Robert Thomsen agrees that Bill W.'s "simple kitchen-table style" (*BW*, 337) may at times seem "stereotyped," but it nonetheless conveys his spellbinding exuberance: "He did not bother about style. The result was a plain prose, the tone and timbre of which was as true as the sound of the wind whistling through his Vermont trees, as straightforward as talk in a general store" (*BW*, 278).

Over time, as general stores have yielded to Wal-Marts, Wilson's writing has dated accordingly. The cracker-barrel philosopher now sounds like a cornball yokel from a vanished American past when goods were packed in wood instead of packaged in shrink wrap. Take, for instance, Wilson's washday metaphor for the experience of one high-bottom drunk: "He had felt only the first nip of the wringer. Most alcoholics have to be pretty badly mangled before they really commence to solve their problems" (*AA*, 43). Having seen, as a child, an old-fashioned washing machine in action in my Irish grandmother's kitchen, I know exactly what Wilson is talking about. But I would guess that most younger readers draw a blank; almost certainly, they miss the pun on "mangle."

Wilson employs such figurative language sparingly; more often he resorts to clichés and jargon, mainly from business and sports. For example, both the wording of Step Four ("Made a searching and moral inventory of ourselves") and Wilson's commentary on the Step draw explicitly from the vocabulary of commerce. The "personal inventory" is no different, Wilson says, from any shopkeeper's ascertaining "the truth about the stock-in-trade." The point of this "fact-finding" and "fact-facing" process is to "disclose damaged or unsalable goods, to get rid of them promptly and without regret. If the owner of the business is to be successful, he cannot fool himself about values" (*AA*, 64). In other words, the fact that the inventory is personal does not mean it cannot also be disinterested: strictly business. The commercial language serves to counterbalance the rhetoric of religion ("searching and moral"); its materiality brings the step's spirituality down to earth.[16]

The main features of Wilson's style may be seen in the following sample, from the second chapter. In this and a few other key passages to follow, I shall quote *Alcoholics Anonymous* as published in 1939, but I shall also indicate in brackets any differences between the first book edition and the earlier multilith draft. Most of the changes have to do with Wilson's switching narrative voice from second-person singular ("you") to first-person plural ("we"). The rhetorical effects of this shift are subtle and cumulative. The book as a whole seems less "Oxfordishly" preachy; the parts that were *not* revised in this manner, however—notably, sections of "Working With Others" (on the Twelfth

Writing the Big Book 125

Step) and "To Wives"—seem, as a consequence, all the more pre-scriptive.

> Therefore, the main [real] problem of the alcoholic centers in his mind, rather than in his body. If you ask him why he started on that last bender, the chances are he will offer you any one of a hundred alibis. Sometimes these excuses have a certain plausibility, but none of them really makes [make] sense in the light of the havoc an alcoholic's drinking bout creates. They sound [to you] like the philosophy of the man who, having a headache, beats [beat] himself on the head with a hammer so that he can't [couldn't] feel the ache. If you draw this fallacious reasoning to the attention of an alcoholic, he will laugh it off, or become irritated and refuse to talk.
>
> Once in a while he may tell [you] the truth. And the truth, strange to say, is usually that he has no more idea why he took that first drink than you have. Some drinkers have excuses with which they are satisfied part of the time. But in their hearts they really do not know why they do it. Once this malady has a real hold, they are a baffled lot. There is the obsession that somehow, someday, they will beat the game. But they often suspect they are down for the count. (*AA,* 23)

Aside from "usually" and "alcoholic" itself, no word in this excerpt exceeds three syllables (most have one or two), except for the ones—"plausibility," "philosophy," "fallacious"—that might require looking up (along with "malady" and "obsession"). There's that funny bit of folk humor about curing a headache with a hammer. There's a buried trope about boxing: "drinking bout" leads in the next paragraph to "down for the count." There are trite phrases: "creates havoc," "laugh it off," "strange to say," "in their hearts," "beat the game." The writing is, on the whole, perfectly serviceable but utterly unremarkable, although it does "sing" with a graceful lilt that reminds us of Wilson's good ear as an avid, if amateur, musician. (Not only his violin and baby grand piano may be seen at Stepping Stones, but also his cello.)

What saves this prose from banality is its wisely knowing tone. This narrator has been there. He knows the drunk's game from the inside, and he has mastered every mental move. No ordinary, or even extraordinary, alcoholic alibi will fool him. He brings his psychological insight to bear pragmatically. It doesn't matter *why* this fellow took the first drink. There is no answer; no answer is required. But once the "insanity" of such drinking is labeled a "malady" and an "obsession," it becomes medicalized and psychologized. But only minimally.

"Obsession," derived from Silkworth's "allergy" theory, also had psychoanalytic connotations in 1939. But the Freudian theory of alcoholism is irrelevant to Wilson's purposes because of his hard-boiled skepticism about the efficacy of introspection alone: "But the actual or potential alcoholic, with hardly an exception, will be *absolutely unable to stop drinking on the basis of self-knowledge* (AA, 39). As for "malady," we have seen that Wilson carefully avoided "disease" to characterize alcoholism. The word appears just once in his section of the Big Book, in the context of his describing alcoholism as "a progressive illness" (*AA*, 30), seen to be symptomatic of a deeper "spiritual malady" (*AA*, 64): an "illness which only a spiritual experience will conquer" (*AA*, 44). This "spiritual disease" (*AA*, 64)—or soul-sickness, as William James would have called it—is closer to an existential "dysease" than a somatic "disease." Here is the counterpoint to Wilson's bringing the spiritual down to earth: his elevating the material to a spiritual plane.

On balance, the upward lift is stronger than the downward drag. As the medical reviewers of *Alcoholics Anonymous* pointed out, its religious impulses are much stronger than its scientific ones. The book *is*, in fact, a "curious combination of organizing propaganda and religious exhortation," with little or no "scientific merit or interest"—except insofar as one may be interested, as William James and Carl Jung were, in the vital relationship of science to religion.

Rhetorically, the best chapter (also the one most indebted to the proselytizing literature of the Oxford Group) is "We Agnostics," in which Wilson rehearses all his old doubts about the existence of a Higher Power and then assaults them with an evangelical fervor designed to convert any but a case-hardened skeptic. His trump card is the assertion that religion is "as old as man himself" and therefore inseparable from humanity; "for deep down in every man, woman, and child, is the fundamental idea of God. It may be obscured by calamity, by pomp, by worship of other things, but in some form or other it is there" (*AA*, 55). Logically, then, the unconverted are always potential believers unless they are hopelessly inhuman. More narrowly, Wilson insists that no alcoholic can ever stop drinking without a "spiritual experience" of the sort Jung had recommended to Rowland H. More narrowly still, he avers that he himself could not have been saved without a religious conversion.

To see how profoundly Wilson's religious faith infuses *Alcoholics Anonymous*, we need only remember the clarifying appendix on "Spiritual Experience" that was added to later editions of the Big Book, along with the softening of Step Twelve from "spiritual *experience*" to "spiritual *awakening*." In the realm of belief, Bill W. was sufficiently atypical of alcoholics that when he expressed his own spiritual convictions, he risked setting too pious a tone and losing their identification with him. Not everyone in A.A. could or would experience a "hot flash." In fact, it's when Wilson draws most fully upon his own experience in the Big Book that we catch a glimpse of his life story apart from its generalized and generic A.A. retelling.

We get another such look beneath Wilson's narrative mask when he deals with the very personal and very touchy subject of sex, which comes up far more often and more urgently in *Alcoholics Anonymous* than one might suppose. For instance, in the famous fifth chapter, from the first three pages of which comes "How It Works" (a passage often read aloud at A.A. meetings), the last three pages center on the alcoholic's special need for an "overhauling" about sex (a passage never read at meetings!).

What's a drunk to do, Wilson asks, in the midst of a culture war between Puritans, who damn sex as "a lust of our lower nature, a base necessity of procreation," and Free Lovers, who "cry for sex and more sex; who bewail the institution of marriage; who think that most of the troubles of the race are traceable to sex causes. . . . One school would allow man no flavor for his fare and the other would have us all on a straight pepper diet" (*AA*, 68–69). While wishing to escape the heat of controversy, Wilson finds no way to avoid the need of alcoholics, who are no less perplexed than nondrinkers, "to shape a sane and sound ideal for our future sex life." Sex, indeed, can provide a good opportunity to apply the spiritual lessons of recovery: to subject "each relation to this test—was it selfish or not?" Ideally, sex can be treated like "any other problem" in A.A.: "In meditation, we ask God what we should do about each specific matter" (*AA*, 69).

What's clear, however, is that sex is not just "any other problem"

for Wilson. We have already seen (Chapter 3) that romantic scrapes
are mentioned in passing in "Bill's Story." In "How It Works," he
addresses, more directly but still obliquely, the topic of marital infidelity:

> Suppose we fall short of the chosen ideal and stumble? Does this mean
> we are going to get drunk? Some people tell us so. But this is only a
> half-truth. It depends on us and on our motives. If we are sorry for
> what we have done, and have the honest desire to let God take us to
> better things, we believe we will be forgiven and will have learned our
> lesson. If we are not sorry, and our conduct continues to harm others,
> we are quite sure to drink. We are not theorizing. These are facts out
> of our experience. (AA, 70)

If sex should become "very troublesome," then the sober alcoholic
should throw himself more vigorously into Twelfth-Step work; acting
selflessly "quiets the imperious urge, when to yield would mean heartache" (AA, 70).

In glossing the Fifth Step (in which alcoholics admit "to God, to
ourselves, and to another human being the exact nature of our
wrongs"), Wilson cautions that "we cannot [you should not] disclose
anything to our wives [your wife] or our [your] parents which will
hurt them and make them unhappy" (AA, 74). Later in the same chapter, "Into Action," there is a frank discussion of how "drinking does
complicate sex relations in the home." "Perhaps we are mixed up with
women in a fashion we [you] wouldn't care to have advertised." Maybe
the husband has exhausted the patience and compassion of his long-
suffering wife—"a loyal and courageous girl who has literally gone
through hell for him"—and when she turns resentfully cool, he self-
pityingly seeks "a secret and exciting affair with a 'girl who understands' ['the girl who understands me']" (AA, 81). Just what does honesty require in such a situation?

> If we [you] are sure our [your] wife does not know, should we [you]
> tell her? Not always, we think. If she knows in a general way that we
> [you] have been wild, should we [you] tell her in detail? Undoubtedly
> we [you] should admit our [your] fault. She [Your wife] may insist on
> knowing all the particulars. She will want to know who the woman is

and where she is. We feel we [you] ought to say to her that we [you] have no right to involve another person. . . .

Our design for living is not a one-way street. It is as good for the wife as for the husband. If we can forget, so can she. It is better, however, that one does not needlessly [you do not needless (*sic*)] name a person upon whom she can vent [her natural] jealousy. (*AA*, 81–82)

In its scrupulous desire to protect the "innocent" third party, such a passage seems remarkably self-serving: exculpatory of the husband's "wild" behavior, but admonishing of the wife's "natural" (but potentially hysterical) "jealousy." If *we* choose to forget the offense, then why shouldn't she? Much the same bias is apparent in Wilson's treatment, in "The Family Afterward," of the effects of alcohol on sexual relations: "Alcohol is so sexually stimulating to some men that they have overindulged. Couples are occasionally dismayed to find that when drinking is stopped the man tends to be impotent" (*AA*, 134). The emphasis falls here on the wife's need for patience in the face of her husband's difficulties.

What's truly incredible in Wilson's handling of adultery is his impersonation of a woman's point of view in the chapter that he would not permit Lois to write. "To Wives" opens with three brief paragraphs that ostensibly turn the ball over to the women, who then appear to speak in a first-person plural voice, which is really Wilson's ventriloquism. "Sometimes there were other women," he writes as if he himself were one of those loyal and courageous girls. "How heartbreaking was this discovery; how cruel to be told they understood our men as we did not!" (*AA*, 106). Later, still in narrative drag, he seems to hold women accountable if their men should stray. "The first principle of success is that you should never be angry." Even if your husband becomes so unbearable that you have to leave him temporarily, you must try to "go without rancor." You should definitely *not* tell him what to do about his drinking; for he will dismiss you as "a nag or a killjoy" and use your interference as an excuse to drink all the more—or worse! "He will tell you he is misunderstood. This may lead to lonely evenings for you. He may seek someone else to console him—not always another man" (*AA*, 111). The menacing coyness of this threat is calculated to put any uppity wife in her place, which is to be seen, perhaps, but definitely not to be heard.

Of course, Wilson's assumptions about gender and gender roles are typical for men of his generation; if anything, he was far *more* understanding of women's needs and sensitive to their rights than most of his male literary contemporaries. His preoccupation with infidelity, however, likely sprang from his own history of philandering, no trace of which, unsurprisingly, is to be found in official A.A. publications.

Although hints of Bill W.'s compulsive womanizing have long circulated through A.A.'s gossip mill,[17] the first break in the wall of silence came in Robertson's controversial book, *Getting Better* (1988). Robertson wrapped herself in the authority of the recently deceased Lois Wilson in order to justify revealing that Bill had chased skirts throughout his sober years. "His flirtations and his adulterous behavior filled him with guilt, according to old-timers close to him, but he continued to stray off the reservation." Robertson alleges that Wilson's "last and most serious love affair" involved a woman at A.A. headquarters. To this "last and most enduring mistress," he bequeathed 1.5 percent of the royalties on the Big Book, while Lois got 13.5 percent.[18] While there is apparently no question that such payments were made to "Helen W." (actually Helen S.), who outlived Bill by only a few years, her family has denounced the allegations as slanderous scandalmongering. Wilson's motivation has been explained in terms of his kindness; he was merely repaying a loyal assistant who had always worked for peanuts and who deserved fair, if belated, compensation for her selfless dedication. Maybe so, but maybe not.

Another alleged mistress has been outed by novelist Carolyn See in a memoir of her familial drinking life. It seems that Wynn C., See's father's second wife (he was her fifth husband), had once "come within a hair-breadth of becoming the First Lady of AA." For a while during the late 1940s or early 1950s, "she and Bill had been a mighty item." A tall and buxom beauty, with pale skin, high cheekbones, red hair, and turquoise eyes, Wynn "was a knockout, and she knew it, and dressed like a chorus girl." Unfortunately, Bill was already married, but he struck "a hard but loving bargain" with Wynn: "He wouldn't, *couldn't* marry her, but he'd put her in the Book."[19] That is, he included her story, "Freedom From Bondage," in the second edition of *Alcoholics Anonymous.*[20]

Bill W. would no doubt have agreed with Wynn C.'s assertion that "A.A. has taught me that I will have peace of mind in exact proportion to the peace of mind I bring into the lives of other people. . . . For the only problems I have now are those I create when I break out in a rash of self-will" (*AA*, 551). The treatment of sex in the Big Book reveals a man, stung by guilt, struggling to confront his self-will and to overcome it.

Perhaps the most revealing evidence of Wilson's sexual infidelity is his April 1953 letter to his Jesuit confidant, Father Edward Dowling, whose influence on Bill was so strong that he nearly converted him to Roman Catholicism. The two men had met for early mass and breakfast, and later that day Bill wrote to thank Father Ed for his compassion: "however you may dislike the sin (about which you said nothing) you surely make the sinner feel understood and loved as no other mortal in my life can." Robert Fitzgerald, S. J., editor of the Wilson-Dowling letters proposes that "the 'sin' Bill speaks of might be his overdependence on women. This would fit the 'confessional' tone of the letter." Fitzgerald says nothing about Wilson's philandering. On the contrary, he suggests, discreetly but implausibly, that Bill's entire experience with "dependency relationships with women" was limited to his marriage and his adolescent affair with Bertha Bamford.[21]

It seems obvious, however, that what Wilson was really doing, with Dowling's help, was working through those emotional issues, including his "sins" of the flesh, that had come to seem concomitant to his chronically dark moods. "I am beginning to see that all my troubles have their root in a habitual and absolute dependence upon my personal prestige, security, and romantic attachment," Bill W. wrote to a fellow A.A. the same month as his note to Dowling. "When these things go wrong, there is depression" (*NG*, 214).

It is not accidental that such ruminations coincided with the appearance of *Twelve Steps and Twelve Traditions* (1953), Wilson's sounding of A.A.'s vigor, the greatest threats to which were an institutional lust for prestige and security, and the fellowship's unhealthily "romantic" attachment to its cofounder.

Forging the Traditions

E I G H T

Early in 1961, Bill W. wrote two letters to Carl Gustav Jung, the famous Swiss psychiatrist. In the first he belatedly thanked Jung for his "critical [if entirely unwitting] role in the founding of our Fellowship" (*PIO*, 382)—by virtue of what Sam Shoemaker called Jung's "simple declaration" to Rowland H. that science alone "had no answer" to the riddle of alcoholism (*AACA*, 262). In reply, Jung recalled that Rowland's craving for alcohol had been "the equivalent on a low level of the spiritual thirst of our being for wholeness, expressed in medieval language: the union with God." "Alcohol in Latin is *spiritus*," he pointed out, "and you use the same word for the highest religious experience as well as for the most depraving poison. The helpful formula therefore is: *spiritus contra spiritum*" (*PIO*, 384).[1] (Roughly, holy spirit versus ardent spirits.)

In his second letter Wilson embraced this idea: "Your observation that drinking motivations often include that of a quest for spiritual values caught our special interest" (*PIO*, 385). During the formative years of A.A., he reported, many members had found great benefit in reading *Modern Man in Search of a Soul*, a sampler of Jung's most accessible writings that appeared in 1933, a year before Bill's conversion experience. He likely read it soon after Ebby had mentioned Jung in late 1934, when Bill was also prompted to read *The Varieties of Religious Experience*. These two books, indeed, are fundamental texts of Alcoholics Anonymous: the sources of many of Wilson's profoundest ideas about religion, philosophy, and psychology.

In one key essay, titled "The Stages of Life," Jung postulated a psychic watershed at the age of forty, when a person's deepest currents change direction and his or her submerged traits often rise to the surface. This midlife reversal, which is sometimes subtle and sometimes quite dramatic, usually involves a man's exploration of his "womanliness" (his *anima,* in Jungian terms) and a woman's corresponding exploration of her "manliness" (her *animus*). Jung compares the course of human life to the transit of the sun from dawn to dusk. Once the zenith is reached, however, the downward curve of the sun, which is the mirror image of its ascending arc, demands a different set of truths and ideals. "We cannot live the afternoon of life according to the programme of life's morning—for what was great in the morning will be little at evening, and what in the morning was true will at evening have become a lie." It is regrettable, says Jung, that "colleges for forty-year-olds" do not exist to prepare them for "their coming life and its demands as the ordinary colleges introduce our young people to a knowledge of the world and of life.²

Religion once performed this task, but religion has lost its force in the modern, secular world. For Jung and his disciples, the function of religion was consigned to their practice of Analytical Psychology, with its increasingly mystical trappings. The process of "individuation" through Jungian analysis was what allowed a person to "go forwards with the stream of time," rather than "backwards against it," and thus "to discover in death a goal towards which one can strive" and to realize that "shrinking away from it is something unhealthy and abnormal which robs the second half of life of its purpose."³

What compelled Wilson's closest attention in this essay was Jung's conviction, as Bill paraphrased it,

> that most persons having arrived at age 40 and having acquired no conclusions or faith as to who they were, or where they were, or where they were going next in the cosmos, would be bound to encounter increasing neurotic difficulties; and that this would be likely to occur whether their youthful aspirations for sex union, security, and a satisfactory place in society had been satisfied or not. In short, they could not continue to fly blind toward no destination at all, in a universe

seemingly having little purpose or meaning. Neither could any amount of resolution, philosophical speculation, or superficial religious conditioning save them from the dilemma in which they found themselves. So long as they lacked any direct spiritual awakening and therefore awareness, their conflict simply had to increase.

These views of yours, doctor, had an immense impact. . . . We saw that you had perfectly described the impasse in which we had once been, but from which we had been delivered through our several spiritual awakenings. (*PIO*, 385–86).

This summary of Jung's argument omitted his reference to a specific neurotic difficulty, the one urgently germane to Wilson himself. "Statistical tables," said Jung, "show a rise in the frequency of cases of mental depression in men about forty."[4]

Depression was the nightmare of Bill Wilson's afternoon. Although he suffered debilitating bouts of melancholia during adolescence, and although his drinking exacerbated his depressive tendencies, still he had escaped the dark night of the soul that fell upon him in sobriety. Whatever the gains of not drinking—and they were incalculable for Bill Wilson—he could not banish prolonged visitations of despair even in the midst of his triumphs. For about a decade, between the mid-1940s and the mid-1950s, chronic depression crushed him, sometimes to the point of mental paralysis. Nell Wing remembered days when all that Bill could accomplish at the office was to cradle his head in his hands as he teetered on the verge of weeping. Another associate recalled how hard it had been on Bill's bad days to make any contact through the forbidding ring of pain: "He'd try and cooperate if you had a question, but to try and sit down and do any planning with him at that time was useless. His whole face would fall; he looked sad, sad, very sad" (*PIO*, 294).

Wilson made a point of commiserating with other depressed A.A.s who would write for help to New York Headquarters. In one 1960 letter, he recalled how the disciplines of simple walking and deep breathing had once presented insuperable challenges: "I sometimes told myself that I couldn't do even this—that I was too weak. But I learned that this was the point at which I could not give in without becoming still more depressed." So Bill took it literally one step at a time, counting each breath, nudging himself forward for a quarter-mile, and then a half-mile more, and then another half-mile until "the false sense of physical weakness," which depression had induced, would leave. "The walking and especially the breathing were powerful affirmations toward life and living and away from failure and death."[5]

'Pass It On' suggests that because there are so "many and varied accounts of Bill's recurrent depression, and almost as many opinions about its nature, its causes, its intensity, its dynamics, and its manifestations," it is "virtually impossible to isolate a definitive account" (PIO, 292–93). Even the chronological boundaries of Wilson's misery are somewhat in dispute. Although Robert Thomsen links the start of Bill's "blackest depression" to the winter of 1940–41 (BW, 315), Ernest Kurtz believes the worst came later; and "Pass It On' seems to agree, placing the onset in 1944 and the nadir in the first two years of an eleven-year siege that persisted until 1955.

The timing matters insofar as it suggests a connection between Wilson's mental state and his emotional stake in A.A. His depression was certainly "overdetermined" in the psychoanalytic sense that symptoms express a confluence of multiple and disparate etiologies. One major cause, however, was Bill W.'s total immersion in the fellowship as it rapidly and often chaotically expanded during the 1940s, the period when A.A. history became inseparable from Wilson's life story.

In the aftermath of writing Alcoholics Anonymous, Wilson endured a series of setbacks that led up to the worst years of his depression. First, as we have seen, the book sold poorly, despite vigorous attempts to promote it. Then Bill and Lois became homeless. The row house at 182 Clinton Street, the Burnham homestead for nearly sixty years, had never actually been owned by Lois's father. After his death the Wilsons were allowed to stay on, paying a modest rent against the mortgage, but in May 1939 they were evicted in favor of a buyer. Most of the family heirlooms were unceremoniously dumped at the Salvation Army; a few precious items went into storage. Until 1941, when they managed to buy a house in Westchester County, Bill and Lois were set adrift for two years of hand-to-mouth vagabondage. They lived wherever they were welcome, surviving on a pittance (thirty dollars per week) from the trust fund the Rockefellers had established in support of the cofounders. The regular Tuesday meetings of the New York A.A. group were also displaced from one site to another until permanent quarters were found on West Twenty-fourth Street. A con-

verted stable was fitted out as a clubhouse, and the Wilsons were en-
sconced upstairs in one of the tiny bedrooms.

Lois recalled it was ten feet square, with one window, a door to the
fire escape, and a useless but massive dumbwaiter to the kitchen below. "We painted the walls and curtained two orange crates to use as
dressers. From an old friend we bought a bed without a footboard, so
Bill could hang his feet out. We had to crawl over the bed to reach our
clothes, which hung on hooks on the wall" (LR, 131). The Twenty-
fourth Street Clubhouse was "a rare and special place," as Thomsen
calls it (BW, 305), a shrine for generations of A.A. pilgrims, and it allowed Bill to work his program day and night. But it afforded precious
little space and privacy, especially for Lois. The situation must have
revived Bill's doubts about his adequacy as a provider.

Wilson absorbed another blow to his pride early in 1942, when at
the age of forty-six he tried to join the war effort by enlisting in Army
Intelligence. He was offered instead a much less appealing commis-
sion as captain in the Quartermaster's Corps, and then he flunked his
physical because of ulcers. "One can only guess," says Thomsen, "at
what his innermost feelings were when he learned that he, a patriot,
a Vermonter, a veteran of the First World War, wasn't even acceptable
to his country as an old retread" (BW, 325).

During this same period Wilson suffered a bitter falling out with
Hank P., his erstwhile buddy and business partner. Their joint ven-
tures, including the Big Book, were all failures; and sometime in 1939
Hank got drunk again.[6] The proximate cause, evidently, was a love
affair involving Ruth Hock, who entertained and then spurned Hank's
offer to leave his wife for her. Hank blamed Bill for the alienation of
Ruth's affections, "charging that she was more committed to A.A. and
Bill than she was to him" (PIO, 229). She did indeed accompany Wilson, after the collapse of Honor Dealers, to the new A.A. Headquarters in Manhattan, where she continued to work for many years.

Hank's resentment was compounded by what he took to be Bill's
enrichment at his own expense. Early in 1940, when the Alcoholic
Foundation was buying up all shares in the Works Publishing Company, Hank refused at first to cooperate. But when he showed up
"completely broke and very shaky" at the New York office one day,
Bill took advantage of Hank's condition and cajoled him into signing
the necessary papers. In return Hank received $200, ostensibly in pay-

ment for office furniture A.A. had appropriated from the New Jersey office.

This turned out to be a mistake of huge financial proportions—on the same order of folly as Esau's selling his birthright to his brother Jacob for a mess of pottage—for "it was not long after this incident that Bill was granted a royalty on the book, similar to one that had already been voted for Dr. Bob. While this royalty was at first very modest, it eventually became substantial and provided both Bill and Lois a lifetime income." Understandably, Hank always felt he had been cheated out of "any future share in the book's profits" (*PIO*, 236).

Deeply into debt, divorce, and drunkenness, Hank fled to Ohio, where he spread slanderous tales in A.A. about Bill's alleged malfeasance and his supposed collusion with the Rockefellers. The rumors fell on receptive ears in Cleveland, where A.A. had established its largest base of operations and where the prickly and egomaniacal Clarence S. was vying with the cofounders for power and prestige. Local discontent—there was even talk of Cleveland's secession—ultimately sparked a star-chamber investigation of A.A. finances. In June 1942, Bill W. and Dr. Bob both were humiliatingly called on the carpet to answer allegations about their ill-gotten gains. (Instead they documented their actual penury.) "It was an ugly and painful episode" (*BW*, 323). Wilson later wrote that he had left this A.A. kangaroo court "with a great feeling of emptiness, futility, and heartache." The experience, of the sort he had "never expected to meet in life," had been a severe test of his spiritual fitness (*PIO*, 257).

In April 1940, Wilson had become embroiled in yet another controversy in Cleveland, where Rollie Hemsley, star catcher of the baseball Indians, broke his anonymity and extolled A.A. at a news conference. As the story of Rollie's recovery (he had a year's sobriety) attracted national coverage, it generated a wave of new members. Cleveland A.A., which guarded anonymity jealously, deplored all the buzz, but it seems to have tickled Wilson's competitive instincts. Not only did he defend Hemsley's actions as a possible blessing in disguise, a means to mass recruitment for A.A., but he also began to court the same kind of celebrity for himself. "He'd accepted Rollie's challenge and was proving that he could command as much publicity as a ballplayer" (*BW*, 301).

"Soon I was on the road," Bill recalled in 1955, "happily handing out personal interviews and pictures."

> To my delight, I found I could hit the front pages, just as he could. Besides, he couldn't hold his publicity pace, but I could hold mine. I only needed to keep traveling and talking. The local AA groups and newspapers did the rest. I was astonished when recently I looked at those old newspaper stories. For two or three years I guess I was AA's number one anonymity breaker.
> So I can't really blame any AA who has grabbed the spotlight since. I set the main example myself, years ago. (*LH*, 212)

As Wilson's head swelled, A.A.'s rank and file indicted him for grand-standing and begged him to get off his "dry drunk."

Bill W. later used himself, with his "strong tendencies toward the pursuit of prestige, wealth, and power" (*AACA*, 135–36), as the chief example of why anonymity was essential to Alcoholics Anonymous. It's telling that even in chastising himself, Wilson betrayed an inverted pride; he claimed to be a Number One man even in the A.A. dog-house! This proved to be a common rhetorical and pedagogical strategy in the cofounder's writings, in which the life of Bill Wilson effectively merged with the legend of Bill W.

We can follow this process in the renderings of the Hemsley incident in the standard A.A. histories. Closely following Bill W.'s 1955 *Grapevine* account, Thomsen associates Wilson's "alcoholic grandiosity" with the period 1940–41. Kurtz follows Thomsen's lead while expressing doubt about the chronology and citing contrary evidence in his notes—evidence that suggests that Wilson did little or no traveling at this time and that his *Grapevine* story may have been a "didactic distortion" (*NG*, 286 n. 32). Kurtz speculates that Wilson was projecting his later lust for publicity, manifest during the mid-1940s, back upon this earlier period.

"*Pass It On*,' confirming Kurtz's suspicions, finally sets the record straight, attributing the discrepancies among the sources to "an endearing—and important—facet of Bill's character":

> When Bill told this story on himself, he was speaking figuratively, in metaphor, rather than relating events as they actually happened. He did not at this time become "A.A.'s number one anonymity breaker";

indeed, the anonymity breaks he did make came two years later, not directly following the Rollie H. publicity in May of 1940. But Bill was never likely to pass up the opportunity to deliver a parable where he thought it could do some good, never afraid to use himself as a negative example (something he would not do to anyone else) when he thought he could make a point or highlight a principle, and never reluctant to stretch a fact for the sake of emphasis. . . . Rollie's anonymity break may have aroused Bill's old competitive and envious feelings. But the truth is that he did not act on those feelings. (*PIO*, 237–38)

He didn't act in 1940, that is. By the fall of 1944, however, Bill W. had become a Number One man road show, with appearances before A.A. groups in Chicago, Omaha, Saint Louis, Little Rock, Denver, Dallas, Fort Worth, Houston, Tucson, San Francisco, and points in between. During this same period he was giving a series of invited lectures to medical societies and forging an enduring relationship with the Yale School of Alcohol Studies, to the first publication of which he contributed a piece on "The Fellowship of Alcoholics Anonymous." Here Wilson appeared as "W. W. (One of the founders)."[7] But when a comparable lecture was published in the *N.Y. State Journal of Medicine* (1944), the author was identified as "W. G. Wilson." This was, according to Kurtz, "the only occasion on which Wilson's full name was published crediting any of his writings" (*NG*, 292 n. 17).

The use of Wilson's full name caused a uproar in 1946, when he permitted Marty Mann, a fellow A.A. and the founding director of the National Committee for Education on Alcoholism, to list him (as well as Dr. Smith) as sponsors on N.C.E.A. stationery. Mann, the first woman in the New York group and the first woman to attain long-term sobriety in A.A., was a promotional virtuoso who used her personal charisma and her colorful drunkalog to sell the American public on the "disease" concept of alcoholism. Having decided to sacrifice her own anonymity to what she deemed the higher cause of making converts, she routinely divulged her A.A. membership during her barnstorming publicity campaigns. Apparently she persuaded Wilson and Smith that if they preferred not to go quite this far publicly, they might still make a fine but legitimate distinction between being alcoholics and being members of Alcoholics Anonymous and lend their names to her solicitations. But in a 1946 fundraising letter, Mann went beyond merely including the A.A. cofounders among supporters of the N.C.E.A.; she also implied a direct relationship between the organizations.

When A.A. members got wind of Mann's letter, a dangerous crisis erupted. Within hours the New York office was "flooded with calls and wires of question and protest, and two days later the office staff telegraphed Wilson: 'A.A. can split if Marty carries your backing'" (*NG*, 119). Wilson and Smith saved the day by immediately dissociating themselves from Mann and reaffirming A.A.'s fundamental principle of anonymity.

During the furor, Wilson was away in Hollywood, consulting with producer Hal Wallis on a proposed movie about A.A.—a project that was soon obviated by Billy Wilder's production of *The Lost Weekend* (1945). This California junket was also motivated by Bill's seeking a geographical cure for his depression, which was at its steepest between 1944 and 1946.

It was no coincidence that this span of time coincided with the years when Wilson was most acutely in conflict with himself and with A.A. about the bounds of his leadership and the degree of his personal anonymity. The relationship between his own mental suffering and the growing pains of the fellowship was something Bill came to understand through psychotherapy. During earlier troubles Bill had found solace in the spiritual ministrations of his unofficial sponsor, Father Ed Dowling. In 1945 or 1946, however, he finally sought professional help, from Dr. Harry M. Tiebout, a psychiatrist who operated a Connecticut sanitarium for alcoholics. (He had also steered Marty Mann to Alcoholics Anonymous and helped to finance the Big Book; later he served as an A.A. trustee.)

Tiebout was of the strictly Freudian persuasion—these were salad days for psychoanalysis in American medicine—and his twice-weekly treatments of Wilson, which stopped short of being a full-dress analysis, stressed the party line on the "regressive" dynamics of alcoholism. The doctor urged Bill to accept that he was in the grip of his own immaturity, "that both in his active alcoholism and in his current sobriety he had been trying to live out the infantilely grandiose demands of 'His Majesty the Baby'" (*NG*, 126–27). Although the sessions with Tiebout sharpened Bill's self-awareness and reduced his fear about losing his mental balance altogether, he found them not to be "especially curative" (*PIO*, 296). Wilson's depression continued, at a lower level of intensity; and after leaving Tiebout's care, he sought other, nonpsychological means of relief, including vitamins and hormones, as well as osteopathic remedies.

He also found a new analyst: Dr. Frances Gillespy Wickes, a devout Jungian. Jung, in fact, had written a commendatory introduction to her first book, *The Inner World of Childhood* (1927).[8] One philosophical difference between the Freudian and the Jungian approaches to psychotherapy is that whereas the former encourages excavation of the childhood roots of neurosis, the latter centers more on present conflicts and the process of adult "individuation."

This difference is clearly reflected in an important 1947 letter in which Wilson mentioned his recent interest in Jung, no doubt inspired by Dr. Wickes:[9]

> Her thesis is that my position in A.A. has become quite inconsistent with my needs as an individual. Highly satisfactory [as it is] to live one's life for others, it cannot be anything but disastrous to live one's life for others as those others think it should be lived. One has, for better or worse, to choose his own life. The extent to which the A.A. movement and individuals in it determine my choices is really astonishing. Things which are primary to me (even for the good of A.A.) are unfulfilled. I'm constantly diverted to secondary or even useless activities by A.A.'s whose demands seem to them primary, but are not really so. So we have the person of Mr. Anonymous in conflict with Bill Wilson. (*PIO*, 335).

This analysis was, he added, "more than an interesting speculation—it's homely good sense." In fact, Wickes cut to the quick of Wilson's depression, which could now be understood, at least on one level, as the turning inward of anger aroused by outward causes, a symptom of his resentment of A.A.'s exorbitant demands upon his psychic autonomy.

Wilson was forced to confront a painful paradox. While he willfully endeavored to make himself synonymous with Alcoholics Anonymous, A.A. correspondingly apotheosized him as "Bill W.," who was thought to be virtually infallible when he spoke ex cathedra as the cofounder. But standing for A.A. also meant never standing apart from A.A. The wages of celebrity—the dues Bill Wilson paid for being Mr. Anonymous—turned out to be the loss of his private life and, to a degree, of his personal identity. As a result, he suffered excruciating self-denial. When he felt most "himself" as Bill W., reveling in the role of the revered cofounder, Wilson also felt his true individuality dissolving into a cult of personality that he himself had coveted and helped to create. As he complained to a correspondent in 1948, "If the A.A. movement knew me as I really am, I agree no one would care very much what I did. But unfortunately, that is not the case. They believe in me as the symbol of the whole" (*PIO*, 284).

For a person in Wilson's vulnerable position—"a founder of a life-saving program that promised its adherents 'a new happiness'"—to seek psychiatric help at all, and to do so openly, was "an act of cour-age" (*PIO*, 295). Some members of A.A., perhaps the same ones who clamored for Bill W.'s attention to their (nonprimary) needs, were quick to take the cofounder's inventory. They wondered aloud if the explanation for Bill's depression wasn't really very simple: he was not working the Steps. Wilson himself considered this explanation, la-menting his "inability to practice the program in certain areas of my life" (*PIO*, 299), and thus piling guilt upon depression and redoubling his misery.

This was, however, a form of blaming the victim: A.A.'s equivalent of the classic Freudian double-bind by which "resistance" to the claims of psychoanalysis is interpreted only as evidence of an acute need *for* psychoanalysis. In the A.A. variation, doubt that the Twelve Steps are the panacea for any and all problems in a member's life is read only as evidence of a defective program, a failure to work the Steps hard enough. But, as *'Pass It On'* shrewdly remarks, Wilson discovered from his own trials "that alcoholic drinking may in some people mask deeper psychological and emotional disturbances. . . . that the A.A. program might not be the answer for every alcoholic. There might be people who could not 'get' the program because of various perceptual or psychological obstacles" (*PIO*, 299).

Insofar as such disturbances may lie on a biochemical level[10]—as part of a person's "hard-wired" genetic encoding—it seems neither just nor reasonable to hold him or her morally accountable for supposedly spiritual deficiencies. But, of course, this was the pre-Prozac era, when the nature/nurture pendulum had swung heavily toward cultural rather than somatic explanations of mental disorders and also when the successful treatment of clinical depression was rare. Although we certainly cannot know if any of the antidepressant drugs now available might have banished Bill Wilson's gloom for good, there's no doubt, given his proven willingness to go to any lengths for a possible cure, that he would have given them a try.

With his wariness of medicalizing alcoholism, Wilson never completely bought into Dr. Tiebout's Freudian theory of his case, which implicitly condemned alcoholics to a permanently infantile state in which they would always require some form of "adult" supervision, even in sobriety. Hence the ambivalent "parental" projections upon Bill W. by A.A. members who both craved and challenged his potently "paternal" authority. Wilson's strategy was to use the practical wisdom of Tiebout's perspective on alcoholism without acceding to its reductive portrayal of alcoholics as childishly "dependent."

Wilson *was* prepared, however, to adopt the idea of "immaturity" to describe a parallel he perceived between his own defects of character and the structural problems of A.A. Kurtz suggests, using appropriately Jungian language, how Bill W. set a double agenda during the early 1950s. Whereas his own articulation of "the A.A. way of life"[11] represented the "introverted *program*-developing accomplishments" of Alcoholics Anonymous, the "extroverted, *fellowship*-developing task of A.A. was its selfconscious effort at 'Coming of Age'" (NG, 126). That is, both Bill W. and A.A. would grow together toward a stage of maturity that would then allow them to live freely apart. The eventual separation of A.A. from its cofounder would be to their mutual advantage.

To bring both A.A. and himself into fuller maturity, Bill W. thought that organizational reform was imperative; throughout the late 1940s, he worked obsessively to create a democratic governing body that could ultimately supplant the authority of the cofounders. Wilson recognized that "so long as 'Bill W.' lived, even his remote presence inhibited the development of any organizational bureaucracy that could stifle A.A.'s original vision and zeal under a haze of self-serving process." But the cofounder's presence also impeded A.A.'s "development of any kind of truly autonomous, self-renewing authority" (NG, 135).

Wilson pushed so obstinately for an elected General Service Conference that he exasperated some nonalcoholic members of the A.A. Board and alienated those members of A.A. who preferred Bill the storyteller to Bill the power-driving politician. It was as if their easygoing and indulgent "father," who had always been ready to assure them with his own "bedtime story," had been transmogrified into a rigid disciplinarian, lecturing recalcitrant adolescents about their need to act more responsibly. In a sense, that was exactly what he *was* about. Bill W. believed that if A.A. were to survive him, it needed to "grow up."

During the grey-flanneled 1950s, such "maturity" was the watchword for a pervasive concern in postwar America with rising to its solemn historical destiny as "the leader of the free world." To be other than "mature" in the dawning "American Century" was tantamount to being un-American. In the "post-Repeal era," from the mid-1930s to the mid-1960s, the last vestiges of old-time Prohibitionism melted away; as Lori E. Rotskoff remarks, "alcohol acquired a new set of cultural meanings as it melded into the dominant culture's recreational life." The idea of "maturity" now included the advocacy of "mature" and "responsible" drinking. A cocktail (or two) was just the thing, it seemed, to take the edge off, to ease the strain on Americans after a hard day of shouldering the weight of global challenge. Drinking became more acceptable and drink more ubiquitous than at any time since the nineteenth century.

> Catalyzed by the unique circumstances of the Great Depression and World War II, the beverage industries and a supportive coalition of wet advocates successfully "normalized" social drinking—aided by countless advertisers, filmmakers, entrepreneurs and writers. By the 1950s, the paradoxical nature of alcoholic culture—one that alternatively celebrated and denigrated alcohol's effects—signified a larger set of cultural predicaments endemic to the Cold War era.[12]

A.A. was shaped by cold war ideology no less than any other American institution; but since recovering alcoholics necessarily could *not* conform to the mores of an increasingly bibulous society, they had to prove their maturity otherwise. As Kurtz says, "Alcoholics Anonymous could not combat directly an advertising industry that presented the drinking of alcohol as the hallmark of maturity, but it could and did launch an attempt to demonstrate in its own existence that abstinence from alcohol was not in itself a sign of immaturity" (*NG,* 127).

Bill W.'s chief means to A.A.'s "coming of age" was the formulation and dissemination of the Twelve Traditions, which were the culmination both of A.A.'s turbulent youth and of Wilson's depressive years. Like many things in A.A., the Traditions developed initially out of a practical need. As the groups multiplied exponentially during the 1940s, and as many new groups recapitulated the disputes of early A.A., the volume of queries to New York Headquarters overwhelmed the skeletal office staff. "It seemed," Wilson recalled, "as if every contestant in every group argument wrote us during this confused and exciting period" (*AACA*, 203).

Bill W. handled hundreds of these letters himself, offering nonbinding suggestions for this dilemma or that. When he noticed that the problems reported were falling into patterns—mainly questions of leadership, money, and authority—he took the efficient route of dispensing similar advice for similar situations. From there it was a short step to his abstracting A.A.'s collective wisdom, hard won by trial and error, into a set of "Twelve Points to Assure Our Future," published in the April 1946 issue of the *Grapevine*.

Before laying out the twelve points (yet to be called officially the Twelve Traditions), Bill W. implored the membership to eschew codification: "Should we ever harden too much, the letter might crush the spirit. We could victimize ourselves by petty rules and prohibitions; we could imagine that we had said the last word" (*LH*, 20).[13] It was "a testament to Bill's genius," says *'Pass It On,'* that he called these principles "traditions" rather than "laws" or "by-laws" or "rules" or "regulations": "Bill knew his fellow alcoholics well; he knew that no self-respecting drunk, sober or otherwise, would willingly submit to a body of 'law'—much too authoritarian!" (*PIO*, 306).

Although some of the Traditions did arise from A.A.'s field experience, some of them were not really in place at the level of local group custom. Wilson was, to a degree, legislating for the future on the authority of an imaginary past. He was also appealing to the mandate of A.A.'s group conscience whether or not he was actually guided by it. "He was selective, using only those experiences that went to the heart of A.A. problems. Since his desire was always the best interest of A.A., his so-called manipulations always worked for the good of the Fellowship." As Wilson himself put it, "My personal life may not be exemplary, but I have never made a mistake about A.A." (*PIO*, 322).

Here we have the official A.A. biography, with help from the cofounder himself, putting the best possible face on the infallible Bill W.'s leadership; because his ends were always good, his slipperier means may be glossed over. But Wilson's boast may have been warranted,

after all, at least in regard to the Twelve Traditions and his later emphasis on Service as A.A.'s Third Legacy (along with Recovery and
Unity). Certainly, A.A. owes much of its continuing success to the organizational gifts of Bill Wilson, who installed a durable institutional
design, sometimes over strenuous objections, that proved to be good
for A.A. even when A.A. wished to define its best interests otherwise.
What's most impressive about the Twelve Traditions, perhaps, is how
inevitable they came to seem in the long run, how truly traditional.

Throughout 1948, in a series of monthly commentaries in the
Grapevine, Bill W. took up each of the Traditions in turn and explained
its historical background and its significance to A.A.'s practices, which,
he stressed, were still evolving and ideally ever would be. For instance,
there was a subtle but important change in the wording of Tradition
Three: "The only requirement for membership is an honest desire to
stop drinking." Derived from the foreword to the Big Book (*AA*, xiv),
this sentence did not appear in the 1946 long form of the Traditions,
as written by Bill W. In 1949, when it became the entire text of the
short form (the version read at meetings), *honest* was omitted on the
grounds that a maturing A.A. had come to recognize "that it is nearly
impossible to determine what constitutes an 'honest' desire to stop
drinking, as opposed to other forms in which the desire might be expressed" (*NG*, 106).[14] This change was, in effect, a reconfirmation of
Wilson's original conception of this Tradition: that A.A. should have
no membership requirements whatsoever beyond anyone's desire to
belong. "Our membership ought to include all who suffer alcoholism.
Hence we may refuse none who wish to recover . . . .Any two or three
alcoholics gathered together for sobriety may call themselves an AA
group" (*LH*, 22).[15]

The Twelve Traditions were officially adopted in Cleveland in June
1950, during A.A.'s fifteenth anniversary celebration, which was also
its first international convention. The other main event that year was
the moving farewell speech by Dr. Bob, whose cancer was to kill him
soon afterward. With the mortality of one cofounder so painfully in
plain sight, the membership, perhaps, better appreciated the other cofounder's pains to provide for A.A.'s future without him. In Wilson's
mind, the event constituted A.A.'s "'coming of age' party." That mile-
stone is generally thought to have been reached not in 1950, but rather
in 1955, at the second international convention in Saint Louis, when

Bill W. retired from his leadership role, leaving A.A. completely in the hands of the governance system he had devised so carefully. "But Bill's inner timetable was, as usual, five years ahead of other people's" (*PIO*, 338).

Wilson's sense of urgency had much to do with his need to gain some healthy distance from A.A. The recognition of this need had come from his efforts to combat his depression, and formulating the Traditions had been part of the therapy. "Sometimes I could be quite paralyzed," he wrote to a female A.A. in 1953, "other times I could get a good deal done. Actually, this was very good for AA. It kept me off the big-time speaking circuit; it made me sit home and wonder what was going to become of me and of the fellowship. This was the beginning of the formation of the AA traditions."[16] As he told journalist Jack Alexander a year later, "The whole A.A. Tradition is, in a sense, a result of my gradual adjustment to reality" (*NG*, 290 n. 7).

Once Wilson had discharged his duties, the dark clouds finally lifted. "After 1955, the year he declared A.A. of age, pronounced the service structure complete, and turned the fellowship over to its members, he was free of depression" (*PIO*, 303). That is, once Wilson had tamed the conflict between the demands of A.A. and his own needs as an individual, the root of his depression was extirpated. Once he became "entirely sure that Alcoholics Anonymous was at last safe—even from me" (*LH*, 165), he too became surer that he was safe at last—even from A.A.

In *Alcoholics Anonymous Comes of Age*, Wilson related the Twelve Traditions to his individual growth:

> Because I myself have always had strong tendencies toward the pursuit of prestige, wealth, and power, all of A.A.'s Traditions have borne down upon me with great force. . . . With nearly every Tradition much the same thing has happened. At first, I obeyed because I had to; I would have lost my standing in A.A. if I had not. After a while I began to obey because I saw that the Traditions were wise and right. While I conformed because it was right to do so, I still resisted inwardly.
>
> This was particularly true of anonymity. Today I hope I have come to a time in my A.A. life when I can obey because I really *want* to obey, because I really want the Traditions for myself as well as for A.A. as a whole. (*AACA*, 135–36)

As the author of the Traditions, Wilson spoke of and to himself in speaking for A.A. The Traditions were thus more "personal" than they might seem. Conventional A.A. wisdom has it that whereas the Steps are meant for the individual, the Traditions are meant for the group. But it's also possible to think of the Traditions as having a secondary, individual application. Like the cofounder, any A.A. member can apply these principles to all of his or her affairs. Each Tradition, as Bill W. wrote, is really about "the deflation that each of us has to take, of the sacrifice that we shall all have to make in order to live and work together" (*AACA*, 136). In this sense, the Twelve Traditions might be regarded as a second set of Twelve Steps[17]—perhaps the advanced course insofar as the Traditions, concerned as they are with renunciation and humility, seem to demand a more fully seasoned sobriety.

This was the ultimate lesson of the Traditions for Bill Wilson himself, who continually sought relief from depression in the same way he had found reprieve from alcoholism: through a liberating spiritual awakening—or, as Wilson put it to Carl Jung in 1961, "a remotivating conversion experience' (*PIO*, 386). The spiritual quest, which was the motive force of Wilson's later years, helps to explain certain aspects of his private life that, as we shall see, became scandalous to uncomprehending A.A. members.

The Sage of Stepping Stones

By the 1950s, Bill W. had become the most famous unknown man in America. As everyone knew who he "really" was, he had attained the oxymoronic status of being an "anonymous" celebrity. Although Bill had officially withdrawn from A.A. leadership, he made it known he could still be called back in an emergency, and he continued to commute to the New York office once a week. His duties there were light; he was merely keeping his hand in. The new center of his life was his Westchester retreat, Stepping Stones, which became a mecca for A.A. pilgrims seeking enlightenment directly from the cofounder. From his hand-built study there, Wilson carried on an ambitious writing program that included books, *Grapevine* columns, and numerous letters to fellow alcoholics. All the while his fusion with A.A. in the eyes of its members and of the world at large became all the more complete. As Wilson realized, his personal autonomy was hostage to his fame as Bill W.; his private choices were circumscribed by the obligations of his public persona.

Robert Thomsen eloquently sets the scene of Bill W.'s farewell address at Saint Louis in 1955:

> He seemed to have grown, to be somehow a little larger than life, a man who just naturally created memories. If Bill W. had engaged a Madison Avenue PR firm, one old-timer recalled, and if this firm had

worked around the clock on his account, they could never have done for him what he without even trying did for himself that afternoon. There had always been a powerful affinity between Bill and the imagination of alcoholics, and now this could be felt in the farthest corners of Kiel Auditorium. . . .

They were assembled here to honor him for something that had not really been his doing. But that was all right; he had no objections; some people would always want and believe they needed a leader. To them he had become a symbol. He was more than an administrator, more than a cofounder, or the author of the Steps. He was the custodian of their deepest beliefs and of that faith which somehow had created dignity and peace out of their unbelievable hells. (BW, 351–52)

This evocation of "Bill W." in all his exalted majesty—as if (at least metaphorically) he had descended into hell and then arisen from the dead—hints at the ways in which being A.A.'s "symbol" might weigh heavily upon a man who did not always prefer to seem "larger than life." If Bill W., the messiah of sobriety, "naturally created memories," he was also locked into them by worshipers who demanded that he stay just as he was in their adoring vision. Indeed, the reassurance he delivered to the A.A. faithful depended on his never changing, on his being perpetually the custodian of their deepest beliefs.

One side effect of Bill W.'s apotheosis was the petrification of the Big Book, the updating of which was Wilson's last and most important contribution before his retirement. The new edition of *Alcoholics Anonymous* was prepared for publication in the same year, 1955, in which he would hand over the reins of power. Wilson, a habitual tinkerer with mechanical things, had also acquired a writerly itch for revision. But the Big Book proved to be too sacrosanct for even minor alterations. "As to changing the Steps themselves, or even the text of the A.A. book," Wilson remarked sardonically in a 1952 letter, "I am assured by many that I could certainly be excommunicated if a word were touched. It is a strange fact of human nature that when a spiritually centered movement starts and finally adopts certain principles, these finally freeze absolutely solid" (NG, 300 n. 67).[1]

He had no choice, therefore, but to retain the first section intact, as published in 1939. Perhaps in reaction to this constraint, Wilson took a very free hand to the story section; it was nearly a clean sweep. Aside from Smith's (also untouchable) account, "The Doctor's Nightmare"—

now retitled "Dr. Bob's Nightmare," in recognition of his own legendary status—Wilson discarded *all* of the other twenty-eight original narratives, except for modified versions of "The European Drinker," "Our Southern Friend," and "Home Brewmeister." (Along with "Bill's Story" and "Dr. Bob's Nightmare," these are the only stories to appear in all three editions of the Big Book).

In fact, unless one has ready access to the three editions, there is no way to see how much *Alcoholics Anonymous* has changed from one version to the next—but only in the second part, which I have dubbed its New Testament. Even in the Big Book's Old Testament, however, a few small changes have silently crept in. Ernest Kurtz notes that when, in a later printing of the first edition, "spiritual awakening" was substituted for "spiritual experience" in Step Twelve, the phrase was made "more consistent in other scattered references." In addition, "the words *disease, cure,* and *ex-alcoholic* were more carefully avoided, the first generally replaced by 'illness' and the second and third by circumlocutions adverting to the persistence of the condition" (*NG*, 132). Without a full collation of all the many printings of the Big Book—the kind of scholarly scrutiny ordinarily reserved for Scripture and highly canonical literary texts—it is impossible to say what other emendations, if any, have been made over the years.[2]

To replace what was omitted from Part Two, Bill W. inserted thirty-three new stories, most of which were carried over into the third edition of 1976. The criteria for inclusion sprang from a desire to reflect the current membership more accurately and also to display a diversity that might attract an even wider range of people. Thus whereas women in A.A. were represented by only one story in 1939, the revised edition included eleven; the proportion of female stories was higher, in fact, than the actual proportion (15 percent) of female membership (*AA*, xx). The subtitle of *Alcoholics Anonymous* was also revised to include women among the "many thousands who had recovered from alcoholism." In recognition that many new members had not plumbed the depths of degradation to which early A.A.s had characteristically sunk, the Big Book now offered a dozen 'high-bottom" stories ("They Stopped in Time"), in addition to a dozen "low-bottom" ones ("They Almost Lost All").

As in the original edition, there was some editorial sleight of hand in order to downplay the homogeneity of membership. These distortions were largely subliminal. As one old-timer later reflected, although A.A. "certainly has turned out to be a middle-class, largely white phenomenon," this trend was not so pronounced in 1955 that the editors were aware of it or "concerned with it as a problem." On the contrary, "I think in those days we felt that our spread was pretty broad and democratic" (NG, 301 n. 71). Nonetheless, as Kurtz reports, the editors "tended to understate employment status" in the interests of occupational diversity. In one case, an entrepreneur was presented merely as an artisan; whereas this supposed "upholsterer" actually "owned his own fairly large firm even though he continued to work as a craftsman" (NG, 132).

What A.A.'s leaders, including Wilson, wished to minimize was that few members came from the ends of the socioeconomic spectrum; neither the rich nor the poor tended to stay.

> Most regulars at meetings had hit the rocks of alcoholism from one of two related directions: the frustrations of efforts at upward mobility—preeminently a lower middle class affliction; or the pains of perceived downward mobility—a torment of especially the children of the upper middle classes who had not successfully internalized the values (or the luck) of their forebears. (NG, 133)

Whether A.A.'s members were rising from below or falling from above, they met in the epicenter of the American middle class. Throughout its history A.A.'s ideology has remained inveterately bourgeois.

During the early 1950s, before revising the Big Book, Wilson had published a new series of *Grapevine* columns on the Traditions. He then undertook a matching set of commentaries on the Steps. Eugene Exman, who once had encouraged the (then) nameless bunch of drunks to publish the Big Book by themselves, now cooperated in a joint venture. *Twelve Steps and Twelve Traditions* (1953), the so-called *12 & 12*, was issued both by A.A. for its members, and also by Harper and Brothers in a higher-priced (by fifty cents) trade edition, distinguished by its green rather than blue dust jacket. (The same dual publication was arranged in 1957 for *Alcoholics Anonymous Comes of Age*.)

Twelve Steps and Twelve Traditions was impelled, in part, by Wilson's frustration that the text of the Big Book had become "too 'sacred' for even its principal author's taste" (NG, 132).[3] The *12 & 12* was also written while Bill W. was still in the throes of his depression, to the point where he "apparently felt obliged to add an explanation—or apology—near the end of his essay on Step Twelve: ' . . . it may appear that A.A. consists mainly of racking dilemmas and troubleshooting. To a certain extent, that is true'" (*PIO*, 353).

Even after 1955, Wilson had moments when he feared that darkness was descending again. In "The Next Frontier: Emotional Sobriety," a *Grapevine* article from 1958, Bill revealed he had recently caught a whiff of his old demon and dreaded he "was in for another long chronic spell." Despite his efforts to work the program, the thickening gloom almost took him, he said, "to the cleaners," until he was freed by an inspiration:

> I kept asking myself, "Why can't the Twelve Steps work to release depression?" By the hour, I stared at the St. Francis Prayer . . . "It's better to comfort than to be comforted" [Wilson's ellipsis]. Here was the formula, all right. But why didn't it work?
>
> Suddenly I realized what the matter was. My basic flaw had always been dependence—almost absolute dependence—on people or circumstances to supply me with prestige, security, and the like. Failing to get these things according to my perfectionist dreams and specifications, I had fought for them. And when defeat came, so did my depression.

Thanks to his "emotional sobriety," Bill now had the capacity to forestall depression, by swiftly and ruthlessly severing "these faulty emotional dependencies upon people, upon AA, indeed, upon any set of circumstances whatsoever." Only then would he "be free to love as Francis had" (*LH*, 237).[4]

Such freedom was the fruit not merely of Wilson's not drinking for more than twenty years, but also of his searching and fearless self-scrutiny. "Emotional sobriety" lay beyond mere abstinence, Bill asserted in the same *Grapevine* column. Neither alcoholics nor neurotics have, after all, any monopoly on the problem of "how to translate a right mental conviction into a right emotional result, and so into easy, happy, and good living." This is "the problem of life itself for all of us who have got to the point of real willingness to hew to right principles in all our affairs." Echoing an insight from psychoanalysis, he added: "How shall our unconscious—from which so many of our fears, compulsions, and phony aspirations still stream—be brought into line with what we actually believe, know, and want! How to convince our dumb, raging, and hidden 'Mr. Hyde' becomes our main task" (*LH*, 237).

The Jekyll-Hyde analogy, which had also been used in the Big Book,[5] appeared as well in Karen Horney's explanation of psychic conflict in *Neurosis and Human Growth* (1950), a book that Wilson read with great enthusiasm and that was formative of his ideas about "emotional sobriety." As he wrote in a letter of 4 January 1956:

> I have the highest admiration of her [Horney]. That gal's insights have been most helpful to me. Also for the benefit of screwballs like ourselves, it may be that someday we shall devise some common denominator of psychiatry—of course, throwing away their much abused terminology—common denominators which neurotics could use on each other. The idea would be to extend the moral inventory of AA to a deeper level, making it an inventory of psychic damages, relieving in conversation episodes, etc. I suppose someday a Neurotics Anonymous will be formed and will actually do all this.[6]

Although what became N. A. was *Narcotics* rather than *Neurotics* Anonymous, something close to Wilson's idea has been widely adopted by the Recovery Movement in recent years. Wilson himself was quick to adopt Horney's insights and some of her terminology in explanations of his own case.

Horney, a renegade German psychoanalyst who had split off from Freud, fashioned her own theory, which rejected certain Freudian ideas and incorporated, without explicit acknowledgment, certain Adlerian ones. In particular, Horney shared Alfred Adler's criticism of Freud's "overemphasis on biology and his disregard of cultural factors." She also followed Adler in dismissing the Freudian theory of libido development through psychosexual phases; instead she traced all neurosis to "an effort to ward off anxiety."[7] After emigrating to the United States during the 1930s, Horney published a series of popular books designed for general readers, including the one Wilson evidently read.

According to Robert Fitzgerald, "Bill's use of the words 'neurosis' and 'absolute dependency' referring to his drive for approval and glory seem to come from the first chapter" of *Neurosis and Human Growth*. He may also have borrowed from a later chapter on "Morbid Dependency."[8] Certainly, one passage that held his attention concerns "the alienation from self" as the "nuclear problem" in all neurotic developments, a passage that recalls Adler's theory of the "inferiority" and "superiority" complexes (see Chapter 1). "In his conscious way of experiencing himself," Horney writes, "a neurotic may shuttle between a feeling of arrogant omnipotence and of being the scum of the earth. This is particularly obvious in (but by no means restricted to) alcoholics, who at one moment may be up in the clouds, making great gestures and grandiose promises, and at the next be abject and cringing." Severe conflict is bound to arise from a neurotic's incompatible identifications with "his superior proud self" and "his despised self":

> If these two ways of experiencing himself operate at the same time he must feel like two people pulling in opposite directions. . . . There is not only a conflict, but a conflict of sufficient impact to tear him apart. If he does not succeed in diminishing the resulting tension, anxiety is bound to arise. He may then, if so disposed for other reasons, take to drinking to allay his anxiety.[9]

This is Horney's most direct treatment of alcoholism in the book, and she goes on to explain the alcoholic's dilemma, as Wilson does, in terms of *Doctor Jekyll and Mr. Hyde*:

> Dr. Jekyll recognizes that there are two sides of him (roughly presented as the sinner and the saint, with neither of them being himself) at perennial war with each other. . . . If the story is divested of its fantastic garb, it represents the attempt to solve the conflict by *compartmentalizing*. Many patients veer in this direction. They experience themselves successively as extremely self-effacing and as grandiose and expansive without feeling disquieted by this contradiction, because in their minds the two selves are disconnected.
>
> But as Stevenson's story indicates, this attempt cannot be successful . . . it is too partial a solution. A more radical one follows the pattern of *streamlining*, which is . . . the attempt to suppress permanently and rigidly one self and be exclusively the other. A third way of solving the conflict is by withdrawing interest from the inner battle and *resigning* from active psychic living.[10]

Wilson might have read here the history of his own attempts to resolve his nuclear conflict. For Wilson, however, *resigning* did not mean an end to active psychic living. Instead, resigning from A.A. leadership was the beginning of *acceptance* in its deepest sense: a healing embrace of human frailty and insufficiency. Wilson believed that attaining acceptance was impossible by means of psychotherapy alone; it required the cultivation of a spiritual program. As Bill W. wrote to a fellow A.A. in March 1953, "Since I have begun to pray that God may release me from absolute dependence on anybody, anything, or any set of circumstances, I have begun to do so much better that it amounts to a second conversion experience" (NG, 214).

Thus through the ordeal of his depression and the interior voyage of exploration it induced, Wilson came to realize that in cases like his own "the A.A. way of life" needed to expand beyond abstinence to "a quest to find greater enlightenment, to find healing for sober alcoholics for whom sobriety alone, even when they worked the Steps, was insufficient to provide a comfortable life." This quest would eventually lead him "in a direction apparently away from A.A., and would have consequences of major proportions" (PIO, 299).

To some members of A.A., the controversial new directions suggested that William Griffith Wilson, like Poe's William Wilson, might have a shadowy double, that the supreme arbiter of A.A. orthodoxy might be twin to a subversive A.A. heretic. Bill W. and Mr. Wilson; Dr. Jekyll and Mr. Hyde. The more timorous trustees felt that Bill was acting so weirdly that A.A. itself needed protection from his potentially damaging folly. "They—and he—carefully shielded from public scrutiny three areas among the cofounder's many activities," says Kurtz. These were "Wilson's interest in spiritualism, his experimentation with LSD, and his promotion of the Vitamin B-3 therapy" (NG, 136).[11] To this list one might add, as does 'Pass It On,' his flirtation with Roman Catholicism.

What matters about the Wilson "scandals" is that all of them arose directly from Bill's quest for spiritual enlightenment, a quest that was intertwined at first with his search for relief from depression and later for an end to "neurosis," understood in the broadest sense as any human conflict. In that sense, Wilson was not far from Freud, who also looked into parapsychology and wrote several clinical papers on telepathy. "It was evidence of intellectual courage," says sociologist Philip Rieff, that Freud was "willing to extend his theory of the unconscious and his therapeutic method even into areas of speculation where misunderstanding is especially likely."[12] What similarly seemed so threatening and embarrassing to some A.A. conservatives might, from another angle, have been regarded as evidence of the evolving wisdom of the Sage of Stepping Stones.

Soon after their arrival there in 1941, the Wilsons set aside one small downstairs room, jokingly known as the "spook room," in which to conduct séances and experiments with other spiritualistic phenomena, such as clairvoyance, spirit rapping, levitation, and the Ouija board. As Bob and Anne Smith were also avidly interested in such things, and as "there are references to séances and other psychic events" in the letters Bill wrote home to Lois during the Akron summer of 1935 (PIO, 275), it might be said that for the cofounders at least, A.A. was entangled with spiritualism from the very beginning.

For Wilson the bond endured until the very end. Late in the 1940s, he was "drawn through friendship with philosopher-mystic Gerald Heard into the ambit of the later-life interests of Aldous Huxley" (NG, 136), whose mystical investigations were well known. In 1957, Bill W. told a fellow A.A. that in his quest for faith, "I've had the advantage of what seems to have been a very genuine and illuminating spiritual experience, together with many later encounters with the psychic realm, both personal and by observation" (NG, 302 n. 3).

Tom P., a friend and neighbor of the Wilsons who, despite his skepticism, was a regular participant in the "spooking circle," witnessed the intensity of their sessions. "Now these people, Bill and Dr. Bob, believed vigorously and aggressively. They were working away at the spiritualism; it was not just a hobby. And it related to A.A., because the big problem in A.A. is that for a materialist it's hard to buy the program." Tom, a confirmed atheist, was speaking for himself here; he recognized Wilson's hope that spiritualism might play some part in bringing A.A. unbelievers into contact with a Higher Power: "So the thing was not at all divorced from A.A. It was very serious for everybody" (PIO, 280).

Wilson himself seems to have been an "adept," that is, "gifted" in the psychic sense; and he served as a medium for a variety of "controls," some of them recurrent. "Controls," in the lingo of spiritualism, are the discarnate entities who seem to usurp a medium's identity and literally to speak through him or (far more usually) her. Sometimes the control answers questions; sometimes a spirit seems to materialize. In fact, according to the account published in 'Pass It On,' Bill had one such experience during a trip to Nantucket in 1944: a breakfast

conversation with a succession of ghosts. After his long session with
the shades, Bill claimed he had found local evidence of their earthly existence.

> Therefore, the record shows that I had picked up pretty accurate de-
> scriptions of three quite obscure and long-dead Nantucket citizens,
> names no doubt gone from the minds of living people. There isn't even
> a remote chance that I had at some earlier time read or heard about all
> three of them, *ordinary* former *inhabitants* of the island. Maybe *one,* but
> certainly not *three.* (*PIO,* 278).

In this instance, Wilson was witness to what would have been called
a "veridical phantasm" by the Society for Psychical Research, the organization that, since the 1880s, had promoted scientific investigation
of spirit survival and other higher mysteries.[13] The magnum opus of
the S.P.R.—Frederic Myers's *Human Personality and Its Survival of Bodily
Death* (1903)—is still in the bookcase in the "spook room," along with
a small library of related books, including Jung's *Flying Saucers* (1958).

The very existence of the S.P.R. suggests how central—and also
how intellectually respectable—spiritualism had become in Victorian
culture since its first manifestation in the eerie rappings of the Fox
sisters at their family farm outside Rochester, New York, in 1848. (Like
many psychical celebrities, the Fox sisters were later exposed as frauds;
the uncanny noises were produced by cracking their toe joints!) Any
number of prominent people took an interest; indeed, spiritualism was
so pervasive in the late nineteenth century that its presence is now
nearly invisible. That is, it was so ordinary a part of everyday life that
it was taken for granted, and then it vanished without leaving much
of a historical trace.

Noting that the "era of great mediums lasted from about 1880 to
1925," Rieff shrewdly suggests that "this terminal date coincides fairly
with the end of the Protestant era":

> Perhaps survivalist experience was the genteel form of revivalist experi-
> ence, fit for those rare creatures who could not otherwise express their
> sense of the over-all meaning of life in a culture that, in both its waning
> religious and waxing scientific phase, denied the legitimacy of mystical
> modes of understanding.[14]

This insight goes far toward explaining Bill Wilson's spiritualistic pro-clivities. As a institutional vestige of evangelical Protestantism, A.A., for all its earthy pragmatism, was also committed to "mystical modes of understanding" as a means to enduring sobriety.

In taking these modes seriously, Wilson was not alone. In fact, he was in good company. As we have seen, Sigmund Freud, whose high-est ambition was to put psychoanalysis on a scientific footing, none-theless took notice of psychical phenomena—much to the chagrin of his closest disciples, who felt (as did some A.A.s about Wilson) a need to bury the offending facts or else to explain them away. An entire chapter of Ernest Jones's monumental biography is dedicated to Freud's "open-mindedness" about "occultism" (he was even a member of the S.P.R.) and his publication, over Jones's protestations, of his papers on telepathy. Jones took this to be just one more regrettable example "of the remarkable fact that highly developed critical powers may co-exist in the same person with an unexpected fund of credulity."[15]

More to the point, both the men Wilson considered forefathers of Alcoholics Anonymous were deeply involved with spiritualism. Wil-liam James, who was a friend and admirer of Frederic Myers and who himself served as president of the American Society for Psychical Re-search, spent innumerable hours, in the course of twenty-five years, in séances with Mrs. L. E. Piper, the marvelous trance medium whom the S.P.R. kept practically under house arrest in Boston.[16] It was pre-cisely James's openness to spiritual manifestations in *The Varieties of Religious Experience* that made him simpatico with Wilson. Carl Jung, too, took occultism seriously, beginning with his doctoral dissertation, "On the Psychology and Pathology of So-Called Occult Phenomena" (1902: the same year as *Varieties*). This was a psychoanalytic study of his cousin Hélène ("Helly") Preiswerk, whom Jung had encouraged to practice as a medium. Throughout his career, to a degree that was fully apparent only to a small circle of his intimates, Jung cultivated his own fascination with and susceptibility to occult experience.

If, as Rieff suggests, spiritualism was the last gasp of Protestantism, then it makes intuitive sense that Wilson should have been drawn so powerfully to Roman Catholicism—especially during the late 1940s, when he was taking formal instruction in the faith from Monsignor Fulton J. Sheen, the sleekly brilliant apostle to the masses and grand master of celebrity conversions, whose "Catholic Hour" on the radio drew a million listeners every week. (Later, as Bishop Sheen, he was to host his own weekly television program, a Catholic *half*-hour that I can dimly remember watching, rapt, in my early childhood.) According to Lois Wilson, Sheen "offered to explain Catholicism," but "he didn't say 'converted'"; so Bill "thought it would be very ungrateful not to at least try to learn" (*PIO*, 281). He agreed to meet with Sheen every Saturday for most of a year during 1947–48.

This unlikely story—that Wilson's religious instruction was motivated merely by tact and/or intellectual curiosity—supports one (implicitly anti-Catholic) view of Bill's flirtation with Rome: that he proved too shrewd and too sensible, after all, to fall for Sheen's silver-tongued ministry. Lois was sure that Bill "never really had it in the back of his mind that he would be converted" (*PIO*, 281). There is plenty of evidence to the contrary, however. In his correspondence with Father Ed, Wilson spoke quite fervently of his attraction to "that sweet and powerful aura of the Church, that marvelous spiritual essence flowing down the centuries"; and he wondered, half facetiously, if the Church didn't have "a fellow-traveler department, a cozy spot where one could warm his hands at The Fire and bite off only as much as he could swallow."[17]

Although, as Wilson told Dowling, he felt like a Catholic already, Bill ultimately shied from conversion. He could come to believe in divine mysteries that were "confirmed by experience—the Resurrection and return, the healing miracles, spiritual experiences themselves." But try as he might, he could not swallow "what was beyond human experience":[18] Virgin Birth; the transubstantiation of bread and wine into Christ's body and blood during the Mass; the doctrine of infallibility—"not only the personal infallibility of the Pope, but the infallibility claimed for the effectiveness of the sacraments in Catholic theology." "These excursions into the absolute are rather beyond me," he wrote to a friend. "Though no disbeliever in all miracles, I still can't picture God working like that" (*NG*, 52).

Infallibility was a particular sticking point because it offended all of Wilson's democratic principles and contradicted his vision of A.A.'s self-governance. He knew that his greatest problem in reforming A.A. was precisely the quasi-papal authority that had been thrust upon him as a cofounder and the presumption of "infallibility" that went with it. As Thomsen reports: "Men who worked beside Bill in this period have said that in his private life Bill Wilson could make mistakes, horrendous ones, but as far as AA was concerned he was never wrong" (BW, 326). It would have been at least inconsistent for Wilson to have joined the Catholic Church and submitted to its hierarchy—which was far more exacting of the faithful's compliance during the 1940s than after the *risorgimento* of the Second Vatican Council two decades later—at the same time he was trying to rid A.A. of hierarchical tendencies.

For public consumption, Wilson's standard explanation for his aborted conversion was that he feared it "might adversely affect Alcoholics Anonymous" (NG, 52). This idea was confirmed by one of Bill's closest friends: "I had the impression that at the last minute, he didn't go through with his conversion because he felt it would not be right for A.A." (PIO, 281). But if so, in what way would it not have been "right"? Presumably, Wilson was aware of lingering prejudice in America against ethnic Catholics; even the Irish, the most fully assimilated group, were told they "need not apply" in some quarters; and their large presence in A.A., especially in larger cities, no doubt perturbed those who did not identify themselves with "recovering Catholics."[19] Bill W. must have anticipated that some A.A. members would be as scandalized by his turning to Rome as he once had been by Ebby's getting religion in the Oxford Group. So even at the risk of passive complicity in the bigotry of some A.A.s, Bill W. wished not to stir up any sectarian religious disputes.[20]

There may have been another reason as well. Throughout the 1940s and early 1950s, entering the Church became so common among writers and intellectuals that one might speak of a Roman vogue. Thomas Merton, for example, climbed the best-seller list with the compelling account of his spiritual journey from secular Columbia University to an ascetic Trappist monastery. *The Seven Storey Mountain* (1948), which appeared while Wilson was taking instruction from Sheen, carried Sheen's laudatory blurb on the dust jacket.[21] Merton was inspiration to others who were seeking belief in the seemingly faithless modern world and who were attracted to Catholicism by its very opposition to reigning intellectual orthodoxies, especially worship at the First Church of Karl Marx. The reasons for these conversions, some of which were attended by considerable publicity, were as various as the individuals involved, but faith was sometimes alloyed by the reverse snobbery of Catholic chic.

Although there is no doubt of the sincerity of Wilson's interest in Catholicism, he was always careful not to expose to A.A. his own intellectuality, which he developed in private through extensive reading and contemplative practices. It has often been observed that A.A. ideology, in the service of pragmatism and egalitarianism, exhibits a militantly anti-intellectual strain; whenever Bill W. was perceived to be thinking too big or too much, he was promptly laid low by criticism from the fellowship. In the eyes of those who otherwise distrusted him, Bill W.'s conversion to Catholicism would have been judged to be a deviant and, possibly, a crypto-elitist act.

Better that, perhaps, than Wilson's experimentation with LSD, one common A.A. reaction to which is rolling the eyeballs in disbelief. How could Bill W., Grand Poohbah of sobriety, ever have allowed himself to join the Learyesque acidheads and "turn on, tune in and drop out"? The only explanation, it seems, is hypocrisy—or lunacy! But, here again, Wilson's actions are reasonable enough in the context of his unending search for spiritual enlightenment. For one thing, Timothy Leary's notorious summons to the drug culture was issued in 1966, a decade *after* Wilson had first dropped acid under the careful supervision of two Canadian physicians, Humphry Osmond and Abram Hoffer, who were testing its effects on alcoholics and schizophrenics in a mental hospital setting. The theory was that (1) as some alcoholics react so violently to delirium tremens that they are, in effect, scared straight, and (2) as LSD seems to induce a mental state akin to delirium tremens, then (3) maybe it could be therapeutic to *induce* so bad a trip with LSD that the patient might be deterred from ever risking its recurrence through drinking. This was, in short, a bizarre kind of aversion therapy. And it didn't work as expected. One of the doctors later recalled that LSD had given "pause for thought, not on the grounds of how terrifying it was, but how illuminating it was. Rather different!" (*PIO,* 369).

This difference is what finally interested Wilson, who had initially been skittish about trying the drug. He thought that LSD might be another way of achieving the ego "deflation at depth" that he saw to be prerequisite to the inflowing of higher consciousness. After his trial session in California, late in August 1956, Bill was thrilled with the results: "he felt it helped him eliminate many barriers erected by the self, or ego, that stand in the way of one's direct experience of the cosmos and of God. He thought he might have found something that could make a big difference to the lives of many who still suffered" (*PIO*, 371). Back at Stepping Stones, Wilson carried on his own LSD experiments; he invited his wife and friends, including Helen Wing, Father Ed, and Sam Shoemaker, to join him. Some didn't, but Lois did, although she claimed the drug did nothing for her. "Actually, I could not tell any difference" (*PIO*, 372).

Eventually, Dowling began to question the prudence of Wilson's activities, which were becoming known to A.A. at large and were arousing vigorous remonstration. At first Bill was disgruntled by A.A.'s infringement of his personal freedom, and he complained at length to Shoemaker about A.A.'s misunderstanding of his interests in spiritualism and LSD. But late in 1959, he eventually yielded to pressure and dropped the drug experiments for the sake of A.A. harmony. "You cannot escape being 'Bill W.,'" he was reminded by one of the worried trustees; "nor would you, really, even though at times you will rebel" (*PIO*, 376). Wilson laughed off the controversy in an October 1959 letter to Father Ed: "The LSD business created some commotion. . . . The story is 'that Bill takes one pill to see God and another to quiet his nerves.' No amount of factual information can seem to dispel their fearful doubts. Though one does not like to disturb unnecessarily one's friends, it must be confessed that these recent heresies of mine do have their comic aspect."[22]

Wilson now hatched his last heresy: advocacy of niacin (Vitamin B-3) as therapy for alcoholism. This notion was also advanced by Doctors Osmond and Hoffer, who had noticed a correlation between alcoholism and hypoglycemia and who believed niacin could help prevent disorienting drops in blood sugar. The compulsion to drink, they hypothesized, might be attributable at times to an alcoholic's natural impulse to raise his blood sugar levels. (Hence the common presence of hard candy and other sugary snacks at A.A. meetings and the folk wisdom that eating sweets can kill an urge to drink.) Although the theory was far from proven, Wilson was utterly convinced that the researchers had confirmed Doctor Silkworth's (dubious) old idea of putting alcoholism on a physical basis as an "allergy." Wilson, in fact, got the B-3 bee in his bonnet; his zeal knew no bounds as he took to promoting niacin as a wonder "drug" that was all the more wonderful for not really being a drug. As well as writing three papers to publicize the B-3 research to A.A.'s medical community, Bill also proselytized within the fellowship, and quarrels soon broke out between niacin converts and skeptics. In 1967, Bill was finally persuaded to move his campaign outside of A.A., at least to the extent of receiving niacin-related inquiries at a private post office box in Westchester and of answering all such mail on paper other than official A.A. letterhead. Wilson remained a niacin enthusiast to the last; his final report was finished just before his death.[23]

As Thomsen remarks, some old-timers were so appalled by the co-founder's interest in "drugs" that "he received several letters suggesting that the district attorney's office might like to be informed that Bill W. was now practicing medicine—and without a license" (BW, 359–60). In warning Wilson off LSD in 1959, one good friend had worried: "The greatest danger that I sense to the Fellowship is that you might lose A.A. as it applies to you" (PIO, 376). This possibility had long concerned Bill W., who as early as October 1947 had published a Grapevine column poignantly titled, "Why Can't We Join A.A., Too?" It was time, he urged with Dr. Bob's concurrence, for A.A. to let them retire to the sidelines like other elders in the fellowship. "As private citizens of AA," they proposed, "we shall often wish to come and go among you like other people, without any special attention. And while we would like always to keep the wonderful satisfaction of having been among the originators, we hope you will begin to think of us as early AAs only, not as 'founders'" (LH, 111).

This hope proved to be quixotic, at least for Bill W., special attention to whom swelled to the point where he had no choice but to decline all speaking engagements lest he seem unfair in accepting only the few he could handle. The idea that Wilson might come and go unnoticed at meetings, as merely a private A.A. citizen, was literally the stuff of Hollywood fantasy. At the end of My Name Is Bill W. (1989), the powerful made-for-television movie, James Woods (playing Bill) is shown slipping anonymously into a meeting. At first Wilson is piqued to go unacknowledged as the cofounder, but he quickly suppresses his vanity; after the meeting, as just plain Bill, he lends a sympathetic ear to another suffering alcoholic. As the film fades to black, we see Bill, properly fortified with coffee, beginning what we know will be a long talk with someone who desperately needs his help. Lois, beaming with devotion, understandingly absents herself; she knows Bill must be about A.A.'s business.[24]

In reality, when Bill W. went to meetings, not only was he inevitably recognized, but he was also swarmed by admirers and pressed into telling them his story. Sometimes he would hold audiences for small groups of the faithful. One old-timer remembers waiting for two hours in order to spend twenty minutes with Bill W. at a Boston hotel in 1947. That day more than two hundred A.A.s were placed in groups of fifteen; each group was seated in turn in a large lounge, where Wilson held court. The experience was thrilling; the pilgrim felt as if he "had been in the presence of some spiritual force." Bill's "aura" pervaded the room; he seemed "to be unaware of the phenomenon and even of his part in it, but to me it was real yet unnatural."[25]

As a result of his remoteness from the natural and ordinary life of the fellowship, Bill W. *did,* in fact, come to lose A.A. as it applied to him. Nell Wing has revealed what may be the biggest Wilson "scandal" of all: that for years at the end of his life Bill W. stopped going to A.A. meetings!—although private, house-call gatherings were occasionally arranged for him at the New York office or at Stepping Stones. "To some members," writes Wing, "Bill's failure to attend A.A. meetings regularly was a grievous fault."[26] Wilson himself did not disagree. No one else could better have appreciated the bittersweet irony that the acclaimed cofounder *of* A.A. was, in a real sense, no longer *in* A.A.

Afterword

On my first visit to Stepping Stones, I nearly got a ticket. As I approached Bedford Hills from the north, on one of the winding two-lane roads that serve as thoroughfares in suburban New York, I saw blinks from the headlights of two oncoming cars. Sure enough, I soon passed a radar trap, set by the local constabulary to enforce the speed limit of thirty miles per hour. Maybe I was doing forty-five, but I braked in time and slipped on by.

Such a show of force seemed gratuitous. The coils of the road itself hold speeding within reasonable bounds. The presence of the patrol car, I concluded, had more to do with warning travelers they'd be under surveillance as they breached this privileged domain, where affluent residents provide scarce police business and police act mainly as security guards for a quasi-gated community. Pass at your own risk.

When I was growing up in northern Westchester County during the late 1950s and early 1960s, I had no idea who Bill Wilson was. Certainly I had no more awareness that he was living in Bedford Hills than I did that a distinguished composer, Samuel Barber, was living in Mount Kisco. Although I sometimes went on movie dates to Mount Kisco, I never had occasion to enter Bedford Hills. I knew of it vaguely as one of the poshest suburban enclaves: a horsey place, with white fences, huge houses, and a few celebrity residents. This was certainly nowhere for a kid to hang out on Saturday night.

My old preconceptions were largely confirmed that brisk and sunny October day in 1998. There *are* indeed imposing estates in Bedford Hills, grand houses set well back from the road on either side, largely hidden in the thick woods. Even the air seems to whisper of discreet exclusivity. And when I made the turn into Bill and Lois Wilson's old neighborhood, I invaded a zone of even deeper stillness and seclusion. Such places, which are less about neighborly sociability than aloof co-existence, define the suburban ideal of "private property."

At first glance, Stepping Stones seemed to fit its surroundings. It is a large compound, eight and a half acres in all, consisting of the main house and several outbuildings. Not much is visible from the road. At the mouth of the driveway, which remained unpaved while Bill was alive (Lois had other ideas and later acted on them), stands a rural mailbox stenciled "Wilson" and "Stepping Stones." There's also a historical marker, painted in the official New York State colors, yellow and blue: "Home of Bill & Lois Wilson / 'Bill W' was Cofounder of Alcoholics Anonymous—1935; / 'Lois W' Cofounder of Al-Anon Family Groups—1951."

Off to the right lies the archive, built since Lois's death in 1988. Straight ahead is the garage, added around 1950, where a vintage Volkswagen Beetle rests in a state of partial disassembly (it belongs to a former archivist). To the left and down the hill, the main house faces east, with a broad veranda overlooking a densely wooded ravine.

Stepping Stones is a barnlike Dutch colonial, painted chocolate brown, with white trim, sky-blue doors, and an hexagonal attic window. A large white stuccoed chimney rises from the draping roof. The house is surrounded by rhododendron. A rock garden contains a birdhouse, a bird feeder, and a birdbath. Up the hill to the right of the driveway, a hundred paces from the house, stands Bill W.'s study, wittily dubbed "Wit's End," a simple cinderblock cabin, with a fireplace and lots of windows, that Wilson built from scratch in 1949. He also installed a furnace in the main house, which had not been equipped for winter use.

Stepping Stones was constructed during the 1920s by Helen Griffith (no relation to the Wilsons) as a summer home for a friend. But it was never occupied by its intended occupant, and when the Wilsons were desperately looking for more permanent quarters in 1941, they were rescued by Mrs. Griffith, "whose husband had died of alcoholism and whose best friend had been retrieved by the Jersey group" (*PIO*, 260). She offered them the house and its one and a half acre lot on extremely generous terms: a mortgage of $6,500, with no interest, nothing down, and small monthly payments of forty dollars (merely double what the Wilsons were already paying for storage). At first they called the place "Bill-Lo's Break." They later acquired the adjoining seven acres, and it became "Stepping Stones."

The interior retains the integrity of its original design for simple country living. It's here, inside, that Stepping Stones departs from more typically stylish and lavish homes in Bedford Hills. For one thing the furnishings are decidedly old-fashioned: a lot of heavy, dark, Victorian pieces. The house is also unpretentious; especially in the kitchen and on the second floor, it feels like a rustic camp, the kind of place in which Lois's family used to summer on Emerald Lake.

The downstairs consists of an enormous common room with ceiling beams, a huge stone fireplace, and French doors facing onto the screened-in porch, as well as four small rooms, one in each corner. Two of these are guest bedrooms, one of which was often occupied by Nell Wing, Bill's longtime secretary. Next door is the "spook room," where the Wilsons staged séances. Opposite that, at the other end of the house, nestles the tiny eat-in kitchen. Upstairs, a small balcony overlooks the common room, the focal point of which is the same baby grand piano (recently reconditioned) that Bill bought in flush times for their oversized Brooklyn apartment. The balcony makes the clearance to the staircase so low that Bill (at six feet, two inches) must have had to duck every time he went upstairs.

The upper story has two rooms: a large open space at one end of which (over the kitchen) is Lois's study and all along the walls of which are many well-stocked bookcases, photographs, and A.A. memorabilia. In one of the dormer alcoves is Lois's antique Willcox and Gibbs sewing machine, on which she made all the drapes and curtains for the house. There's also a tiny half-bath papered entirely in shellacked maps from *National Geographic*. At the other end of this floor is the Wilsons' modest bedroom.

Nothing much has been changed at Stepping Stones since Bill's death in 1971. The pine-paneled kitchen, in particular, seems stuck in time; most of the furnishings and appliances, including an old-fashioned Chambers stove, were imported from Brooklyn in 1941. An

ancient (and currently unoperational) dishwasher is the only sign of
modern convenience. Dishes are stacked on open shelves. Amid A.A.
knickknacks there's a silver sugar bowl monogrammed "W & W." In
the middle of the kitchen, at the spiritual center of the house, lies the
famous table—gray painted legs, white porcelain top, with patches in
the finish—at which Bill and Ebby sat in November 1934.[1] There's no
gin bottle, of course, but five coffeepots, of varying size, stand ready
to serve.

Inside Bill's office, his desk remains just as he left it; a few books and
wall hangings add color to an otherwise austere ambience. Outside, at
the rear of the structure, a magnificent black birch leans perilously but
protectively over "Wit's End," its roots inextricably intertwined with a
large rock. Pretty soon, I am told, the tree will have to be cut down.

I've come to this A.A. shrine to get a better feel for Bill and Lois
Wilson as living, breathing persons, a sensory impression to supple-
ment the documentary profile I've drawn from books and also from
the archives here and in New York. I later spent a pleasantly desultory
afternoon at A.A. Headquarters, nosing around the papers, the sheer
tonnage of which could keep any researcher busy for months on end.
I was scouting the collection, getting an overview of its contents,
and dipping into it here and there, not quite at random. At Stepping Stones, however, where Bill and Lois lived together for thirty
years (Lois alone for seventeen more), it was easier to imagine their
"presence."

What I sensed in Bedford Hills and what I read in New York combined to raise my regard for Bill Wilson, whom I had always respected
as a great man who did much good in the world, but whom I had also
suspected of being too slick by half: a hustler and a self-promoter.
What I came to understand was that Wilson himself was intensely
aware of his own shortcomings and that he made heroic efforts to
surmount them through self-awareness and spiritual discipline. Although Bill W. certainly envisioned Alcoholics Anonymous as a monument to his highest human aspirations, he struggled long and hard
against any desire for his own monumentalization. The keys to the
kingdom, he stressed again and again in his later writings, were humility and sacrifice; self-abnegation opened the door to deflation at depth
and thus to "the influx of God's grace" (*PIO*, 372).

As he wrote in "Why Alcoholics Anonymous Is Anonymous," his important *Grapevine* column for January 1955:[2]

> Gradually we saw that the unity, the effectiveness—yes, even the survival—of AA would always depend upon our continued willingness to sacrifice our personal ambitions and desires for the common safety and welfare. Just as sacrifice meant survival for the individual, so did sacrifice mean unity and survival for the group and for AA's entire Fellowship.
>
> Viewed in this light, AA's Twelve Traditions are little else than a list of sacrifices which the experience of twenty years has taught us that we must make. (*LH,* 211)

Such principles, Wilson asserted, set AA "against nearly every trend in the outside world."

> We have denied ourselves personal government, professionalism, and the right to say who our members shall be. We have abandoned do-goodism, reform, and paternalism. We refuse charitable money and prefer to pay our own way. We will cooperate with practically everybody, yet we decline to marry our Society to anyone. We abstain from public controversy and will not quarrel among ourselves about those things that so rip society asunder—religion, politics, and reform. We have but one purpose: to carry the AA message to the sick alcoholic who wants it.

The bedrock of A.A., Bill W. declared, is anonymity: "the greatest single protection" that A.A. can ever have, "our greatest symbol of personal sacrifice," and "the spiritual key to all our Traditions and to our whole way of life" (*LH,* 211).

I have suggested in this book that, to a considerable degree, Bill Wilson was swallowed up in his fame as Bill W. As an anonymous celebrity, he was also a nonentity, in the sense that he was scarcely acknowledged by A.A. to exist outside of his symbolic identity. But Wilson found a way to take advantage of this paradoxical situation in which the flip side of fame was self-abnegation. He was free to be "himself," as it were, as long as he kept his A.A. persona firmly in place, protecting "himself" from public scrutiny. All the while that Bill W. was gaining ever more notoriety, Mr. Wilson was seeking ever more personal anonymity.

The issue of Wilson's control over his own life extended to his control over the representation of "Bill W." at the level of press, radio, and films. Consider his dealings with Yale University, which wished to grant him an honorary Doctor of Laws degree at its 1954 commencement. As Wilson told an A.A. correspondent in 1961, he had been highly flattered to be offered "the highest degree—the LL.D.—that a layman can receive, a degree reserved by large universities for only the world's great." He wanted that degree, he admitted. "In fact, quite humanly speaking, I felt that I had earned it."[3]

Wilson thought at first that he might indeed accept, especially since Yale was willing to respect his anonymity by awarding the LL.D. to "W. W." and by excusing him from ceremonial photographs. And he had the enthusiastic support of every member of the A.A. Board—save one. This was Archie Roosevelt, son of Theodore, who argued for his father's presidential example of always turning down such honors "because he feared their effect on himself and on the country. He did not believe that public officials should take them." This advice, Bill reported, "marked a great turning point for A.A., and for me." He immediately knew that Roosevelt had "hit the nail on the head"; there was really no choice but to refuse the degree.[4]

In an eloquent letter to Reuben Holden, Yale's secretary, Wilson explained why he finally felt "obligated to decline such a mark of distinction" (PIO, 311). Although the honor and the accompanying coverage would undoubtedly boost public approval of A.A., and although "none but the most compelling of reasons could prompt my decision to deny Alcoholics Anonymous an opportunity of this dimension," there was, in the end, no way around the implacable force of the Eleventh Tradition (PIO, 311–12).

Yes, he had survived the horrors of alcoholism, Wilson continued, but he knew "that the dread neurotic germ of the power contagion has survived in me also. It is only dormant, and it can again multiply and rend me—and A.A., too" (PIO, 312–13). Even the use of "W. W.," he had come to discern, was ultimately a subterfuge. Although this device might protect his anonymity for the present, "it would surely appear on the later historical record that I had taken an LL.D.," and his identity would then be unmasked. "So, while I might accept the degree within the letter of A.A.'s Tradition as of today, I would surely be setting the stage for a violation of its spirit tomorrow. This would be, I am certain, a perilous precedent to set" (*PIO*, 313).

In the moral exactitude of Wilson's reasoning, we get a glimpse of his affinities to the tradition of Jonathan Edwards and other Puritan divines. We can also see a sober alcoholic who has attained an exceptionally high level of "getting honest with himself," so as to leave no opening for dry-drunken self-seduction. Having renounced such great temptation in this instance, Wilson then used it to explain his subsequent, and relatively easier, refusals to participate in vehicles of potential self-promotion.

He declined, for instance, to cooperate with *Reader's Digest* on a biographical piece. When *Time* approached him about a cover story—only the back of his head would have been shown—he said no, even though he worried that he might, for refusing, have blood on his hands:

> For all I know, a piece of this sort could have brought A.A. a thousand members—possibly a lot more.
>
> Therefore, when I turned that article down, I denied recovery to an awful lot of alcoholics—some of these may already be dead. And practically all the rest of them, we may suppose, are still sick and suffering. Therefore, in a sense, my action has pronounced the death sentence on some drunks and condemned others to a much longer period of illness. (*PIO*, 314)

Wilson's reasoning here might seem to have carried him beyond scrupulosity into a kind of moral megalomania, in which he supposed himself to have power over life and death. But in a 1961 letter to one prospective biographer, he applied the same logic to a sanely utilitarian calculation of the costs of his resistance to publicity.

> About proposals such as yours there is always a certain amount of ordeal. One can see the immediate benefit, and then one tries to make an estimate what the long time result will be. When one turns down a good thing, some will die and others will suffer longer. On the other hand, if we start precedents that could alter the whole character of our society in the future, then in the long run we might not, after all, be doing the greatest good for the greatest number.[5]

One of Wilson's correspondents hounded him for years about a biographical screenplay she hoped to get produced. "I would certainly hate to see," she cozened, "your life's work ruined by a motion picture that gives as bad a portrayal of the truth of AA as did A Day at a Time or I'll Cry Tomorrow, or even Wine and Roses."[6] Then, echoing Wilson's own compunctions, she begged him to think of all the lives that could be saved instead of lost if he would only authorize her to make the movie. At least two other such scripts were in circulation during the 1960s; one author claimed already to have lined up Dana Andrews for the part of Bill. This same person did not wait four days after Bill's death before crassly importuning Lois for support of his project.

As it happened, no film biography appeared during the lifetimes of either Bill or Lois. But My Name Is Bill W. finally came to ABC television in 1989.[7] By then, as Norman K. Denzin points out, its appearance was "almost after the fact, for A.A. and its understandings of alcoholism are now established presences in American popular culture." In a criticism that recalls Marxist critiques of A.A., Denzin argues that the fusion in the film of Bill W.'s life with the story of A.A. results in nothing other than "a piece of official A.A. ideology that reproduces this organization's version of its place in American society." Like other narratives that recapitulate and propagandize "origin myths," says Denzin, My Name Is Bill W. ultimately resorts "to the biographical form that places Wilson and the organization he helped create outside history, politics, and power."[8] The life of Bill W. becomes, in this view, an agreeable fairy tale for the New-Agey Twelve-Step Recovery communities of the 1980s and 1990s.

Although one of my own purposes in this book is to resist any such ahistorical reading of Bill W.'s life, I have no illusions that Wilson would have liked my approach any better than the others. In fact, he had no patience for any attempts to appropriate Bill's story, even for a good cause. As he wrote to Mary C., the pushy screenwriter, in 1966: "Of course I hold with your view that someday biographies will be written. Were there any legal way to prevent this, I would take steps."[9]

In this same letter, Wilson says something that jolted me when I read it, because it seemed to take full measure of Bill W.'s capacity for sacrifice, to epitomize his willingness to go to any lengths to preserve the principle of anonymity. As he often did, he was using his refusal of the Yale degree as an explanation for his reluctance to endorse Mary C.'s proposed biographical film: "Despite the fact that this [the LL.D.] could have raised the status of A.A. in the public eye, and might conceivably have led to Stockholm, I declined because I did not think it wise to be made a public figure—even minus my last name and picture—because in a spiritual sense this would amount to broken anonymity."[10]

Stockholm. What was at stake, at least in Wilson's own mind, in his decision not "to be made a public figure" was nothing less than his chance for a Nobel Peace Prize! Who knows what basis he had, beyond his own ambition, to suppose he was or ever would have been considered by the Swedish Academy. Whether it was realistic or not, he nonetheless gave up the idea out of a spiritual conviction that was unnatural and antithetical to his self-aggrandizing nature. Lois, who knew Bill better than anyone else, once remarked of his character:

> Bill felt very strongly that of all things, he should not set himself up as superior in any way to other alcoholics. So to emphasize this, he took every opportunity reasonable to exaggerate his own defects. He was a tremendous egotist. But he recognized this, and I believe that the triumph of his life was his victory over himself and his becoming truly humble. (*PIO*, 313)

Bill Wilson carried that humility literally to his grave. He had been deeply impressed that Dr. Bob, as he approached his death, had denounced the idea of erecting "a suitable monument or mausoleum erected in honor of him and his wife Anne [who had died in 1949], something befitting a founder." When Bob got wind of this project, he immediately insisted that all funds already raised should be returned. "For Heaven's sake," he told Bill, "why don't you and I get buried like other folks?" (*LH*, 217). Smith, in fact, left nothing to chance. He arranged for a plain double headstone with his and Anne's names and dates.

When he visited the Akron cemetery during the summer of 1954, Bill wept with joy over the eloquent silence of Bob's anonymity:

> Did this wonderful couple carry personal anonymity too far when they so firmly refused to use the words "Alcoholics Anonymous," even on their own burial stone?
>
> For one, I don't think so. I think that this great and final example of self-effacement will prove of more permanent worth to AA than could any spectacular public notoriety or fine mausoleum.
>
> We don't have to go to Akron, Ohio, to see Dr. Bob's memorial. Dr.

Bob's real monument is visible throughout the length and breadth of
AA. Let us look again at its true inscription—one word only, which we
AAs have written. That word is sacrifice.[11] (*LH,* 217–18)

Bill kept the pact. In the family plot in East Dorset, Vermont, a flat
footstone gives his exact dates of birth and death and records his military service. A thin rectangular headstone reads simply: "William G.
Wilson / 1895–1971." There's no mention of Alcoholics Anonymous.

In 1999, *Time* finally had its way with Bill W. In an issue that appeared the week of Founders' Day, Wilson was counted—face forward and by name—among the *"Time* 100": the supposedly most influential figures of the last hundred years. Susan Cheever, daughter of
a notorious literary drunk who has recently put her own drinking and
recovery on the record, recapitulated all the standard legends of Bill
W. as "The Healer," seconding Aldous Huxley's estimate of him as "the
greatest social architect of our century." At the end of her sketch,
Cheever mentions the Yale incident as evidence of Wilson's clinging
to "the principles and the power of anonymity."[12]

It's worth remembering that Bill W. refused the Yale doctorate only
insofar as it was an *individual* honor, of the sort epitomized by this
recent spread in *Time* (in which, not incidentally, the other A.A. cofounder is barely mentioned). In declining the honorary degree in
1954, Wilson held out the possibility of its being awarded instead to
the entire fellowship. "Though it might be a novel departure," he
wrote to Reuben Holden, "I'm wondering if the Yale Corporation
could consider giving A.A. itself the entire citation, omitting the degree to me. In such an event, I will gladly appear at any time to receive
it on behalf of our Society" (*PIO,* 313). Yale evidently demurred.

Wilson's gesture might be interpreted, ungenerously, as a desperate
gambit to evade the iron law of anonymity, a way for him to gain in
some fashion the recognition and reward he coveted. But I would prefer to think that Bill W. was motivated primarily by a desire to set
another of his good examples. He was reminding himself, as A.A.s
often remind each other in their everyday meetings, that the first word
of the First Step is *We.*

Notes

Founders' Day 1998

1. "Dr. Bob's Last Talk" (Sunday, 30 July 1950), quoted in *Alcoholics Anonymous: Birthplace, Akron, Ohio* (Akron Area Intergroup, 1996).

2. The recent history of this symbol says a lot about the uncorporate culture of Alcoholics Anonymous. Having already blundered into losing U.S. copyright to the first two editions (1939, 1955) of *Alcoholics Anonymous* (the indispensable "Big Book"), New York Headquarters was not about to give up its cherished symbol without a fight. Virtually (but not actually) a trademark, the encircled triangle was being brazenly infringed by non-A.A. enterprises. Money was not the issue, as A.A. Traditions proscribe the profit motive; principle was at stake. But after going to court to stop the rip-offs, Headquarters amazingly elected to release the logo outright, lest A.A. become embroiled in litigation and lose its spiritual way over matters of property and prestige. Officially, then, the triangle within the circle is no longer an A.A. symbol.

3. Nan Robertson, *Getting Better: Inside Alcoholics Anonymous* (New York: Morrow, 1988), p. 30.

4. Ibid., p. 78.

5. *As Bill Sees It: The A.A. Way of Life (Selected Writings of A.A.'s Co-Founder)* (New York: Alcoholics Anonymous World Services, 1967), pp. iii–iv. This book was originally titled *The A.A. Way of Life*.

6. Robertson, *Getting Better*, p. 85. My approach is analogous to that taken toward Jesus by Marcello Craveri: "The aim that I have set myself is that of

never losing sight of Jesus as an individual born into a clearly defined society at a clearly defined point in history, and hence of striving to understand his life, his ideas, his behavior as the product of a particular culture and unique historical circumstances." *The Life of Jesus,* trans. Charles Lam Markmann (New York: Grove, 1967), p. v.

Chapter 1: Bill's Elusive Childhood

1. Although I asked A.A. Headquarters in advance for permission to hear the tape and read the transcript during my research trip, neither of these important items could be produced the day I was in New York. It was not entirely clear why not. The tape, which I gathered was brittle, required a reel-to-reel player, and none was in working order. The transcript was not locatable. This might mean it was temporarily misplaced; it could also mean it has been lost. According to Ernest Kurtz, who used both the tape and the transcript, Robert Thomsen often quotes verbatim from both in *Bill W.*

2. Paul Murray Kendall, *The Art of Biography* (New York: Norton, 1965), p. 21.

3. Although Thomsen consistently uses "Billy" as Wilson's childhood nickname, Wilson's own extant letters from the period are signed "Willie." Perhaps he answered to both names; perhaps the adults in his life had different preferences. Here, in the context of my analysis of *Bill W.,* I follow Thomsen's usage.

4. Ernest Hemingway, *The Nick Adams Stories,* ed. Philip Young (New York: Scribner, 1972), p. 14. The deleted opening of "Indian Camp" was first published here under a separate title, "Three Shots."

5. Ibid., p. 21.

6. In his stress on the elder Wilson's jug, Thomsen seems to go beyond the testimony of Bill W. himself: that although his father was "at times a pretty heavy drinker," he "never became an alcoholic" (*PIO,* 24).

7. Thomsen insinuates that the father's misbehavior finally became intolerable because of some unprecedented affront. Bill W. never knew the lurid details, only the disastrous results.

8. This scene seems to have been inspired by Wilson's retrospective statement: "My mother was a disciplinarian, and I can remember the agony of hostility and fear that I went through when she administered her first good tanning with the back of a hairbrush. Somehow, I never could forget that beating. It made an indelible impression on me" (*PIO,* 25). But Thomsen takes Wilson literally when he was clearly speaking figuratively. If Bill "could never forget" the incident, so Thomsen suggests, then he "must" have re-

membered it on the occasion when his mother revealed that his father had absconded. There is no clear indication, however, whether the memorable thrashing came before or after the parental separation. It is dubious whether Wilson really thought about this event at the moment Thomsen says he did. Wilson's sketchy recollections, moreover, provide none of the suggestive details of Thomsen's rendering, such as the boy's bare bottom draped across his mother's lap.

9. There's no mention in *'Pass It On,'* for instance, of the incident on which Thomsen builds his entire book: the fateful night of Billy's supposed surreptitious outing with his father. This scene may have been Thomsen's extrapolation from a single detail in Bill W.'s taped recollections (as quoted in *'Pass It On'*): that on Sundays his father would rent "a covered buggy with a flat top with tassels all around," and they would go about "in some style and with a great deal of satisfaction" (*PIO*, 14).

10. Although most sources are documented in *'Pass It On,'* this particular quotation is not. We may assume it comes from a letter probably written long after the fact.

11. *The Individual Psychology of Alfred Adler: A Systematic Presentation in Selections from His Writings,* ed. Heinz L. Ansbacher and Rowena R. Ansbacher (New York: Harper and Row, 1964), pp. 257–58, 260. Although "inferiority complex" became widely associated with Adler, especially in America, Adler did not coin the term, which he disliked as too psychoanalytic. Later in her life, Wilson's mother, during a season in Vienna, "studied psychology under Dr. Alfred Adler, the former associate of Freud"; she later, in San Diego, led an Adlerian group for "young people interested in learning more about their own behavior" (*LR*, 106).

12. Thomsen spells Bertha's surname "Banford," an apparent error that has been silently corrected in *'Pass It On.'*

Chapter 2: Bill's First Drink

1. In *'Pass It On'* it is asserted, probably on better authority, that Whalon was nine years older than Bill.

2. "During that first semester, Bill received 94 in chemistry, 86 in French, 75 in drawing, 68 in English, 61 in trigonometry, and 53 in algebra." Aiming, as usual, to please, he had "an outstanding rating of 98 in military duty and 100 in deportment." His overall average of 86 placed him fifth in the class (*PIO*, 44).

3. See the authoritative and influential paper by Freud's faithful disciple, Karl Abraham: "The Psychological Relations between Sexuality and Alcohol-

ism," *International Journal of Psycho-Analysis* 7 (January 1926); repr., *The Dynamics and Treatment of Alcoholism: Essential Papers,* ed. Jerome D. Levin and Ronna H. Weiss (Northvale, N.J.: Jason Aronson, 1994).

4. "Edison on College Men," *New York Times,* 6 May 1921, 4:3.

5. "Grade XYZ," *New York Times,* 8 May 1921, 2:2.

6. "Edison's Questions Still Puzzle City / College Men Pore Over Tomes and Maps—Traffic Menaces Lives of Answer Seekers," *New York Times,* 12 May 1921, 21:1; "Can't Answer Edison / Chicago University Students 'Flunked' by His Questions," *New York Times,* 11 May 1921, 6:2; "Holyoke Youth, Crazed by Test, Asks Police Protection," *New York Times,* 17 May 1921, 19:7.

7. "Edison Dashes Off New Questionnaire / Compiles It Without Assistance in a Few Minutes, According to His Representative," *New York Times,* 14 May 1921, 9:2.

8. Ibid., 9:1.

9. "Edison Questions Stir Up A Storm," *New York Times,* 11 May 1921, 6:1.

10. *Study and Stimulants; Or, The Use of Intoxicants and Narcotics in Relation to Intellectual Life,* ed. A. Arthur Reade, rev. ed. (Manchester: Abel Heywood and Son; London: Simpkin, Marshall, 1883), pp. 54–55.

Chapter 3: Bill's Roaring Twenties

1. Mark Schorer, "The Burdens of Biography" (1962); repr., *Biography as High Adventure: Life-Writers Speak on Their Art,* ed. Stephen B. Oates (Amherst: University of Massachusetts Press, 1986), p. 87.

2. John J. Rumbarger, "The 'Story' of Bill W: Ideology, Culture, and the Discovery of the Modern American Alcoholic," *Contemporary Drug Problems* (Winter 1993): 763, 764, and 769. Rumbarger's questions are derived from E. M. Jellinek's highly influential 1946 study, based on interviews with early A.A. members: "Phases in the Drinking History of Alcoholics: Analysis of a Survey Conducted by the Official Organ of Alcoholics Anonymous." Jellinek became synonymous with the idea of "alcoholism" as a "disease" that was advanced by the so-called Alcoholism Movement during the 1930s. Ironically, Jellinek himself seems to have become skeptical of his own beliefs by the time he produced his ostensibly definitive statement of them in *The Disease Concept of Alcoholism* (New Haven: College and University Press; New Brunswick, N.J.: Hillhouse, 1960).

3. Rumbarger, "The 'Story' of Bill W," p. 761.

4. An associative linkage between Bill Clinton and Bill Wilson was created by the political appropriation of "Friends of Bill": the euphemism, often em-

blazoned on bumper stickers, by which A.A. members identify themselves as such, without (strictly speaking) breaking the anonymity required by the Traditions. On Wilson's extramarital affairs, see Chapter 7.

5. Robin Room, "A 'Reverence for Strong Drink': The Lost Generation and the Elevation of Alcohol in American Culture," *Journal of Studies on Alcohol* 45 (September 1984): 542–43.

6. See *PIO,* 97. Lois Wilson reports that Bill would furiously write letters of protest to President Roosevelt and then tear them up. She saved the scraps and taped them back together.

7. Edmund B. O'Reilly, *Sobering Tales: Narratives of Alcoholism and Recovery* (Amherst: University of Massachusetts Press, 1997), p. 108.

8. Craig Reinarman, "The 12-Step Movement and Advanced Capitalist Culture: Notes on the Politics of Self-Control in Postmodernity," forthcoming in *Contemporary Social Movements and Cultural Politics,* ed. B. Epstein, R. Flacks, and M. Darnofsky (New York: Oxford University Press).

9. John Kenneth Galbraith, *The Great Crash, 1929* (Boston: Houghton Mifflin, 1961), p. x.

10. The exact movements of the Wilsons in this period are quite uncertain. Paul Lang, former archivist at Stepping Stones, "counts fifty-four different addresses for the couple in the early nineteen-thirties." Cited in Andrew Delbanco and Thomas Delbanco, "A.A. at the Crossroads," *New Yorker* (20 March 1995): 51.

11. This is one of the details contested by Rumbarger, who finds it improbable that Wilson would have been dismissed, as he claimed, "as the result of a brawl with a taxi driver" (*AA,* p. 4). "A more likely explanation," Rumbarger supposes, "can be found in the circumstances of the Depression. With very little demand for speculative stocks, Standard and Poor simply reduced its overhead and discharged the now redundant Bill W—a circumstance more than likely to have produced a fight or some such altercation from someone of Bill W's temperament" ("The 'Story' of Bill W," p. 767). This alternative "explanation," however, is a tissue of unfounded speculation, lacking even the possibly questionable authority of Wilson's own recollections.

12. Delbanco and Delbanco, "A.A. at the Crossroads," p. 52.

13. Galbraith, *The Great Crash,* pp. 27, 174.

14. O'Reilly has analyzed the rhetorical patterns of "Bill's Story," showing that the narrative depends on "a terminology of reciprocal motion": "The rise and fall of stocks and money values becomes a leitmotif, replicated in the fluctuations of commercial enterprises, in business successes and failures. As the story progresses, the alternation between sobriety and drunkenness

reflects these first oppositions, but then absorbs their force and takes on a life of its own." Institutional and personal history then coalesce "in the single image of the Crash" (*Sobering Tales*, p. 109).

15. In a letter of 11 September 1906, James complained of the "moral flabbiness born of the exclusive worship of the bitch-goddess, *success*. That— with the squalid cash interpretation put on the word success—is our national disease." *The Letters of William James*, ed. Henry James (Boston: Atlantic Monthly Press, 1920), 2:260.

16. Rumbarger, "The 'Story' of Bill W.," pp. 774, 775, and 777.

17. "The 12-Step Movement and Advanced Capitalist Culture." Reinarman observes that "the 12-step movement is comprised [*sic*] of people who often have in the past and might again participate in movements for social change, yet who are now enmeshed in a self-help movement that ideologically ignores social change in favor of individual change."

18. Ibid. On the radical shift from a drunken to a sober outlook, see Gregory Bateson's brilliant analysis—the best thinking I have ever encountered on this subject—of the psychodynamics of alcoholism and recovery: "The Cybernetics of 'Self': A Theory of Alcoholism," *Psychiatry* 24 (1971): 1–18; collected in Bateson, *Steps To an Ecology of Mind* (1972); repr., *The Dynamics and Treatment of Alcoholism: Essential Papers*, ed. Jerome D. Levin and Ronna H. Weiss (Northvale, N.J.: Jason Aronson, 1994). The importance of Bateson's theory is discussed in O'Reilly, *Sobering Tales*, pp. 19–29.

19. Delbanco and Delbanco, "A.A. at the Crossroads," pp. 52, 59, 63, and 62. Niebuhr is commonly, but erroneously, credited with writing the "Serenity Prayer," which has been widely adopted in A.A.: "God grant me serenity to accept the things I cannot change, courage to change the things I can, and wisdom to know the difference." Niebuhr's 1943 version seems to put more stress on the possibility of change, especially of things beyond the self: "God, grant us grace to accept with serenity the things that cannot be changed, courage to change the things which should be changed, and the wisdom to distinguish the one from the other." The origin of this prayer antedates Niebuhr, who himself attributed it to the German philosopher Friedrich Christoph Oetinger (1702–82). Both the German and English versions are quoted in philosopher Sidney Hook's autobiography, *Out of Step: An Unquiet Life in the 20th Century* (New York: Harper and Row, 1987). According to '*Pass It On,*' the prayer may go back to Boethius in 500 A. D. (*PIO*, 258 n. 6).

20. John Steadman Rice, *A Disease of One's Own: Psychotherapy, Addiction, and the Emergence of Co-Dependency* (New Brunswick, N.J.: Transaction, 1996), p. 29.

21. Ibid., pp. 134 and 106–7.

Chapter 4: Bill and the Oxford Group

1. After Whitman sent Emerson a copy of *Leaves of Grass* in July 1855, Emerson famously praised it as "the most extraordinary piece of wit and wisdom that America has yet contributed." He went on to greet Whitman "at the beginning of a great career, which yet must have had a long foreground somewhere, for such a start. I rubbed my eyes a little to see if this sunbeam were no illusion; but the solid sense of the book is a sober certainty." Quoted in Gay Wilson Allen, *The Solitary Singer: A Critical Biography of Walt Whitman* (New York: Macmillan, 1955), p. 152. Some such words might be used to describe the initial response of some A.A. members to the Big Book.

2. William L. White, *Slaying the Dragon: The History of Addiction Treatment and Recovery in America* (Bloomington, Ill.: Chestnut Health Systems, 1998), p. 127. White goes on to say, however, that "A.A. has a distinctive place in this history" because of its institutional durability, its manifest success, and its worldwide influence.

3. As Milton A. Maxwell points out, the "often repeated" figure of six hundred thousand derives from the 1843 annual report of the American Temperance Union, which states: "A half million hard drinkers often drunken, and a hundred thousand sots . . . may safely be considered as having been brought to sign the total abstinence pledge within the last two years." "The Washingtonian Movement," *Quarterly Journal of Studies on Alcohol* 11 (September 1950): 427. Such figures were likely inflated, but even if allowance is made for exaggeration, Washingtonianism still must be counted among the most remarkable social phenomena of the American nineteenth century.

4. An anthology of highlights from this neglected genre has recently appeared: *Drunkard's Progress: Narratives of Addiction, Despair, and Recovery,* ed. John W. Crowley (Baltimore: The Johns Hopkins University Press, 1999). See also Leonard U. Blumberg (with William L. Pittman), *Beware the First Drink! The Washington Temperance Movement and Alcoholics Anonymous* (Seattle: Glen Abbey Books, 1991).

5. [John Zug], *The Foundation, Progress and Principles of the Washington Temperance Society of Baltimore* (Baltimore: John D. Toy, 1842), pp. 42–43.

6. Wilson, who had a proprietary interest in stressing the errors of the Washington Society as well as its differences from Alcoholics Anonymous, moralized that the movement had been destroyed by individual ambition, institutional arrogance, and political wrangling over issues (abolition, prohibition) irrelevant to the primary purpose of keeping drunks sober. "The original strong and simple group purpose was thus dissipated in fruitless controversy and divergent aims" (*LH,* 5).

7. *Beware the First Drink!* p. 220. The authors nonetheless conclude that because Washingtonian principles were "rediscovered and reapplied in a new sociopolitical context" by Wilson and his A.A. associates, it follows that "only in an attenuated fashion do the two social movements have historical ties" (p. 220).

8. Paul Antze, "Symbolic Action in Alcoholics Anonymous," in *Constructive Drinking: Perspectives on Drink from Anthropology,* ed. Mary Douglas (Cambridge: Cambridge University Press, 1987), pp. 173–74.

9. Daniel B. Shea Jr., *Spiritual Autobiography in Early America* (Princeton: Princeton University Press, 1968), p. xi.

10. Edmund B. O'Reilly, *Sobering Tales: Narratives of Alcoholism and Recovery* (Amherst: University of Massachusetts Press, 1997), p. 105.

11. See Bill Pittman, *AA: The Way It Began* (Seattle, Wash.: Glen Abbey Books, 1988), pp. 192–97. The only other book common to Nell Wing's and Dr. Bob's lists was William James's *The Varieties of Religious Experience* (1902). Another model for "Bill's Story" may have been William Seabrook's *Asylum* (1935), a best-selling account of his treatment for alcoholism in a mental ward. The book, based on Seabrook's experiences early in 1934, appeared soon after Bill W.'s first meeting with Dr. Bob. An analogous account is F. Scott Fitzgerald's essay, "The Crack-Up," published in *Esquire* in three installments during early 1936, and collected in *The Crack-Up,* ed. Edmund Wilson (New York: New Directions, 1945).

12. Mel B., *New Wine: The Spiritual Roots of the Twelve Step Miracle* (Center City, Minn.: Hazelden. 1991), p. 27.

13. Pittman, *AA: The Way It Began,* p. 123.

14. See Walter Houston Clark, *The Oxford Group: Its History and Significance* (New York: Bookman Associates, 1951), p. 27.

15. Ibid., p. 55.

16. L. W. Grensted, *What Is the Oxford Group?* (New York: Oxford University Press, 1933), p. 3.

17. Clark, *The Oxford Group,* pp. 28 and 108. Mel B. traces these tenets also to a 1934 article in the *Atlantic Monthly* by the theologian Henry P. Van Dusen. "These six points," Mel B. remarks, "although not mentioning alcohol, were surprisingly similar to the word-of-mouth program that was developed by Bill Wilson and his friends in the years immediately preceding publication of the book *Alcoholics Anonymous* with its Twelve Step program." *New Wine,* p. 41. See also Wilson's version of the same six "steps" in *AACA,* 160.

18. Sources differ on exactly when and how often Wilson was admitted to Towns Hospital. I am taking Ernest Kurtz's view to be authoritative (*NG,* 254 n. 26).

19. White points out that a recent review of Rowland's papers "reveals no

evidence that Rowland was treated by Jung and suggests that, if such treatment did occur between 1930–1934, it was for a much shorter period (a few weeks)" than the year or more stated in A.A. accounts. *Slaying the Dragon,* p. 128 n. 2. That Rowland really *was* treated by Jung seems not to be in doubt, as Jung himself later confirmed it in his correspondence with Bill Wilson.

20. It has recently been suggested that Bill W. misremembered the date of Dr. Bob's last drink. Ernest Kurtz remarks: "Thanks to the research and evidence turned up by a New Jersey attorney [about the date of the medical conference that Dr. Bob attended during his final bender], it seems probable that June 17th is the correct date, and the same evidence suggests how naturally such a memory error might have occurred." "Spirituality and Recovery: The Historical Journey," in *The Collected Ernie Kurtz* (Wheeling, W.Va.: Bishop of Books, 1999), p. 112.

21. *Letters of William James,* ed. Henry James (Boston: Atlantic Monthly Press, 1920), 1:147.

22. William James, *Pragmatism: A New Name for Some Old Ways of Thinking* (1909); repr., *Pragmatism and Other Essays,* ed. Joseph L. Blau (New York: Washington Square, 1963), p. 89. See also James's 1896 essay, "The Will to Believe," where he defended "our right to adopt a believing attitude in religious matters, in spite of the fact that our merely logical intellect may not have been coerced." *William James: Writings, 1878–1899,* ed. Gerald E. Myers (New York: Library of America, 1992), p. 457. On the Jamesian connection to A.A., see "The Spirituality of William James: A Lesson From Alcoholics Anonymous," in *The Collected Ernie Kurtz,* pp. 63–76.

23. Howard M. Feinstein, *Becoming William James* (Ithaca: Cornell University Press, 1984), pp. 307–8 n. The traditional story of James's 1870 "crisis" of faith, attributable mainly to Ralph Barton Perry, a devoted Jamesian disciple, suggests that James attained the "philosophic cure" of his despair through his saving, pragmatic insight about free will. Feinstein argues, however, that although "Perry's version provides a pleasing literary structure for the biography of an important philosopher," it falsifies the sources, which show that the "'crisis' was not unique, nor did it mark a change in William's beliefs, and it had no dramatic impact on his health."

24. Despite Bill's apparent dislike for Cornell, the Wilsons continued to socialize with him, and Shep regularly attended the Tuesday open house for alcoholics at 182 Clinton Street. There was also a cordial exchange of letters in 1946, in which Wilson and Cornell brought each other up to date about themselves and mutual friends. Hearing from Shep, as Bill told him, "stirred up happy recollections of that time more than 10 years ago when you and Ebbie paid me the visit that changed my whole life—in fact saved it." Letter of 22 March 1946.

25. V. C. Kitchen, *I Was A Pagan* (New York: Harper, 1934), p. 39. That Wilson might have conflated the writings of William James with those of the Oxford Group is not surprising, given the latter's highly pragmatic approach to religion. Kitchen himself approvingly quotes from James; see p. 69.

26. *The Complete Works of Ralph Waldo Emerson*, 12 vols., Centenary Edition (Boston: Houghton Mifflin, 1903), 1:10.

27. Andrew Delbanco and Thomas Delbanco, "A.A. at the Crossroads," *New Yorker* (20 March 1995): 62. There is no evidence, however, that Wilson himself ever read Edwards or was directly exposed to his theology.

28. Or, perhaps, a creed as "vague and visceral" as that of "American civil religion," which Leroy S. Rouner has defined as "not what we believe in our heart of hearts about the destiny of our immortal souls," but rather "the beliefs we share with our fellow citizens about our national purpose and about the destiny of our national enterprise. Vague and visceral it may be, but there is an American creed, and to be an American is to believe the creed. America is, in this sense, a religious venture." The capacity for such belief lies in our ability to be converted to any particular creed and, by embracing it, to become a full member of that credal community. "Civil Religion, Cultural Diversity, and American Civilization," *Key Reporter* 64 (Spring 1999): 3. By analogy, A.A.'s singleness of purpose may be said to provide the basis for a nondoctrinal "civil religion" of sobriety.

Chapter 5: Bill's Hot Flash

1. Bill Wilson to Robert J. Roth, S. J., 12 November 1965. This letter, but without the crucial first sentence, is published in *NG*, 257 n. 53. Kurtz identifies Roth as a professor of philosophy at Fordham University; his article appeared in the Jesuit magazine, *America* 113 (1965): 48–50.

2. In Wilson's 1954 talk in Syracuse, New York, which provided the draft of his story for *Alcoholics Anonymous Comes of Age*, he states that "somebody, (I don't know now who it was), brought that book to me in the hospital." Robert Thomsen asserts that Wilson "could never recollect if it had been Ebby or Rowland who gave him a copy" (*BW*, 230). The official A.A. biography, however, unequivocally identifies Ebby as the bearer of *Varieties*: "Ebby, who came to see him on the third day, was not quite prepared for Bill's description of what had happened—he himself had neither seen bright lights nor stood on a mountaintop. But he brought Bill a book that offered further clarification. . . . Ebby had not read the book, but it had been recommended by Oxford Group members" (*PIO*, 124). The authority for these assertions is not cited, but it may have been the oral history tape Ebby made for the A.A. archives.

3. John Gough's 1845 *Autobiography* is generously excerpted in *Drunkard's Progress: Narratives of Addiction, Despair, and Recovery,* ed. John W. Crowley (Baltimore: Johns Hopkins University Press, 1999).

4. V. C. Kitchen, *I Was A Pagan* (New York: Harper, 1934), p. 43. In his study of masculine adult development, Daniel J. Levinson refers (without exact citation) to Carl Jung's version of this idea: "Jung speaks of 'ego inflation,' when a man experiences his internal hero figure as all-powerful. The inflation is followed, says Jung, by a period of 'deflation' in which the hero is badly wounded. Painful as it is, deflation is a necessary step in overcoming the internal dominance of the hero and forming a more integrated self during the Mid-Life Transition." Levinson et al., *The Seasons of a Man's Life* (New York: Knopf, 1978), pp. 247–48.

5. Bill Pittman, *AA: The Way It Began* (Seattle, Wash.: Glen Abbey Books, 1988), p. 170. According to Kurtz, *Varieties* "heads the list of six titles of 'Spiritual Reading Bill and early A.A.'s found helpful'" (*NG,* 256 n. 52). This may be a version of the same list, arranged in alphabetical order, that appears as an appendix to Pittman's book.

6. Clapp, who wrote two later books on alcoholism, said he met Bill Wilson in October 1935. See *Drunks Are Square Pegs* (New York: Island, 1942); cited in Charles Bishop Jr. and Bill Pittman, *To Be Continued: The Alcoholics Anonymous World Bibliography, 1935–1994* (Wheeling, W.Va.: Bishop of Books, 1994), item 1089. In his letter of 22 March 1946 to Shep Cornell, Wilson mentions that Clapp "began to flounder heavily" after his discharge from the army but has sobered up since.

7. Charles Clapp Jr., *The Big Bender* (New York: Harper, 1938), pp. 120–24 and 127–28.

8. Kevin McCarron, "*Spiritus contra spiritum:* The Recovery Narrative and 'Spirituality,'" *Dionysos: Journal of Literature and Addiction* 9 (Winter 1999): 35, 34, and 40.

9. On the Keeley Cure, see William L. White, *Slaying the Dragon: The History of Addiction Treatment and Recovery in America* (Bloomington, Ill.: Chestnut Health Systems, 1998), pp. 50–63.

10. Pittman, *AA: The Way It Began,* pp. 164 and 166. Known as the Towns-Lambert Cure, the belladonna method was first developed in 1906 as a treatment for addiction to opium and other narcotics; a 90 percent cure rate was claimed. Lambert, personal physician to President Theodore Roosevelt, dissociated himself from Towns when "he began to notice that people kept coming back for the cure, cure after cure, for years on end," and when Towns, whose background was in insurance rather than medicine, began "billing his cure as guaranteed to work for *any compulsive behavior,* from morphinism to nicotinism to caffeinism, to kleptomania and bedwetting." See Dean Latimer

and Jeff Goldberg, *Flowers in the Blood: The Story of Opium* (New York: Franklin Watts, 1981), p. 249.

11. White, *Slaying the Dragon*, p. 86.

12. Pittman, *AA: The Way It Began*, p. 169.

13. James derived the idea of the "subliminal self" from Frederic W. H. Myers, a researcher into spiritualism and a prominent member, with James, of the Society for Psychical Research. See also James's enthusiastic report on Pierre Janet's theory of hysteria, in "The Hidden Self," *Scribner's Magazine* 7 (1890): 361–73.

14. William Seabrook, *Asylum* (New York: Harcourt, Brace, 1935), p. 142.

15. Ibid., pp. 147–48. Unfortunately for Seabrook, he became convinced that if, as his psychiatrists were telling him, a drinking problem was "always a symptom of some other underlying psychic disorder," then in principle a real cure might remove the underlying cause and thus enable an alcoholic to drink again. "I said that I still hoped to be really 'cured,' cured so well that I would be able not only to take a highball with my friends, but even on appropriate occasions to take several and cut up high jinks" (p. 260). At the end of *Asylum,* Seabrook reports that he has, in fact, taken up drinking on rare occasions: "I seem to be cured of drunkenness, which is as may be" (p. 263). It didn't last, however. He was soon drowning in the bottle again, and he eventually took an overdose of sleeping pills after years in and out of mental hospitals. On Seabrook's colorful life, see his autobiography, *No Hiding Place* (Philadelphia: Lippincott, 1942) and also the memoirs of his ex-wife: Marjorie Worthington, *The Strange World of Willie Seabrook* (New York: Harcourt, Brace, 1966). Bill Wilson, who very likely read *Asylum,* once mentioned Seabrook in the context of recalling Ebby T., during a 1959 address in Akron commemorating his twenty-fourth sobriety anniversary.

16. Mel B. *New Wine: The Spiritual Roots of the Twelve Step Miracle* (Center City, Minn.: Hazelden, 1991), p. 78.

17. By coincidence, the man in charge at the Twenty-third Street Mission was Henry Harrison Hadley, son of S. H. Hadley, the story of whose salvation Bill had just encountered in *The Varieties of Religious Experience*. On the reform careers of S. H. Hadley and his brother Henry H. Hadley, see the latter's memoir, *The Blue Badge of Courage* (Akron, Ohio: Saalfield, 1902). On the Calvary Mission, see Mel B., *New Wine,* pp. 52–55.

18. Lois reports that she did *not* join such a team. In an interview with Ernest Kurtz, she confessed, "Well, I didn't have much use for the Oxford Group: I didn't think I needed 'conversion'" (*NG,* 258 n. 58).

19. It is not clear whom Thomsen is quoting here, but presumably it is Wilson paraphrasing Silkworth. Wilson's retrospective account implies that

the term "hot flash" originated with Silkworth in 1935. If so, it was also adopted by Bill himself. The earliest use I have found in Wilson's writings dates from a 1944 lecture at Yale, where he joked about his conversion experience: "Down in New York, where they know me pretty well in the A.A. [sic], they facetiously call these sudden experiences that we sometimes have a 'W. W. hot flash.' I really thought that I had been endowed with the power to go out and produce a 'hot flash' just like mine in every drunk." "The Fellowship of Alcoholics Anonymous," in *Alcohol, Science and Society: Twenty-Nine Lectures with Discussions as Given at the Yale Summer School of Alcohol Studies* (New Haven: Quarterly Journal of Studies on Alcohol, 1945), p. 465.

20. The A.A. archives have called this untitled and unpaginated document "Talk by Bill at Le Moyne College, Syracuse, N.Y." It is a transcript of Wilson's extemporaneous remarks on 11 March 1954, when he participated in a lecture series on alcoholism, organized by Raymond J. H. Kennedy, S. J., a professor at Le Moyne College in Syracuse. The lecture itself took place not at the college but rather in Grant Junior High School, which could better accommodate the crowd.

21. Lori E. Rotskoff, "Sober Husbands and Supportive Wives: Gendered Cultures of Drink and Sobriety in Twentieth-Century America," Ph.D. diss. (Yale University, 1999), chap. 4. I am grateful to Rotskoff for providing me with a copy of her excellent study.

22. June Arnold, *Sister Gin* (1975), ed. Jane Marcus (New York: Feminist Press, 1989), p. 28.

23. Ibid., pp. 11–12.

Chapter 6: Bill W. Meets Dr. Bob

1. Walton Hall Smith and Ferdinand C. Helwig, M. D., *Liquor, The Servant of Man* (Boston: Little, Brown, 1939), p. 174. This epigram is attributed to "America's greatest rhetorician" [H. L. Mencken?].

2. Mel B., *New Wine: The Spiritual Roots of the Twelve Step Miracle* (Center City, Minn.: Hazelden, 1991), pp. 62–63.

3. Ibid., pp. 65–66.

4. Quoted in *New Wine*, p. 71.

5. Carl G. Jung, "On Synchronicity," in *The Portable Jung*, ed. Joseph Campbell (New York: Viking, 1971), p. 505. Jung's exhaustive exploration of unconscious processes had led him, he wrote elsewhere, "to look around for another principle of explanation, since the causality principle seemed to me insufficient to explain certain remarkable manifestations of the unconscious. I found that there are psychic parallelisms which simply cannot be related to

each other causally, but must be connected by another kind of principle altogether." *The Spirit in Man, Art, and Literature,* trans. R. F. C. Hull (Princeton: Princeton University Press, 1966), p. 56.

6. Smith quoted in the taped recollections of Henrietta Seiberling; for a transcript, see *New Wine,* pp. 69–71.

7. *New Wine,* p. 176 n. 9. *Silent* has been silently emended to *secret* in A.A.'s official biography; see *DB,* 58.

8. Nan Robertson, *Getting Better: Inside Alcoholics Anonymous* (New York: Morrow, 1988), p. 66.

9. Without speaking directly to such representations, Wilson was careful to acknowledge his indebtedness to Mrs. Seiberling. See, for instance, his fulsome tribute in *Alcoholics Anonymous Comes of Age:* "Right here I want to set on record the timeless gratitude that A.A.'s will always have for Henrietta Seiberling, she who first brought Dr. Bob and me together. . . . What Alcoholics Anonymous owes to her will always be beyond anybody's reckoning. And Dr. Bob's debt and mine are the greatest of all" (*AACA,* 73).

10. On the break with the Oxford Group, see also *NG,* 43–45; *DB,* 156–70 and 212–19; *PIO,* 171–74.

11. Kurtz adds that Wilson's concern was not entirely misplaced. He explained in 1953 why he had omitted all reference in the Big Book to the Oxford Group's "four absolutes" (which continued to be part of A.A. tradition in some Midwestern chapters): "Just at that juncture, the Pope had decreed that no Catholics could come to Oxford Group meetings. Therefore, if we used any of their words or phrases, the same sentence might fall on us" (*NG,* 52). In fact, the Pope took no such action, although it was hinted that he might.

12. Buchman quoted in Charles Bufe, *Alcoholics Anonymous: Cult or Cure?* (San Francisco: See Sharp, 1991), p. 23. Buchman also visited with Heinrich Himmler during a trip to Germany that same year, and he allegedly introduced the Gestapo commander to a British M. P. at the 1936 Berlin Olympics as "a great lad" (p. 25). As Bufe points out, *'Pass It On'* misrepresents Buchman's remarks by silently deleting words and running different sentences together, without benefit of ellipses: "Buchman's statements are carefully edited to put his best possible face forward" (p. 24). Despite its tabloid title, Bufe's book offers an interesting critique of A.A. from the perspective of Rational Recovery.

13. Walter Houston Clark, *The Oxford Group: Its History and Significance* (New York: Bookman Associates, 1951), p. 78.

Chapter 7: Writing the Big Book

1. Nan Robertson, *Getting Better: Inside Alcoholics Anonymous* (New York: Morrow, 1988), p. 83. Other details in this paragraph are taken from the same source.

2. Nell Wing, *Grateful to Have Been There: My 42 Years with Bill and Lois, and the Evolution of Alcoholics Anonymous* (Park Ridge, Ill.: Parkside, 1992), pp. 60–61. Wing adds that whenever Lois tried to break Bill's monopoly on conversation, "he would shoot a slight frown in her direction" in order to shut her off. When he tried the same tactic on Wing, however, "I pretended I didn't notice and, typically, barged right in with my own comments."

3. Sources differ about when the writing began: March or April 1938 (*AACA*, 153 and *PIO*, 193) or May (*DB*, 151). One early member erroneously placed the start in June (*NG*, 274 n. 25).

4. Quoted in Bill Pittman, *AA: The Way It Began* (Seattle, Wash.: Glen Abbey, 1988), p. 179.

5. In 1940, the Alcoholic Foundation, at Wilson's urging, bought up all the stock for Works Publishing Company and arranged for royalties on *Alcoholics Anonymous* to be paid thereafter to both the cofounders.

6. *Sherwood Anderson's Memoirs,* ed. Paul Rosenfeld (New York: Harcourt, Brace, 1942), p. 194. "Much A.A. myth surrounds the composition of the Twelve Steps," declares Ernest Kurtz, who nonetheless judges Wilson's own account in *AACA* to be "scrupulously accurate" (*NG*, 275 n. 31).

7. Sixteen Akron stories and twelve from New York: this is the breakdown reported in *PIO*, which I am taking as authoritative. There is an unexplained discrepancy between these figures and those given in *AACA* and *NG*, both of which state it was eighteen Akron stories and ten from New York. In his 1954 speech in Syracuse, New York, Wilson noted parenthetically: "Fourteen of those people have not had a drink to this day and six more of them are perfectly all right having had only a sip [sic] or two,—even out of those original tough cases."

According to Bill Pittman, the original last chapter to *Alcoholics Anonymous* was "The Lone Endeavor," the story of a man who had gotten sober alone, with the help only of a multilith copy of the Big Book. That story was dropped from the second printing of the first edition because A.A. lost track of the author and could no longer vouch for his sobriety. This story itself was written by Ruth Hock (*AA: The Way It Began,* p. 181).

8. "The first documented use of the name in the A.A. archives is in a letter from Bill to Willard Richardson [one of the nonalcoholic trustees] dated July 15, 1938. . . . Bill, at that time, was using 'Alcoholics Anonymous' both as the working title of the book and as the name of the Fellowship" (*PIO*, 202).

9. See also *PIO,* p. 200.

10. According to Bill Pittman, Uzzel [sic] was "an accomplished magazine editor and teacher of short story writing at New York University." He is said, on Ruth Hock's authority, to have cut 800 pages in order to reduce *Alcoholics Anonymous* to its published length of 400 pages (*AA: The Way It Began,* p. 181). I have been unable to determine at which college Uzzell (also listed as "Utzell" in the index to '*Pass It On*') really taught. As for the claim that he cut 800 pages to arrive at 400, it ignores the difference between typed and printed pages. A reasonable conversion ratio is two typed pages for every printed page; 800 becomes 400, and thus the book was evidently cut by half, not by two-thirds, as Hock implied.

11. The following quotations are taken from an exact transcription of the multilith text in *The Anonymous Press Edition of Alcoholics Anonymous* (Croton Falls, N.Y., 1994). This "library edition," issued without A.A. cooperation or approval, takes advantage of the copyright blunder that allowed the first two U.S. editions of the Big Book to fall into the public domain. The Anonymous Press claims, however, to be a nonprofit operation that plows all its profits back into the production of more books for alcoholics.

12. Charlie Bishop Jr., the leading authority on alcohol-related books, states that the first printing consisted of 4,730 copies; see *Price Guide to Alcoholics Anonymous "Big Books" & Other AA Literature* (Wheeling, W.Va.: Bishop of Books, 1994), p. 16. This relatively small printing, combined with a burgeoning market in A.A. collectibles, has boosted the average price for first editions of *Alcoholics Anonymous.* According to Bishop, copies without the distinctive dust jacket now sell in the three to five thousand dollar range, depending on condition; the price doubles if the dust jacket is present. (These are retail prices, not what book dealers will actually pay wholesale, which is a fraction of retail value.) Copies even of later printings of the first edition, if pristine, can be worth hundreds of dollars.

13. Wilson remained so grateful to Blackwell for his trust and assistance that A.A. continued "to have the Big Book printed at Cornwall Press for a long time after it became a steady seller, so the venture also became profitable for the company" (*PIO,* 205).

14. Over the years, the Big Book has steadily slimmed down. By the second edition (1955)—in which the first part was reset and the second part expanded to include more stories, pushing the page total past six hundred—*Alcoholics Anonymous* had shed half its original weight and a quarter-inch of its bulk. The third edition (1976), which also runs more than six hundred pages (on thin paper), is a skinny slip of a "Big Book" at one pound and one-and-a-half inches thick.

15. Robertson, *Getting Better,* pp. 72–73.

16. Thomsen makes a similar point about the "in" language of A.A.: "a combination of back-alley barroom jargon and the purest spirituality. Much of the latter came from the program itself and the wording of the Steps. . . . But there was a sound reason for the raunchy reality of their talk. It was almost as though some men consciously used four-letter words in one sentence, knowing that in the next they could then use love, tenderness, humility and even serenity, things they were beginning to understand as basically human, which their drinking had kept them from even thinking about" (*BW*, 292–93). Implicit here is a recognition that concern with love, and so forth, was coded "female" in the culture from which A.A. sprang. Tough and profane talk was an antidote to feminization.

17. For example, one A.A. friend told me that his suspicions were first aroused when he heard a speaker's tape. (There is a free trade in such tapes among A.A. members.) Esther R., a blind, African American, old-timer from Cleveland, was exclaiming, "He was a man, not a demi-god, not a sometime saint. . . . He kissed me on the mouth when I was sober two years. I went to Founders' Day. . . . He kissed another young woman on the lips. . . . She was young too. And there was a young little blonde lady there. You didn't get many young ones way back then. And he kissed *her* on the lips. And there was some old ladies; he shook their hands. [Laughter.] And I knew, I knew I could stay sober 'cuz Bill Wilson was a *man!*"

18. Robertson, *Getting Better,* pp. 36 and 84.

19. Carolyn See, *Dreaming: Hard Luck and Good Times in America* (New York: Random House, 1995), p. 51. During Founders' Day in 1998, I noticed that a copy of *Dreaming* was in the library of the Akron A.A. archives.

20. As the last story in the second edition (1955), "Freedom From Bondage" became the matching bookend for "Bill's Story." The narrative was retained in the third edition (1976) but shifted to the penultimate position. At one point the author quips that her history of multiple marriages (she admits to four) "caused the rather cryptic comment from one of my A.A. friends . . . that I had always been a cinch for the program, for I had always been interested in mankind, but that I was just taking them one man at a time" (*AA,* 548–49).

21. Robert Fitzgerald, S. J., *The Soul of Sponsorship: The Friendship of Father Ed Dowling, S. J. and Bill Wilson in Letters* (Center City, Minn.: Hazelden, 1995), pp. 70–71.

Chapter 8: Forging the Traditions

1. The framed original of this letter is displayed at Stepping Stones as one of the Wilsons' most prized possessions. Jung died on 6 June 1961, before he could answer Wilson's second letter.

2. *Modern Man In Search of a Soul* (1933; repr., New York: Harcourt, Brace and World, 1966), p. 108.

3. Ibid., p. 112.

4. Ibid., p. 104.

5. *As Bill Sees It: The A.A. Way of Life (Selected Writings of A.A.'s Co-founder)* (New York: Alcoholics Anonymous World Services, 1985), p. 92.

6. The timing of Hank's relapse is in dispute. Thomsen places it in early 1940 (*BW*, 299). *'Pass It On'* sets no date but implies that Hank slipped during the summer of 1939. Hank, who subsequently enjoyed sober respites in A.A., eventually died from drinking, according to Lois Wilson; see *PIO*, 243 n. 1.

7. See *Alcohol, Science and Society: Twenty-Nine Lectures with Discussions as Given at the Yale Summer School of Alcohol Studies* (New Haven: Quarterly Journal of Studies on Alcohol, 1945), pp. x and 461–73.

8. Wickes later published *The Inner World of Man* (1950) and *The Inner World of Choice* (1963). Wickes is incorrectly identified in *'Pass It On'* as "Frances Weekes" (p. 335).

9. The text of this letter appears in *'Pass It On'* without identification or date, but in a context that might suggest it was written in 1949. Part of the same letter, however, is quoted by Kurtz (*NG*, 214), who cites it as being from Wilson to Margarita L., 14 July 1947. Kurtz's version also includes the three words in square brackets, which are missing in *PIO*.

10. According to Nell Wing, Wilson was certain his depression was "biochemical"; he also described his condition as manic-depressive (bi-polar): "It did seem to be true that his most crippling depressions followed periods of intense emotional and physical activity, when he was expending enormous amounts of psychic and spiritual energy." *Grateful To Have Been There: My 42 Years with Bill and Lois, and the Evolution of Alcoholics Anonymous* (Park Ridge, Ill.: Parkside, 1992), p. 53.

11. Ernest Kurtz points out that the spiritual dimension of "the A.A. Way of Life" had been "implicit in its Oxford Group origins, but only in 1967 did this precise phrase become enshrined in the title of a collection of Bill Wilson's writings" (*NG*, 124). As if in belated recognition of a distinction between the life of A.A. and the life of its seemingly indispensable cofounder, the title of *The A.A. Way of Life* was changed, after Wilson's death, to *As Bill Sees It*.

12. Lori E. Rotskoff, "Sober Husbands and Supportive Wives: Gendered Cultures of Drink and Sobriety in Twentieth-Century America," Ph.D. diss. (Yale University, 1999), chap. 6.

13. In *LH*, this article is retitled "Twelve Suggested Points for A.A. Tradition."

14. Kurtz is quoting the official statement on the Third Tradition in the "Final Report of the 8th General Service Conference of Alcoholics Anonymous, 1958," p. 20.

15. Wilson's 1946 long form of this Tradition was later amended to read: "Any two or three alcoholics gathered together for sobriety may call themselves an A.A. group, provided that, as a group, they have no other affiliation" (*AA*, 565).

16. Quoted in *The Soul of Sponsorship: The Friendship of Father Ed Dowling, S. J. and Bill Wilson in Letters*, ed. Robert Fitzgerald, S. J. (Center City, Minn.: Hazelden, 1995), p. 41.

17. On the strict parallelism between the Twelve Steps and the Twelve Traditions, Kurtz notes that when the short form of the Traditions was written, the total number of words used purposely matched the two hundred used in the Steps.

Chapter 9: The Sage of Stepping Stones

1. At a 1954 A.A. conference in Fort Worth, Texas, speaking about "How the Big Book Was Put Together," Wilson referred ironically to "the good old book, *Alcoholics Anonymous*": "Some people reading the book now, they say, well, this is the A.A. Bible. When I hear that, it always makes me shudder because the guys who put it together weren't a damn bit biblical."

2. In the handy *Anonymous Press Edition of Alcoholics Anonymous* (Croton Falls, N.Y., 1994) five textual variants are noted between the first edition and later editions. None is significant except for the change in Step Twelve from "spiritual experience" to "spiritual awakening." The Anonymous Press editors have overlooked another (also insignificant) variant noted by Ernest Kurtz (*NG*, 300 n. 67): "ex-alcoholic" became "ex–problem drinker" in the eleventh printing (June 1947) of the first edition (see p. 18 in the second and third editions).

3. Kurtz also reports Wilson's later dismay, expressed in a 1961 letter, that the *12 & 12* was likewise turning to stone: "As time passes, our book literature has a tendency to get more and more frozen—a tendency for conversion into something like dogma. This is a trait of human nature which I'm afraid we can do little about. We may as well face the fact that A.A. will always have its fundamentalists, its absolutists, and its relativists" (*NG*, 300 n. 67).

4. Slightly revised, the same letter appears in *As Bill Sees It: The A.A. Way of Life (Selected Writings of A.A.'s Co-founder)* (New York: Alcoholics Anonymous World Services, 1985), p. 63.

5. "Here is the fellow who has been puzzling you, especially in his lack of control. He does absurd, incredible, tragic things while drinking. He is a real Dr. Jekyll and Mr. Hyde" (*AA*, 21).

6. Quoted in *The Soul of Sponsorship: The Friendship of Father Ed Dowling, S. J. and Bill Wilson in Letters*, ed. Robert Fitzgerald, S. J. (Center City, Minn.: Hazelden, 1995), p. 41.

7. Henri F. Ellenberger, *The Discovery of the Unconscious: The History and Evolution of Dynamic Psychiatry* (New York: Basic Books, 1970), p. 640. Horney is most famous for her attack on Freud's notorious doctrine of "penis envy" in women.

8. *The Soul of Sponsorship*, pp. 113 n. 74 and 114–15 n. 87.

9. Karen Horney, *Neurosis and Human Growth: The Struggle Toward Self-Realization* (New York: Norton, 1950), pp. 187 and 188.

10. Ibid., pp. 189–90.

11. During the 1970s, when Kurtz was writing *Not-God*, these three areas were placed off-limits: "the only archive restriction beyond the obvious one of anonymity was imposed by A.A. on this research" (*NG*, 302 n. 2). In 1984, however, '*Pass It On*,' the official biography, aired out these matters publicly—though not in any great detail.

12. Philip Rieff, *Freud: The Mind of a Moralist* (1959; repr., Garden City, N.Y.: Doubleday, 1961), p. 8.

13. On the history of the S.P.R., see Alan Gauld, *The Founders of Psychical Research* (New York: Schocken Books, 1968). On the presence of spiritualism in American culture, see Howard Kerr, *Mediums, and Spirit-Rappers, and Roaring Radicals: Spiritualism in American Literature, 1850–1900* (Urbana: University of Illinois Press, 1972); and *The Haunted Dusk: American Supernatural Fiction, 1820–1920,* ed. Howard Kerr, John W. Crowley, and Charles L. Crow (Athens: University of Georgia Press, 1983).

14. Philip Rieff, introduction to Sigmund Freud, *Studies in Parapsychology* (New York: Collier Books, 1963), pp. 12–13.

15. Ernest Jones, *The Life and Work of Sigmund Freud* (New York: Basic Books, 1957), 3:375.

16. See *William James on Psychical Research,* ed. Gardner Murphy and Robert O. Ballou (New York: Viking, 1960). This volume contains all of James's studies of psychical phenomena, including his investigation of Mrs. Piper.

17. *The Soul of Sponsorship*, p. 47.

18. Ibid., p. 51.

19. This is a common A.A. joke: that a strict upbringing in the American Catholic Church, especially in the hellfire and guilt-trip atmospherics of the "bad old days" before Vatican II, is another "disease" that requires a Twelve-Step recovery program.

20. In like manner, he tried not to inflame racial tensions in A.A. by uneasily tolerating the segregation practiced in many parts of the South, where Negroes (the term at the time) had no choice but to hold "separate but equal" meetings. Kurtz reports that Wilson, rumored to have been "discomfited by black people," refused to takes sides in disputes between segregationists and integrationists. Although such exclusionary discrimination seemed

flagrantly at odds with the Third Tradition, his advice was to "obey the law; do not make A.A. too odd for any community." He also pleaded powerlessness over racial injustice, which he chose to treat as an "outside issue"— and, therefore, as great a threat to A.A.'s "singleness of purpose" as any other social or political cause. He also kept in mind the example of the Washingtonians, who failed in part because they *did* become involved in such divisive matters as prohibition and abolition. "Alcoholics Anonymous would never print 'whites only' or 'blacks only' in a listing of meetings, but if the community understood such from the listed meeting place, well, that was reality— part of the 'things I cannot change'" (*NG*, 148–49).

21. "The autobiography of Thomas Merton is a Twentieth Century form of the *Confessions of St. Augustine*," said Sheen. See Thomas Merton, *The Seven Storey Mountain* (New York: Harcourt, Brace, 1948).

22. *The Soul of Sponsorship*, p. 95.

23. A facsimile reprint of Wilson's three "communications" has been issued in a limited edition as *Bill Wilson & The Vitamin B-3 Therapy, 1965–1971* (Wheeling, W.Va.: Bishop of Books, 1993).

24. According to William G. Borchert, author of the screenplay, this incident is based on a true story told him by Lois Wilson, about a meeting she and Bill had attended during the early 1940s in Barstow, California. Borchert moved the scene forward chronologically to 1950, in a way that makes it dramatically effective but undercuts its historical plausibility. Borchert also told me that he too was aware that the scene in the Mayflower lobby (see Foreword) could not have happened the way it has been written. But the legend had become so deeply entrenched, he felt he had no choice but to follow the myth rather than the facts.

25. Freeman Carpenter (pseudonym), *60 Years an Alcoholic; 50 Years Without a Drink* (Newtown, Pa.: Unique Educational Services, 1996), p. 372.

26. Nell Wing, *Grateful To Have Been There: My 42 Years with Bill and Lois, and the Evolution of Alcoholics Anonymous* (Park Ridge, Ill.: Parkside, 1992), p. 63.

Afterword

1. In '*Pass It On*' (p. 227) appears a photograph of Bill W. sitting at this table in the Stepping Stones kitchen along with Ruth Hock, his first secretary.

2. In a revised form, the same essay appeared as an appendix to *AACA*, 286–94.

3. Bill Wilson to Mary C., 18 March 1961.

4. Ibid. Wilson went on to say: "I hope and believe that this decision was right, but history will tell."

5. Bill Wilson to Max W., 13 October 1961.

6. Mary C. to Bill Wilson, 9 September 1966. She is referring to *I'll Cry Tomorrow* (1955), based on singer Lillian Roth's best-selling (but anonymity-breaking memoir) of her drinking career, and *Days of Wine and Roses* (1962), derived from a television play by J. P. Miller. The latter was, in fact, endorsed by A.A.'s information committee. Of *A Day at a Time,* I can find no record. On the portrayal of A.A. in American films, see Norman K. Denzin, *Hollywood Shot by Shot: Alcoholism in American Cinema* (New York: De Gruyter, 1991).

7. This film was made with Lois Wilson's knowledge and cooperation. The screenwriter, William G. Borchert, told me that he read the final script to Lois in her final days; she did not live to see the completed picture.

8. Denzin, *Hollywood Shot by Shot,* pp. 228, 231.

9. Bill Wilson to Mary C., 5 October 1966.

10. Ibid.

11. This part of "Why Alcoholics Anonymous Is Anonymous," unfortunately, was not included in the *AACA* version of the essay. Perhaps Wilson decided it was too "personal" to be consistent with the strict ideal of anonymity.

12. Susan Cheever, "Bill W.," *Time,* 14 June 1999, pp. 201–4. Her fascinating alcoholic memoir is *Note Found in a Bottle: My Life as a Drinker* (New York: Simon and Schuster, 1999).

Index